ESCOFFIER

Escoffier

The King of Chefs

Kenneth James

Hambledon and London

London and New York

Hambledon and London

102 Gloucester Avenue
London, NW1 8HX

838 Broadway
New York
NY 10003–4812

First Published 2002

ISBN 1 85285 396 4

A description of this book is available from the
British Library and from the Library of Congress.

Typeset by Carnegie Publishing, Lancaster

Printed on acid-free paper and bound in
Great Britain by Cambridge University Press

Contents

Interludes

Illustrations

Preface

Auguste Escoffier (1846–1935) was the first great modern celebrity chef. He changed the way we eat and, in partnership with the eminent hôtelier César Ritz, the way we live. *Escoffier: The King of Chefs* sets out to tell the story of his life as he expressed himself through his cookery. The steps in his career are interspersed with interludes on a variety of the foods and dishes on which he held views and which he influenced, from the well-known *Pêche Melba* to *Caneton Rouennais en Dodine au Chambertin*. He left us thousands of meticulously described recipes and it would be difficult to find a modern recipe that owes nothing to his influence.

My wife Peggy was my constant companion in the research for this book, which led us to many unusual places and allowed us to meet a range of remarkable people. Pierre Bresson and Pierrette Boissier gave us the run of the extensive library and archives of the Fondation Auguste Escoffier in Villeneuve Loubet, also helping us find our way through the vast amount of material. My thanks are due to the staff of the Swiss Gastronomy Museum, Schadau Castle, Thun, Switzerland, and to Miss Ashbee, archivist of the Savoy Hotel, London, who went to a lot of trouble digging out material for us. Her successor, Susan Scott, kindly provided two photographs from the Savoy Group's archive. The late Maurice Ithurbure worked with Escoffier and we had the great pleasure and benefit of talking to him about *Le Maître*. Timothy Shaw, an expert on Escoffier, and his enchanting wife Maryse, who has family connections to the Escoffiers, provided guidance and hospitality in Monte Carlo. I owe much to Pierre Escoffier for his delightful company on many occasions when he added a great deal to my understanding of his grandfather. Finally my thanks are due to Martin Sheppard, my publisher and an eagle-eyed editor.

'La bonne cuisine est la base du véritable bonheur.'

Auguste Escoffier

1

Origins

'Youth, what man's age is like to be doth show
We may our ends by our beginnings know.'

Sir John Denham

The village of Villeneuve-Loubet on the French Côte d'Azur is fifteen kilometres from Nice on the left bank of the River Loup, and was previously known as Gaudelet. It grew on the site of a Roman camp below a pentagonal tower erected in the ninth century as a lookout point against Saracens invading from the sea.[1] The village was renamed Villeneuve-sur-Loup probably when the present château was built around the watch-tower in the twelfth century by one of the Grimaldi family, still today a sovereign family but squeezed into the tiny state of Monaco. The river in summer, when the snowmelt from the mountains has gone, is low, clear but sluggish. The reflection in its surface is of the old village climbing steeply to the skyline, which is doubly pierced by the ancient tower of the château and the red-roofed tower of the church nearby. Half way up the hill, on the road leading from the village square, is the old forge and the house in which Auguste Escoffier was born at ten o'clock in the morning of Wednesday, 28 October 1846.[2]

Soon after Auguste's birth, his grandfather, Antonin Escoffier, fell ill. He had started a smithy some forty years earlier while still recovering from a wound acquired in one of the Little Corporal's adventures – he was always likely to pull up his smock to show the scars where the ball had gone into his chest and out the back.[3] His eldest son, Jean-Baptiste, Auguste's father, took over the business which continued to thrive – the villagers had no need to go all the way to Grasse for parts for agricultural implements, or to import them from Nice across the border; Jean-Baptiste could make them better and cheaper at his forge. He also found time to be the schoolteacher, the village locksmith and its mayor, and to supplement his income growing tobacco, ensuring that Auguste grew up in comfortable circumstances. Auguste wrote a little about Jean-Baptiste's four younger brothers. Two brothers followed in their father's footsteps working in iron. Honoré learned the business travelling around France working as a *compagnon*, but gave it up to run an *auberge*. Victor with artistic talent in working iron, was called up in 1855 to help the British fight the Crimean War: he died of the plague in Constantinople. The other two boys went into the restaurant business. The youngest of the family was a girl, Marie-Camille. Auguste doesn't mention her name and says only that she married an Italian. In fact, Auguste wrote very little about his family and, while prolific on the subject of women of the world, he makes short shrift of women of the family. An exception was his grandmother whose cooking he labelled as *cordon bleu*. He records his mother's name Magdeleine but nothing more, and he scarcely mentions his wife – except to describe the odd way in which he came to marry her and, briefly, near the end of her life when she was very ill. He wrote of having a brother he doesn't name, with whom he was taught manners at table by Jean-Baptiste.[4] As for the rest of Auguste Escoffier's family, only tombstones and church records present their incomplete and coldly brief testimony to having lived.

The family house now looks too prim to suit its history – it has become a museum, the Musée de l'Art Culinaire, mostly dedicated to the memory of Auguste Escoffier. The only sign of the old forge is the hitching ring which is still there on the wall at the entrance to the yard.

Auguste stayed at school until he was nearly thirteen, a little unusual for a French country boy in the mid nineteenth century. He found *les beaux-arts* attractive and had been set on becoming a painter or a sculptor. There seems to have been no suggestion that he should join his father in his business: his small stature scarcely suited him for work at the forge. But by this time he was well aware of his father's view that artistic talent did not point the way to a respectable career, and Auguste undoubtedly expected to be pointed away from the future he wanted. The idea of cooking for a living had not occurred to him. 'But', he was to say later, 'I was not indifferent to it', and quoted his interest in his grandmother's work in the kitchen. He claimed that he had saved her *véritable cordon bleu* recipes for *délicats ragoûts* and used them throughout his long career.[5]

In October 1859, the day after his thirteenth birthday, he took his first communion. It was the end of childhood, and his father told him he was to be a cook. As Auguste recalled in old age, 'There was nothing I could do but obey'.[6]

In October 1859 Jean-Baptiste Escoffier took his son Auguste to his first job, as a cook apprentice to his Uncle François. They travelled the rough road along the coast to Nice in the cart that Jean used to carry his tobacco harvest to Antibes. We now know Nice as a French Mediterranean tourist centre, thirty-two kilometres from the Italian border, with not much evidence of its great antiquity. Yet it was founded 350 BC by a group of Greek sailors who probably had to fight for the territory: they named it *nike*, victory, from which the modern name derives. The Romans took over in the first century. Subsequently, it passed back and forth between the Counts of Provence and Savoy. Nice was still formally under Victor Emmanuel II when Auguste went to work there. But not for long: Nice was part of the price Napoleon III received for helping the Italians oust the Austrians from the kingdom of Piedmont-Sardinia.

François Escoffier, already well known in Nice as a restaurant proprietor, had opened his Restaurant Français in 1856. It was pleasantly situated on a corner in rue Paradis facing the public gardens, Jardin Albert Ier.[7] The restaurant hid from the world a commercial kitchen of its day, a 'devil's forge' Victor Hugo might have known. 'This den, this source of indigestion, this terrifying kitchen, is filled with noise day and night.' It was stiflingly hot: one coal-fired range for the entrées; another for the sauces, the soups, the stews and the fries; and another with its turning spits – and all the doors and windows closed so that draughts did not cool the meals being dished up. Then there was the kitchen staff toiling, sweating and swearing in a frenzied turmoil to obey the *chef de cuisine* shouting and cuffing for obedience.

Young Auguste was cast into this, fresh from his healthy and peaceful country life. A mere apprentice, small in stature, his face just inches above stove level despite built-up shoes, he was bullied by his hardened, uncouth colleagues. He had little better treatment from his uncle. He recalled the experience calmly in later life: 'the kitchen then was no bed of roses for the apprentice, and my uncle was a hard man to please'.[8] There is, however, no doubt about the deep impression it made on him – kitchen reform was to become an obsession.

Auguste in his mid sixties ascribed to himself in his early teens views more statesmanlike than one might expect in one so young.[9] 'Those years were quite hard going', he wrote, 'but a desire and a determination which grew led me to accept the situation without the least discontent. After some months, I had already realised the importance of cooking and the role a conscientious cook could play in life.' He also recognised, he went on, that the *chef de cuisine* had for too long been classed among the ordinary servants of an establishment. That should not be so, since 'cooking is a science and an art, and the man that puts all his heart into satisfying his fellow man deserves consideration'.

He pointed out that it was so under the old monarchy when many high-placed people indulged in cooking. There was the *Régent de France,*

Philippe d'Orléans, nephew of Louis XIV, who would sneak off into the country to see his mistress, the Comtesse de Farabère. Sporting a linen apron over his silk trousers, he would cook supper, which they would eat in company with the Comtesse's farm workers, singing bawdy songs, telling spicy stories and playing the fool. Louis XV when young often cooked for himself in his own apartments. In later years, he had a name for preparing excellent coffee for his mistresses. Some, perhaps in envy, were apt to say there was little else he could do – but Auguste would not have broadcast such a remark. Some of the elite, indeed, achieved lasting fame only from their cooking. As Auguste noted, 'if the Marquis de Béchamel had not invented his divine sauce, he would long ago have been forgotten'.[10]

Auguste seems to have been able to recall clearly across the span of half a century:

> Having realised that in cooking there was a vast field of study and development, I said to myself: 'Although I had not originally intended to enter this profession, since I am in it, I will work in such a fashion that I will rise above the ordinary, and I will do my best to raise again the prestige of the *chef de cuisine*.' That was always my objective, and I believe I have given sufficient proof of my devotion to the cause.

Of course, we expect successful people to exude altruism, while recognising that often such idealism comes second, following the primary urge of the need to succeed. Auguste was probably no exception. As he said himself, he was apprenticed to the culinary trade because he saw no alternative but to obey his father. Clearly, however, once started on that road, some inborn drive to perfection, so obvious throughout his later career, exerted itself. One might doubt that young Auguste dedicated himself so early to the improvement of kitchens and the life of those who worked in them, but there is no room for doubt that he himself later worked hard and long to achieve those ends.

When Auguste joined the Restaurant Français it was already popular. Nice, before the railways from the north, was not the bustling tourist centre it was to become, but already it had a 'season', attracting those least able to sustain the hardships of a northern winter and who could pay for the relief. The air of Nice, it was said, was 'agreeable to the constitution of those who labour under the disorders arising from weak nerves, obstructed perspiration, relaxed fibres, a vascidity of lymph, and a languid circulation'.[11] Rich invalids were attracted and they told their friends. Nice was also a select meeting place for cosmopolitan high society on the way to Italy and Greece.

It was not long before François, with the need for more room, took an

opportunity to move his restaurant to a more prestigious address, 7 quai
Masséna.[12] His international clientele moved with him. So, at the beginning
of his career, Auguste met moneyed people demanding cooking of the
highest quality and able to pay for it. It was an atmosphere he worked in
for most of the rest of his life.

The officers of Russian naval vessels, which spent the winter season every
year in the deep-water harbour of nearby Villefranche, were enthusiastic
customers at the Restarant Français and fond of good living. They were
keen not to lose the taste of some of their national dishes. Anxious to meet
the need, François included a Russian cook in the restaurant's *brigade de
cuisine.*[13] Auguste was intrigued with this exotic cooking, which at the time
found favour in Nice. He served many dishes throughout his career derived
from his experience of Russian cooking at the Français. Recipes based on
his *Coulibiac de saumon* (or *Koulibiak*) are used in Britain today,[14] although
the tendency is to do without the *vésiga,* the spinal cord of the sturgeon
Auguste liked to use.

Côtelettes de saumon Pojarski is another survivor Auguste brought us from
the days of the Tsars. They are upper-class fish cakes, often crowned with
a garnish of oysters or prawns and a *Sauce Newburg.* Pojarski was the chef
of a restaurant near the railway station in Torjok, a small town on the
Moscow to St Petersburg line – trains would stop there for passengers to
get a meal.

There was no collective bargaining in those days to restrict working hours
in the kitchen, but perhaps Auguste did a little better than most in occasionally escaping from the toil and sweat. There is little evidence of what
the young man did in his sparse free periods, but François, it appears,
sometimes became the uncle rather than *le patron.*

Auguste refers to one occasion – he was fifteen at the time – when his
uncle took him to the Théâtre Français. His only memory of the play was
of a waiter calling to the kitchen for *Tournedos à la Plénipotentiaire.* He
quoted this in discussing the origins of the word *tournedos* as used to
describe fillet steak. He preferred the word to *médallions* or *noisettes (de
boeuf)*, which are 'not easy on the ear'. His idea was that the name originated
in Paris, where speed of production of a dish was so important and fillet
steak easily fitted the requirement. 'When the sauce and garnish are ready,
it is only necessary to *tourner le dos,* turn your back, and the steak is done.'[15]
The sixteenth-century meaning of *tournedos,* according to the *Larousse
Etymologique* was *fuyard* (shy, timid – of an animal). But it was used by
Labiche to describe a dish in a nineteenth-century comic play – perhaps the
one Auguste saw as a boy in Nice.

Auguste also remembered his uncle taking him to an auction sale of the effects of a deceased English peer. Uncle François bought ten pewter dinner plates, square, with covers.[16] They impressed Auguste: he said that when he had charge of his own restaurant he would feature such tableware. Many years later he did.[17]

The long hours spent at work in far from congenial conditions were over each year by the end of May, when the restaurant closed for the summer. It opened again on 1 September. There were, however, no lazy, carefree summer vacations for young Auguste, as he had to do the cooking for his uncle and family.

Two neighbours, a pastry cook and a confectioner, provided a positive pleasure for him. They were friendly and made Auguste most welcome in their *laboratoire*. He helped the two chefs with their preparations, and they instructed him in the art of preserving fruits.[18] The influence of these interludes can be detected throughout his long career.

Auguste often refers to his uncle as a strict disciplinarian but leaves no doubt that he received excellent grounding at his hands. He recalls: 'In addition to my work in the kitchen I had to busy myself in all the many jobs that go to running a restaurant, and quite early I acquired the knowledge necessary to manage a similar establishment, or at least to understand in some detail how it should all work.'[19]

Auguste completed his apprenticeship in 1863, and in November he became 'first assistant'. He left the following April, before the restaurant closed for the summer, for a job at the Restaurant des Frères Provençaux on the Rue Saint-François de Paul. He was not yet eighteen years old, but because of his broad training he was able to accept a good deal of responsibility. He was given the job of running the kitchen and was able to assume the title of *chef de cuisine*. He also did all the buying.

For the next winter season he moved to Chez Philippe on the Rue de France and for a time he was away from overwintering foreigners. It was a modest restaurant, and cooking was essentially for the locals – there was an irony in this, as we shall see. He recalls also that he got in some practice with his fruit preservation.[20] By this time he was giving serious thought to his future. He was ambitious, with confidence in his abilities. He knew what he wanted to do. Years later he said, 'While realising that I was too inexperienced to know what was best for me, I had my sights set on Paris ...'[21] Perhaps he meant that only in advanced age did he recognise his inexperience in youth. But, whatever his real feelings about his own judgement at the time, there is no reason to doubt his passion to get to the capital.

A Drink to Open the Mind

'Never serve coffee except at the end of a meal.'

Auguste Escoffier

We do a lot that Auguste Escoffier said we should do, although we ignore his coffee commandment derived from a lifetime of experience. His cooking career started with coffee: in 1856, when he was ten years old, he was forbidden it.[1] The drink became immediately desirable. The boy was curious to know what was so special about this mysterious brew the grown-ups kept for themselves.

Auguste remembered an occasion watching carefully as his grandmother prepared her coffee and waiting while she sipped it contentedly. It was an expensive commodity and only to be indulged in on special occasions, and this was one. A day's shopping in Nice, still part of the Kingdom of Sardinia, was an adventure, and the bumpy ride with the local carrier had to be endured. A small cup of the stimulating drink was justifiable. She left, and Auguste set about repeating the brewing process he had seen her use; 'the old method', he later called it without describing it. His first sip was disappointing, bitter, but he persisted, eager to experience the stimulating effect he had heard about. By the end, whether or not he felt any different, he had started to acquire a taste for coffee that remained an enthusiasm all his life.

Sometime later, on Christmas Eve, he was sitting in front of the fire listening to his grandmother and some women, family friends, talking about the ways they favoured of making coffee. Each had some little secret to reveal without which it was not possible to make good coffee. They made it sound so complicated and difficult that the boy felt he had to speak up. 'It's not all that clever to make coffee', he burst into their conversation, and almost ran off when they all turned to stare in surprise. Then, boldly, he went on to tell them of his clandestine adventure in his grandmother's kitchen. They were shocked at first but they all joined in when his grandmother laughed. She kissed him and whispered, 'You'll make a good cook', quite a prophecy on such slender evidence.[2]

Auguste never lost his love of coffee. He wrote an article about it in 1883, almost a spiritual text, in which he said the beverage was the necessary complement to all meals.[3] He records that the drink was discovered by the Mullah Chadly, who would fall asleep reading the Koran. The mullah felt that such impiety would irritate Mahomet. Watching his lethargic goats one day, the mullah noticed that after eating from a certain tree they made off in leaps and bounds, revivified. 'Blessed be the great Allah,' he cried, 'that's what I need.' And so it proved to be. An infusion prepared from the fruits of the tree kept him awake during his holy reading and, what was more, it tasted good. The Arab world adopted coffee as a gift from Mahomet.[4] That was one story, although the discovery is now usually attributed to Kaldi, a young Abyssinian goatherd enjoying a similar experience.[5]

Another version concerns Ali bin Omar al-Shadili, who was banished to the Wusab mountains, in what is now the Yemen, for indulging his manly prowess with the king's daughter. He later cured victims of an 'itch epidemic', using a decoction of coffee cherries he found growing locally, and earned himself a pardon and a sainthood. This tale is immortalised in the Algerian word for coffee, *shadhiliye*.[6]

Since the earliest writings mentioning coffee appear to have been in the tenth century, while its first cultivation was probably in the sixth, great precision on its first recognition can scarcely be expected. Certainly, many stories about it were embroidered, if not actually invented, by storytellers employed by the coffee houses in the Middle East to entertain their customers. It is not clear, for example, whether Shadili, the philanderer banished to the mountains by the king, was Shadomer Shadli the ruler of Mocha in the mid fifteenth century. The port of Mocha in the Yemen in fact monopolised the supply of coffee to the world until the eighteenth century.

The word 'coffee' seems to originate from the Arabic *qahwa*, an ancient word for wine, implying affection. It was applied to the new drink when it replaced wine in religious ceremonies in the Yemen. Travelling with its Turkish pronunciation *kahvé* along with the earliest smuggled beans to

Venice, it became the Italian *caffé* and, soon, the French *café*, German *Kaffee*, Dutch *koffie*, which is not far removed from coffee.[7]

The idea of coffee houses originated in the Middle East – the first was established in 1554 in Constantinople. Half a century later, George Sandys, an inveterate traveller and observer of life, wondered whether coffee was the main attraction or the beautiful boys kept for the entertainment of customers.

Escoffier's researches suggested that it was Soliman Aga, an ambassador in France 1669, who had introduced coffee to the court at Versailles. 'The French people, the most alert in the world', said Auguste, 'had no need of it as a remedy, but both the court and the bourgeoisie adopted it as a new gastronomic joy.'[8] Coffee drinking became an expensive fad for the rich. A few years later an Armenian, called Pascal, started to sell the beverage at a more popular price in a little shop in Paris, but coffee didn't really catch on in France until an Italian opened the first successful coffee house in Paris in 1702, the Café Procope. Not everyone favoured the new concoction. The priests in Italy complained to Pope Clement VIII of Satan's drink – but he liked it and had the happy thought of baptising it.[9]

It was a Turk who brought the idea to England, opening premises in Oxford in 1650. The first coffee house in London was opened in 1652 in St Michael's Alley. As in France, it was about half a century before demand for coffee began to grow. It was at the end of the seventeenth century that the East India Company thought potential coffee trade in England worthy of their attention.[10] The company, founded in 1600 by Royal Charter of Queen Elizabeth I, became the greatest commercial power the world had known. As well as its fleet of East Indiamen, it had its own army, and indeed its own currency. In its time, it made India the jewel in the British Crown, founded both Singapore and Hong Kong, and essentially, it could be said, the United States: near bankruptcy, the company was given, by the Tea Act of 1773, taxes on tea sold in the American colonies, thus precipitating the Boston Tea Party. The company also employed William Kidd, a Scottish privateer (better known as Captain Kidd) to deal with the pirates in the Indian Ocean – he wasn't very successful, and after a couple of years returned to the West Indies, became a pirate himself and was hanged.

The company had been the major supplier of coffee to the Far East since its earliest days, and when it turned its attention to the West the future of the coffee trade was assured. Women in England were not happy with the new coffee houses for men only, which kept their husbands away from home. Some went as far as to issue a pamphlet claiming the drink rendered men impotent:

The
Women's
Petition
Against Coffee
Representing
to
Publick Consideration
the
Grand Inconveniences Accruing
to their Sex from the Excessive
Use of that Drying, Enfeebling
Liquor
Presented to the Right Honourable the
Keepers of the Liberty of Venus

By a Well-Willer

London, Printed 1674

This did little to close down the resorts. They survived and were the forerunners of many modern institutions such as the Royal Society, the Stock Exchange and London's clubs for gentlemen.[11] Mr Edward Lloyd's coffee house became Lloyd's of London.

Coffee spread like a tidal wave across the world. Countries with suitable climates set out to grow their own, acquiring seedlings by fair means or foul – mostly foul since countries with coffee jealously guarded their possession from those that did not have it. India first grew coffee from plants smuggled in from the Yemen strapped to the belly of a pilgrim from Mecca. The Caribbean's first seedlings were stolen from Louis XIV of France – who had a pet bush, a present from the Dutch, which he kept in a greenhouse. The story, now a legend in France, tells of the Duc de Clieu bribing the King's gardener to give him some seedlings. He transported them to Martinique, surviving attacks of pirates and Atlantic storms to arrive at the island with one seedling with which he had shared the last of his water ration. Brazil, now with the world's largest coffee plantations, stole their original seedlings from French Guyana. An emissary from the Emperor of Brazil had a liaison with the French Governor's wife and he left the colony with the coffee plants she had given him hidden in a posy of flowers.

Escoffier recorded that 'a fine lady' who wrote kind and sometimes flattering letters claimed that 'le café vivrait ce que vivrait Racine', and said that, without her knowing it, her satire expressed a great truth. 'And so it is,' he went on, 'that while poetic verses are charming and elegant, the essence from the tree of Yemen is suave and delicious.' 12

He is not much help on how to select coffee, or on its preparation. 'The quality of this *liqueur* depends entirely on the extent of roasting, and the least negligence in this respect can spoil the flavour. Grilled exactly right, the bean must be a uniform chocolate colour.' He writes, too: 'Coffee must be served very hot and the gastronome will not add brandy, which totally changes the flavour. But after coffee one may serve various liqueurs. When one cannot offer the delicate products of the West Indies or of Holland, one must be content with an excellent cognac, rum or kirsch'.

Cognac in the coffee was, however, a habit too well established to be much affected by his entreaty. In 1845, Eliza Acton wrote about the French adding brandy to their coffee.13 They called it *le gloria.* 'Make some coffee as strong and as clear as possible, sweeten it in the cup with white sugar almost to a syrup, then pour the brandy on the top over a spoon, set fire to it with a lighted paper, and when the spirit is in part consumed, blow out the flame, and drink the *gloria* quite hot.' Elizabeth David felt that this must be the forerunner of Gaelic – 'perhaps', she says, 'originally Gallic' – coffee.14 On the other hand, you don't have to be a genius to think of adding brandy to sweetened coffee and so invent the *gloria* for yourself, and then, like the Irish, enrich it with cream. Escoffier thought that all real *gourmands* loved coffee because 'it prevented fatigue of the digestion, made for gaiety, opened the mind, inspired flashes of wit, and illuminated the imagination. The man with a sense of humour became a genius after coffee; the dullest intelligence shone; the callous became sensitive, cold beauty came alive, everything changed, it was the triumph of coffee.'

While there are three main species of coffee, *coffea arabica, liberica* and *robusta,* varieties of these are legion. Moreover, they vary in quality depending where they are grown, on altitude, soil and climate, and of course on the weather pattern of the seasons. There are also variations in the manner of their commercial preparation and the blending of varieties which affect price and quality.

Coffee is grown in about thirty tropical or semi-tropical countries, from Angola, around the world and back to Zaïre (now called the Congo – but Zanzibar grows coffee too). It is one of the world's great industries, probably second only to oil in value – some five million tons of it are sold each year. Received wisdom has it that thirty million people are employed in the business across the world. Despite its commercial importance, not everybody knows how it is grown and produced. The evergreen coffee tree will grow to twenty feet or more, but the better varieties are usually kept pruned to about six feet for ease of harvesting. After its delicate white flowers, with a fragrance not unlike jasmine, clusters of green 'cherries' develop which ripen through yellow to a cherry red and become, when ready for picking, almost black. Within the sticky pulp of the fruit is a pair of green beans – sometimes one – protected by an outer and an inner skin. There are various commercial methods for removing the fruit and skin layers to leave the cleaned beans ready for picking over to remove any bad ones, and for sizing, sorting and grading. Finally, the varieties are chosen for blending, roasted to the desired degree and ground to an extent to suit the mode of preparing the drink.

Choosing coffee is, like choosing a dress or a suit, governed by upbringing, habit and fashion, and any advice is likely to come from others with their own sets of constraints. After all, if the choice were simple, lesser options would have disappeared from the market long ago and no selection would be available. We also have to choose a method of making the brew. We can use an Italian espresso machine, to extract the last trace of flavour. Then, there is the delicate filtrate made with mild coffee extracted shortly with scarcely boiling water; or, at the other extreme, there is the boiled up Turkish-style brew you can almost eat with a fork. 'Black as Hell, strong as death, sweet as love', as a Turkish proverb has it.

There are some pointers. The main contending species are *coffea arabica*, the first to be cultivated, and *coffea robusta*. The last, as its name suggests, is tough, resists disease and will survive dramatic weather changes and, moreover, can best be grown at low altitude and needs little tending and so presents formidable price competition. The bulk of the coffee drunk in the world today is *robusta* and it is the coffee sold by auction on the coffee market. It has more caffeine than *arabica*, a stronger flavour, and the bean gives a higher yield – that is, you need to use less of it. *Arabica is* grown at higher altitudes and needs a lot of attention. It is a high-quality, low-yielding coffee, sold direct to the buyers rather than at auction. Such coffees are called the 'milds', but are not necessarily mild to taste. Some have a built-in nutty bitterness much sought in a blend. In the shop, varieties will completely confuse the simple issue of species. There will be Java, Mocha, Medellin, Excelso, Blue Mountain, washed Venezuelan Maracaibo, and so on; but the general species characteristics, although blurred, still apply.

The green beans are roasted to develop aroma and flavour. Four degrees are recognised: pale, medium roast, full roast and continental. The high, or continental, roast gives a strong bitter flavour and the cheaper blends can be used – better ones would be wasted since the finer flavours are driven off. For a long time in Britain, as in America, a medium roast was mostly used, but in recent years many have acquired a taste for continental roast from other places abroad. The tendency now is towards the full roast, a bit down the scale, a compromise solution but a happy one. Most people seem to find this roast satisfactory for coffee at any time of day, but a pale-roasted *arabica* retains all the choice subtle flavours and aroma, a delight at breakfast.

Grinding is decided by the method of brewing. Each of us has a personal preference, often based on vast experience. For those with doubts, a pointer might be that most experts use a jug. Actually, the tasters use bowls, but it amounts to the same thing: the nearly boiling water is poured directly on to the freshly roasted and ground coffee beans. Connoisseurs appreciate the small amount of fine powder left in suspension in the unfiltered liquid, as it adds body to the drink: it is a taste easily acquired.

Choice of grind is easy. Very fine grind, like flour, goes with the 'filter' of the Melitta type, 'Espresso' coffee makers and the French three-part 'drip'. This grind is the most economical since it gives a high yield – there is more extraction from the smaller particles. Next in line is defined as fine – somewhere between salt and granulated sugar in grain size – and is used for the 'vacuum' type machine, or Cona. Medium is for jugs and bloop-bloop percolators. The latter, which have been around since about 1825, are economical in use since the temperature is kept up during the blooping to extract the dregs of flavour – and bitterness. They are not in fashion today. It might be that the increasing tendency to make them in aluminium is the reason. Even though the idea has now been discounted that aluminium from culinary vessels is a significant health risk, the metal does seem to taint the coffee.

A jug needs a strainer to go with it to hold back the grounds – the Melior type cafetière is a jug with a built-in strainer that is pushed down through the brewed coffee – despite its French name, the cafetière is not much used in France. Some would say that you can't do much better than using a cafetière, *arabica*, full roast (not forgetting pale roast for breakfast), medium grind, four rounded dessert-spoonfuls to the pint. Warm the pot, use soft spring water just off the boil (well, try the supermarket bottle if you are in a hard water area), infuse for four minutes and drink hot. Beans should be freshly roasted (but, to be practical, not more than a week from roasting and kept in the fridge in an air-tight jar), and ground just before use. Yet, half the world likes its coffee strong and bitter, using continental roast, a very fine grind, an espresso machine, a bloop-bloop or just boiling it up. Bitterness is an acquired taste and addictive. But the other is good too.

Not to be neglected is the espresso machine, an English invention with a French name, now very much Italian and used all over the world. In this, the beans are extracted rapidly under high pressure and, importantly, at low temperature. This way, subtle flavours are retained. Variations on this theme add a couple of drops of tangerine or almond essence or a slice of lemon. And there is cappuccino, espresso with hot milk topped with a foam of the mixture and dashed on top with cocoa or cinnamon. The espresso process does not work well with the quality coffees used for high temperature methods and the usual machines used at home do not reach high enough pressure. Essentially, then, for the best results we turn to the professional, and the best espresso coffee is exquisite.

Then there is instant coffee. Coffee drinkers are a bit like wine lovers: they know what they like and sneer at the others. Judging from the sales, a lot of people like instant coffee – 90 per cent of coffee drunk in this country is of the instant variety. They even drink it in Mexico and like it, while declaring that it is not coffee. Of course, the ease of preparation is seductive too.

Until recent years, instant coffee, regarded by the marketeers as price tied, was made almost entirely from the *robustas*. It could be said that none really had the fine aroma or subtlety of flavour of well-made coffee from freshly roasted and ground beans. But it is not easy to aspire to such heights, and the best instant versions give some approximation to the real thing. They are certainly preferable as a drink to badly made coffee or stale coffee made from beans. The approximation is perhaps closer now with the newer freeze-dried instant blends using *arabicas*.

No doubt manufacturing methods will continue to improve. It would not seem to be beyond the wit of man to make sure that the tiny quantities of labile essential oils that make up the subtle flavour of good coffee are not lost in the 'instantisation' process. They just need a good alchemist.

There is one more stage: caffeine-free instant coffee. In the old days, if a chemist wanted some of the alkaloid caffeine to use in the laboratory, he would extract it from coffee beans with a solvent such as chloroform or benzene, or perhaps something less toxic. This would leave the beans clean of caffeine, like a suit just back from the dry-cleaners. It was a chemist, Ludwig Roselius, back in 1900, thinking that his father was poisoning himself with too much coffee, who served him the brew from dry-cleaned coffee beans. In this way decaffeinated coffee was invented. It was mostly made that way until the 1980s when it was thought the solvent used, methylene chloride, might be carcinogenic. It does affect the flavour left in the beans, but less than other solvents, and its use is still allowed, provided there are less than ten parts per million left in the decaf.

Another method uses water to leach out the caffeine – but you have to start with some decaf to saturate the water with all the soluble substances you don't want to wash out of the fresh beans. The more technological method is to use carbon dioxide at high temperature and very high pressure.

The extracted caffeine can be washed free of the carbon dioxide with water – the carbonated water can then be sold to soft-drink manufacturers.

Nicely cleaned and pressed in its plastic bag, the aroma and taste of decaffeinated coffee are several pegs down from the full-blown instants. Escoffier would probably not stir in his grave if you pepped it up with some cooking brandy. But a pleasanter way of cutting down on your caffeine intake is to drink better coffee – *arabica* has only half the caffeine content of the cheaper *robustas*.

2

A Foot on the Ladder

'A sauce must fit the roast or fish
as a tight-fitting skirt fits a woman.'

Auguste Escoffier

M. Bardoux, *propriétaire* of the Restaurant du Petit Moulin Rouge in Paris
– not associated in any way with the Moulin Rouge cabaret of Montmartre –
went to Nice in search of promising staff for his restaurant. A friend
recommended he try the *langouste niçoise* at Chez Philippe. He was immediately impressed and called for the *chef*. Auguste Escoffier was presented
to him and he offered the young man a job at the Petit Moulin. That's one
story.[1] Auguste put it differently in a speech he made in 1909: 'In January
1865, I made the acquaintance of M. Bardoux ... who had come to Nice to
get treatment for his daughter who was seriously ill. I asked him if he could
give me a junior post in the kitchen of his establishment, which he very
kindly did.'[2]

The second version rings true. Auguste was extremely keen to get to Paris
and he would not have missed an opportunity to nobble a Parisian restaurant
owner looking for staff. Auguste, his modesty a formality, was not one for
writing himself down: had he been 'discovered' he would have said so.

Auguste arrived in Paris on Wednesday 12 April 1865 to take up his job
as kitchen assistant, as he called it,[3] or second *commis-rôtisseur*, at the Petit
Moulin Rouge.[4] He could scarcely have started lower. Having spent over
five years climbing to his position in charge of the kitchen at Chez Philippe
in Nice, it might have seemed that he was taking a step down. In fact, it
was a step up from a provincial high onto the Parisian ladder that reached
much higher in the profession to which he had committed himself. It was
a measure of his courage and determination that he took the job.

The Petit Moulin Rouge was first opened by M. Amant in the second half
of the eighteenth century at 19 Avenue d'Antin, a hundred yards from what
is now the Rond Point des Champs Elysées. M. Bardoux was Amant's
grandson,[5] and it was mostly under his direction the restaurant flourished,

enticing royalty and the great and the good from all over Europe. And, of course, such a clientele attracted Parisian society and all that hovered around it. One regular client, the notorious Blanche d'Antigny, once drank champagne there continuously for thirty-six hours – it was to console herself when the Shah of Persia on a visit to Paris did not invite her to join him.

The restaurant extended from Avenue d'Antin through to rue Jean-Goujon, with a garden between used as an outside restaurant. It was sufficiently removed from the avenue at least to moderate the stink of horse dung from the roadway, while one could still, wrote Auguste, 'dine under the spell of the music of *Le Concert Musard* playing in the Champs-Elysées gardens just opposite'.[6]

An eccentricity of the house was to reserve tables permanently for special groups.[7] One, kept for artists and authors, was set in the middle of the garden. Another was in the summerhouse where Russian dignitaries, such as Prince Galitzin and Prince Demidoff, gained a sense of privacy while others could still appreciate their presence.

By the time Auguste arrived in Paris M. Bardoux, who had offered him the job at the Moulin, had sold the restaurant. Bardoux's recommendation to the new management held good, however, and Auguste started work on Easter Monday, a few days after his arrival in the capital. Despite the surface glitter of this fashionable restaurant of the Second Empire, the nether world of its kitchen was an inferno. It was a domain ruled by Ulysse Rahaut, the *chef de cuisine*, emphasising his shouted orders with curses and blows rained down on his underlings. Auguste as the newest recruit got more than a proportionate share of this abuse. He had, however, been well trained for the experience under his taskmaster uncle in Nice. The chef's name has also been variously recorded as Rohan, Robaut and Rochaut, but since Auguste had the name literally knocked into him, he probably got it right as Rahaut. In later reminiscences he had nothing but praise for the chef and he went to a good deal of trouble to get him cared for in old age.[8]

At first, working as assistant to the *chef rôtisseur*, Auguste stood for long hours tending the spits in the blazing heat of the great open fire. He was sometimes switched to other menial tasks, but Rahaut, soon aware of Auguste's familiarity with the routines, moved him to work successively in each of the branches of the kitchen. His hours were still long and hard, but he found time and interest to follow what was going on in the restaurant: 'the great lords, kings and emperors passed through at that time', he recalled.[9]

He was proud of his association with such distinguished people, and he was prone in later years to indulge in a little name-dropping. And why not? It was his job, or he had made it so, to serve the greater to attract the lesser. 'It was not rare,' he wrote, 'to see the Prince of Wales, the future King

Edward VII, in company with the French statesman and founder of the Third Republic, Léon Gambetta, and other political figures dining in a private *salon*.' 10 Yet, while dewy-eyed about the upper crust, he did not lose his feeling for those struggling to earn some of the bread beneath. 'In the evening,' he said, 'one would meet the most gracious society ladies and the charming Elisabeth, the flower seller from the Jockey Club, offering her wares.'

It is not surprising that, with little time to roam, at not yet twenty he should notice the women who passed his way, whether bejewelled or with just nature's ornaments behind a basket of flowers. But Elisabeth was a rarity, an obviously unattached girl in a high-class restaurant; even in Paris it was still not quite the thing for a lady to be seen in a public restaurant, and certainly not unescorted. Auguste tells of the private entrance to the Petit Moulin at No. 3 rue Jean-Goujon, where carriages could drive up shielded by an immense lilac tree so that ladies with their consorts – or without – could slip into the restaurant unobserved. Even those bold enough to use the front door would make a great show of covering their faces, a gesture to propriety.

At the end of his first season in Paris, Auguste presumably went back to Chez Philippe for the winter, although there is no direct evidence of this. Towards the end of his next summer season, 1866, at the Moulin, he had completed his *tour* as an assistant on the various kitchen jobs. Then, in September, his number came up for military service. The draw also put him in the category of the reserve for active service so that he had only to do five months training. He went back to Nice for a period of duty with the 28th Infantry Regiment at nearby Villefranche-sur-Mer.11

Auguste does not write about his military training other than to record that he did it. This is of no significance in itself since he wrote little about himself that was not directly connected with his life's work. Later he always expressed patriotic views but, however strong they may have been, the five months enforced hiatus at a critical time in his career must have irked him. Military training in our present age of high technology is doubtless more enlightened, but the square-bashing of this era provided little intellectual stimulus to one dedicated to a career elsewhere.

In the spring of 1867, after his military interlude, Auguste returned to Paris in time for the Universal Exhibition. At the Petit Moulin he became *chef garde-manger* responsible for stock control and the larder. He had mounted another step on the ladder.

The Paris Exhibition brought the culinary arts before the public as never before and attracted visitors to the restaurants. Distinguished foreigners crowded Paris and thronged to the fashionable Moulin to dine. Auguste was much impressed with one diner in particular, the celebrated Emir Abd-el-Kader. The Emir, once a sworn enemy of the French, had set up the state of Algeria and had been at war with France for six years until defeated and imprisoned. Released in 1852, he had lived in Damascus and had learned to love the French. Auguste tells of the stir he caused when he arrived at the Moulin with his guests all in Arab attire. Auguste probably did not create the meal, served in the Chinese pavilion in the garden of the restaurant, but he kept a copy of the menu.[12] He collected menus – they comprised, essentially, his diary and *aide mémoire* – even in his eighties he could recall the circumstances of the earliest of them, the people present and the highlights of the occasion.

The menu for the Emir was:

Melon Cantaloup arrosé de vieux Frontignan
Bisque d'écrevisses
Paillettes diablées
Truite saumonée pochée au vin de la Touraine
Sauce Mousseline
Pommes Bergerette
Selle d'agneau de Béhague poêlée
Petits pois à la Française
Laitues farcies au riz
Fricassée de poulet à l'ancienne en gelée
Salade de pointes d'asperges Rachel
Aubergines au gratin
Bombe Nélusko
Gaufrettes Bretonnes
Pêches et Raisins Muscats
Café mode Orientale
Liqueurs
Grande fine Champagne
Les meilleurs cigares
Vins: Champagne parfum à la fraise des bois
Château Yquem

There is no account of how much of the alcoholic accompaniment the Arabs consumed, but Auguste does say that the Emir, after this splendid meal, wandered off among the crowds in the street amazed at the interest he had aroused.

Auguste used many of his collected menus in his later writing, often telling the stories they conjured up for him. One of the menus of this period was for a dinner given by the Comte de Lagrande to celebrate the victory of his horse, Gladiateur, in the Grand Prix de Paris. The meal was little different from that served to the Emir but it had one dish named for the Comte's racehorse, *Consommé Gladiateur au suc de tomates* and another after the Empress, *Pêches Impératrice Eugénie*. The use of such names to flatter or to add dignity to a dish was not new. Chefs had used the device since early in the century. It was, however, a process Auguste adopted to excellent effect.

He recalls from a menu an occasion when Cora Pearl, a beauty of the day, dined in one of the thirty or so private salons, *cabinets particuliers*, upstairs in the restaurant. She was the guest of 'a young Lord', another of the 'pigeons she was about to pluck', as Auguste expressed it. The menu on the one hand flattered her with *Noisettes d'agneau Cora* but, on the other hand, went a little near the bone with *Pigeonneaux cocotte*.

When the Moulin closed for the winter in 1867 Auguste returned to Nice, this time to the Restaurant Favre. He was given command of the kitchen there; all good practice for later responsibility in grander places. He was able to get back to preparing his own dishes and composing his own menus. Then came a significant career move; he returned to the Moulin in Paris for the 1868 season and was promoted to *chef saucier*. If any period of his training for stardom were to be picked as the most important, this must be it. Aged only twenty-two, he was now number two in a Parisian restaurant of high repute, second only to Ulysse Rahaut, the *chef de cuisine*. But more than that, he was now responsible for the creation and preparation of sauces.

Before Escoffier, even when sauces were emerging from a primitive background, where they were mostly needed to mask undesirable flavours, they were still haphazard concoctions from habit or whim, gravy to moisten the food. True, the great chefs of the past had recognised that sauces should not be neglected, but Brillat-Savarin, perhaps the most analytical of gastronomes early in the nineteenth century, was not easily convinced that sauces should have highest ranking. In his famous list of aphorisms he said that cooks were made but *rôtisseurs* were born.[13] It was near the end of his life when others persuaded him that the aphorism would be truer if it declared that *rôtisseurs* were made but *sauciers* born.

It was not enough for Auguste that a sauce should be just an artistic gesture, an instinctive flourish to a finished dish. It was to be an integral part of the work of culinary art, its constituents prominent on the palette of ingredients from which a dish was created. The sauce was to be not just the fluid body of a dish but part of its very soul. He spent the next two years studying sauces, their structure and form, and the relationships between them, as well as their effects on the final dish. He simplified them and placed them into interrelated categories, making a system of sauces easy to grasp.

At this time, as always in his adult life, he was tied to his work. It is rare in his writings, whether books, articles or letters, that he gives much hint of enjoyment in anything not connected with his job. One exception related to the Cascade Restaurant in the Bois de Boulogne. He liked to lunch there with friends – he does not name them, but they were presumably his working companions, particularly his friends MM. Bouniol and Fagette.[14] They watched the work on the Bois ordered by Napoleon III to turn the rough woodland into a park – Auguste says 'an English park' – which was then well under way. Drays brought in huge stones from Fontainebleau to construct grottoes and a waterfall. Over a thousand workers were engaged for some years, following not only the architect Varé's original plan but also the many subsequent whims and fancies of the Emperor. The Cascade became the afternoon objective of walkers from Paris. It also attracted the so-called *cascadeurs* – young revellers, roisterers, dandies and social celebrities. Auguste enjoyed the passing pageant and, like the other young men, the parading beauties. The restaurant was also a favourite place for Parisians to hold wedding feasts and he was often invited to these. He wrote later regretting the changes that had taken place in the Bois, brought about first by the bicycle and then the motor car. Except on race days at Longchamps, the Cascade restaurant was to become either 'too close or too far from Paris'.[15]

At the end of the 1868 season at the Petit Moulin Rouge, Auguste changed from his usual practice of returning to Nice for the winter. The Comte de North, a natural son of King George IV of England, engaged him as *chef de cuisine*. The Comte, like his father, was fond of good food, and ran a considerable kitchen. At the time, the feeling persisted from the era before restaurants that prestige for a cook came from the status of the private household that employed him as *chef*. Doubtless his sojourn with the Norths made an impressive entry in Auguste's *curriculum vitae*. The Comte went off to Russia in May 1870 and Auguste went back to his old job as *chef saucier* at the Moulin; but not for long. It was a fateful year.

On 3 July 1870 the news leaked that the Prime Minister of Prussia, Otto von Bismarck, had been conspiring with the Spanish to have a Prussian prince, Leopold of Hohenzollern-Sigmaringen, take over their vacant throne. The French objected to the idea of being squeezed between two Prussian camps, and said so. It was rumoured that Bismarck organised the Spanish affair to precipitate war with France. More likely, the move was part of a convoluted scheme to unite Prussia with the southern German states: Bismarck wanted nothing more than to be left alone by France. Things moved fast. Wilhelm, the King of Prussia, was all for placating the French. He reckoned Leopold should give up the idea of mounting the Spanish throne, as he did. Bismarck, however, felt humiliated and reacted belligerently. Napoleon III thought war with the Prussians would restore his fading popularity in France, and declared it on 19 July 1870. As a reservist, Auguste was called to the colours.

Interlude 2

Primeval Soup

'Of soup and love, the first is the best.'

Thomas Fuller, 1732

Not the least of civilisation's gifts is the restaurant, but it is a modern luxury. The Ancient Greeks opened inns, and the Romans spread them across their empire. Then, for two thousand years, eating out went with sleeping out, with no popping in, *à deux*, just for a romantic, candle-lit meal. Up to the middle of the eighteenth century, even as resident guests, you would probably only get *table d'hôte* — literally, potluck at the host's table in the kitchen.

The seed for change was planted in 1765 in the rue des Poulies, Paris, by a certain Boulanger – that was his name, but he might also have been a baker. He set out small tables and served meals chosen from his small list, a menu. His *pièce de résistance* at each meal was to serve an excellent soup which he called a restorative, *restaurant* in the French of the day. Already well known to Parisians, it was a thick soup referred to as *le restaurant divin*, made from minced beef and chicken with barley and perfumed with rose petals. Boulanger's speciality was made from sheep's feet in a cream sauce, which was claimed by one of the professional guilds, the *traiteurs* or caterers, to be a *ragoût*, which only their members were permitted to sell. They sued Boulanger, but he won the case. It was not long before people were going to the *restaurant* on rue des Poulies and, in due course, to other establishments sprouting small, neatly-laid tables and calling themselves restaurants.[1] By 1789 there were about fifty such establishments in Paris.

Then came the French Revolution and the cultural changes in its wake, and the restaurant idea really caught on. Ten years later there were five hundred restaurants in Paris, and they later spread across France, Europe and the world. The soup remained the distinctive feature of that first restaurant, and the idea of a speciality in such establishments persists.

The restaurant with social grace did not appear in France until after the Revolution. The reasons are not far to seek. From at least the thirteenth century there had been an ever-changing and complex system of guilds dividing up the market for the sale of cooked food.[2] Among the earliest were the *cuisiniers*, selling those cooked meats not claimed by other guilds, such as the *oiers* cooking their geese.

The *cuisiniers* split in two in the mid fifteenth century to become the *rôtisseurs* doing hot roasts – in constant altercation with the *poulaillers* disputing their right to cook chickens – and the *chaircuitiers* with their cold, cooked meats. The *chaircuitiers* reinforced themselves with successful take-overs of several other guilds, including the *saulcissiers* and the *boudiniers* with their sausages and black puddings respectively. Latterly the French have found the word *chaircuitier* as unappetising as we would its literal translation, flesh-cookers. The modern term, *charcutier*, is pleasantly amorphous.

All those guilds – and many others, making, for example, pastries, cakes, bread, and sauces – concerned themselves with cooking food for consumption off their premises, selling to the public direct or to caterers, *traiteurs*. For the exceptional meal, you could have collected the constituent cooked dishes, each from the appropriate guild member, the poultry from one, meat from another and so on, and warmed them up on the fire at home – an awkward equivalent of the modern 'take-away'.

Those rich enough had not bothered with all that; they employed their own chefs in house. Many owners of the better houses didn't keep their heads through the Revolution and good chefs became a drug on the market. They gravitated towards Paris and jobs in its restaurants which, once the fervour for *egalité* had died down, they were able to improve and popularise.

Those of the leisured classes who still had heads, but whose chefs had joined the gold rush to restaurant service, now had an alternative to either calling in a *traiteur* or collecting the constituents of a meal from various places: they could go to a new restaurant they didn't have to slink into. The age of the great restaurant had started.

England was late starting with the restaurant: gastronomy was a sin still condemned by the Puritans.[3] In 1798, Thomas Rule started what he called an Oystery in London, which evolved into the restaurant that still flourishes. Rule's was probably London's first restaurant. It was much later that the French influence produced an English gourmand from among those enticed from boiled meat pudding to such a dish as quail stuffed with an ortolan, itself stuffed with truffles – but not at Mr Rule's establishment, which stayed proudly with the best of English cooking, as did Simpson's and Scott's. It was French cuisine that made for the growth of the grand restaurants, like those of the Savoy Hotel, Hotel Cecil, Claridges and the Carlton.

3

Cooking under Fire

'La guerre est l'industrie de la Prusse.'

Mirabeau

'Take a good look as these gates, lads, you might never see them again', the drum-major of the 1st Regiment of Turcos, Algerian riflemen, called out as the company marched from the Bonaparte Barracks in Paris on their way to fight the Prussians.[1] Auguste watched as they left, knowing that he would be following in a few hours.

A few days earlier, on 20 July 1870, all Paris had fêted the garrison troops as they left for the front. Troops and civilians alike, or most of them, were confident of the defeat of the Prussians – train to the border, a simple march to Berlin and a triumphant return. Those who start wars have to make sure their people are confidently behind them. 'To Berlin' shouted the crowd. Once such fervour has set in, it is no longer possible to know, whatever an individual may say, how he actually feels. It is not possible to know Auguste's innermost thoughts on the occasion. He gives no clue. He writes mostly soldier's flat talk – we did this, this happened, and so on. He leaves us, however, a rare view of the Franco-Prussian War, a cook's eye view from among those in command.

As a reservist, Auguste received his call-up papers promptly but had no chance to comply. The Ministry of War was in a hurry to get cooks for the various sections of the General Headquarters of the Army of the Rhine. When the *Société des Cuisiniers de Paris* failed to produce the numbers required, ordnance officers did a bit of direct recruiting. Auguste was plucked from the Petit Moulin Rouge. He was directed to the Bonaparte Barracks to become the *chef de cuisine* of the 2nd Section of the Headquarters headed by Colonel d'Andlau. M. Bouniol, Auguste's friend, was also taken on to be his assistant. Their friend Fagette had already arrived at the barracks and was assigned to the 1st Section HQ.[2]

In the afternoon following the departure of the Algerians, Auguste and Jérémie Bouniol left the barracks with the 6th Company of Remounts, the back up for the cavalry, and entrained for Metz, where they arrived on

25 July 1870. Bouniol was ordered to go immediately to the Hôtel de l'Europe where the Headquarters officers were lodged. He was to act as *maître d'hôtel*, in reality a factotum. The troopers camped in a town square and Auguste stayed with them to do the cooking. It was three weeks before the cavalry moved on, when Auguste could take over the kitchen of the Officers' Mess in the hotel. There were eight members of the mess, officers ranging from captain to general and a civilian interpreter.

Napoléon III left the Empress Eugénie in Paris as Regent and stationed himself with his Headquarters staff in Metz. In the first week of August the French main army under Marshal MacMahon suffered several defeats and fell back towards the same town. Escoffier reports that on 14 August battle was joined at Borny on the eastern outskirts of Metz. The Emperor and his staff retired towards Verdun, stopping first at the village of Moulin-lès-Metz, a matter of four kilometres to the west.[3]

At the height of the battle on the east of the city, Auguste's Headquarters section received orders to move immediately to Moulin-lès-Metz. Auguste had no time even to change from his whites into uniform. In any case, his first thought was for his food supplies. He had to leave most of his precious stocks, but managed to load his wagon with a large piece of beef and some general provisions. The road was so obstructed with troops moving back to new positions that the short journey to Moulin took eight hours. Auguste's section eventually set up camp at the edge of the village near the railway line from Reims – which was under construction.

It was near midnight but he did not feel like sleeping. He worried about how he was going to produce meals in the immediate future, having abandoned the bulk of his stocks. So many troops had passed through, stripping the area, that there was little hope of replenishment from local sources. It was one of those warm nights of the dog days of summer, 'so dear to vagabonds and railwaymen' wrote Auguste. He and Jérémie Bouniol sat outside their tent discussing their culinary difficulties. The immediate problem was what to do about the piece of beef which Auguste had reserved for his *pièce de résistance* the next day. With the enemy all around them, as he put it, they were likely to be moved out at any time; setting up his kitchen with its stove was out of the question.

'My decision was quickly taken', he reports. 'Great dangers give birth to great resolutions.' They immediately set about constructing a primitive spit of thick branches cut from the railway's hedge, and started a midnight cooking session. The fire and the smell of roasting beef gathered spectators, but their intense interest soon had Auguste and Jérémie drawing protective sabres. Jérémie jumped at one, a French soldier of the Algerian Light Infantry, a Zouave, who came too close. He refrained from slicing off his head but lunged with the penetrating thrust of soldierly invective. The Zouave retreated, swearing on his beard that he had only wanted a light for his pipe.

Early in the morning, Auguste procured some eggs from a farm nearby and then, at seven o'clock, the order came that they were to move off at nine. As it might be some time before the next meal, he served a substantial breakfast, pleased with his decision to cook the beef the night before:

Sardines à l'huile
Saucisson
Oeufs à la coque
Le roastbeef cuit à point
Salade de pommes de terre
Café
Fine Champagne

Not bad for a scratch meal in the middle of a field, virtually under the guns of the enemy – but you don't save the champagne for later when it might be the enemy that drinks it.

Soon after breakfast there was a commotion in the village. A division of Prussian cavalry had been seen manoeuvring across the river, the Moselle, near the château de Frescati where the Emperor had his Headquarters. He was in danger of being cut off from the main army. As the Prussian cannon opened up, Napoleon and his staff took to their horses and departed towards Gravelotte.

The alert delayed the departure of Auguste's section until midday. They got to Gravelotte, ten kilometres away, at six o'clock that evening. This time they did set up the kitchen. Bouniol went off to find water. It was a scarce commodity anyway in high summer, and now most wells had been drained dry by the great influx of men and horses. Bouniol found a well that still had a small quantity of muddy water. Its owner, understandably, refused him access until Bouniol mentioned that he was thinking of bringing his companions along with their horses. He took a few litres that Auguste was able to clear with a small filter he had brought with him from Paris.

The problem of the main dish for the evening meal was solved when they spotted a rabbit in a field. Auguste relates how they stalked it like Red Indians. He thought it might have been the last rabbit in the area and named it Le lapin de Gravelotte. He pondered for some time how to cook this delicacy. In the end he decided, 'There's a war on and it's getting late', and got out his frying-pan. He skinned the rabbit, cut it into pieces and fried it in pork fat with six large, finely chopped onions. After suitable seasoning, a glass of cognac and some white wine went to make a sauce – a French cook down to his military bootstraps, Auguste had made his priority the saving of his stocks of wine and brandy. He served chips with the dish. Other courses were: onion soup, tinned sardines and tunny fish, and then cheese and coffee to finish.[4]

The one rabbit would have provided very small portions for each of the hungry officers back to dinner from their engagements with the Prussians. Auguste records only that 'our officers found it delicious'. Their appreciation pleased him, particularly as he recognised their preoccupation with the military situation – as senior officers they were well aware that a large and crucial battle was likely the next day.

Early in the morning, Tuesday 16 August, the Emperor and his staff left for the main army Headquarters at Verdun, leaving Marshal Bazaine commanding the Army of the Rhine. At half past nine Auguste served a lunch in the open air using the remains of the cold roast beef with chips. There was an hors-d'oeuvre, and they finished with cheese and Turkish coffee.[5] As he was serving the coffee, there was a sudden roar of gunfire. The officers abandoned their cups, ran to their horses, mounted and were away at the gallop. The battle went on for twelve hours.

During the day, Auguste's section had to move half a mile along the road towards Verdun to encamp behind a farmhouse, on a hillside facing Gravelotte, next to a field dressing station.[6] The war became real for Auguste. The battle was in sight and wounded men were being brought in. Among the first he saw was a young soldier severely wounded in the arm – who insisted on keeping hold of his rifle despite its badly bent barrel. Auguste gave him a glass of rum and talked to him while he was awaiting attention. The soldier was not only a cook, a *pâtissier*, but also from Auguste's home region.

In the late afternoon some twenty men appeared suddenly on the ridge above the camp and made their way down, firing across the slope as they came. Presumably the enemy were approaching. An officer galloped off to find out what was happening. It turned out though that the riflemen were stragglers from various regiments, malingerers, shooting hares running in panic from the battlefield. Auguste would have been delighted to see wild life still available for the pot, but he wrote: 'I would have preferred to have kept silence about these men of little honour who wasted their ammunition in hunting hare, but I had to emphasise such cowardice in comparison with the bravery of the soldiers of the 43rd who at that moment were charging the enemy with bayonets.'[7]

As all this was going on, three wounded *cuirassiers* rode in; one even had his nose partially shot away. They were excited and could scarcely wait to get back to the battle. No sooner had they been roughly bandaged than they remounted and were away at full gallop shouting *'Vive la France!'*

At ten o'clock that night the battle was at last over and the Germans had been pushed back towards Ars-sur-Moselle. The officers of Auguste's section came back one by one; none had been lost or wounded. Auguste served supper in the open air. It was a dark night and windy, and Bouniol went around 'swearing and cursing like a heathen' trying to keep candles alight. But everybody was in excellent spirits and the officers sat around recounting the events of the day.

One story was that at a critical point in the battle Marshall Bazaine and his staff had suddenly found themselves surrounded by several squadrons of German cavalry, The easy successes these hussars had experienced so far had made them audacious. Undaunted, the officers of the Headquarters staff took their sabres in hand 'like common soldiers' and charged. The hussars scattered immediately. 'If these Teutons had really been brave,' Auguste wrote, 'the Marshal and his staff could have been taken without a blow being struck.' A newspaper commented later that it would have been better for France if Bazaine had been taken prisoner then.[8] At two in the morning, supper scarcely finished, the order was received to fall back on Metz immediately. Auguste wrote that this was Bazaine's misjudgement that lost the war. It would have been better to have reunited the Rhine Army with the main forces under MacMahon at Châlons.[9]

The next day there was a truce of sorts while dead and wounded were collected from the battlefield. Again, Auguste thought this was a mistake. The Prussians, he said, were a dishonourable lot who would simply use the time to regroup and bring in fresh troops. This indeed they did and Bazaine, slow on the uptake according to Auguste, retired towards Metz while the enemy moved to cut them off from the main French forces.[10] The next morning, the 18th, a determined attempt was made to break out from Metz and the battle of Saint-Privat began.[11] The Prussians who won it called it the battle of Gravelotte.

Auguste prepared a generous meal that day, although his officers' thoughts were mostly elsewhere:

Hors d'oeuvres
Oeufs à la poêle
Blanquette de veau
Côtelettes de mouton et pommes frites
Café – Liqueurs

On the 19th, Auguste's section, No. 2 HQ, moved to le Ban-Saint-Martin, at the gates of Metz, where Marshal Bazaine had set up his Headquarters.

They were soon joined by No. 1 HQ and shared quarters in the house of
M. Beaubourg, a Latin teacher. Auguste was pleased to welcome his friend
Fagette, the chef to No. 1 HQ, but he says nothing on how their friendship
survived sharing a kitchen. An outhouse was arranged as a dormitory that
the two chefs, their assistants and the officers' batmen shared.

There were several battles over the next few days, the Rhine Army trying,
without success, to break through the Prussian lines to join MacMahon. By
the 28th it was clear they were shut in. The army had seen to provisioning
the town but, after eight days of blockade, food supplies were low: there
was no butter, and horse was beginning to appear at table. Spirits were high,
however. Most people had no thought of a siege. MacMahon would soon
win through and bring in butter, lamb and tender steaks.

Auguste had been provident. He says he had 'had an intuition of what
was going to happen'.[12] In an enclave at the bottom of the garden, he had
gathered about fifty chickens, some geese, ducks, young turkeys, half a dozen
rabbits, two small pigs, a sheep and a goat. He also had a large stock of jam
– confiture de mirabelles de Metz – he could use as sugar, which was
unobtainable. He had a good stock of tinned sardines and tunny fish. He
did later run out of salt, but he kept going for a time on brine from the
tannery and pure salt from the pharmacy.

Before shortages set in, he had also bought some piglets in the market
that he made into pâté. He served this as Pâté du siège de Metz. Nearly a
quarter of a century later he recalled how he went about this preparation:

> Having treated the animal with the care necessary to render it suitable for cooking,
> I made a well-seasoned forcemeat from the leg meat and the other fatty joints.
>
> The rest of the carcass I boned and cut the leaner parts, including the skin, into
> strips. Having well seasoned all this I quickly browned it and added fine herbes,
> a glass of cognac, vin blanc or Madeira, whichever was available, and some truffles.
> This I left to cool in a terrine.
>
> Then I lined a mould (borrowed from M. Beaubourg, our host) with pastry,
> spread a layer of forcemeat, then one of the truffled meat and skin strips, and
> then another of forcemeat and so on to fill the mould. I then covered the pâté
> with thinly rolled out pastry – slightly moistened, lacking a glazing – and cooked
> it in the usual way.[13]

Auguste was caught up in the last sortie made by the army out of Metz, on
31 August. With the Headquarters staff, he spent the night in the open. 'It
was freezing and we suffered horribly', he said.[14] It was right at the end of
August. In the morning, he and his section were positioned alongside an
artillery battery getting into position. It was no sooner set up than it was
attacked from the flank and put out of action by Prussian artillery. Auguste
acquired a Prussian carbine on this occasion, which he intended to keep as

a war souvenir. He didn't see his officers again until the following lunchtime. He knocked up a scratch meal:

Oeufs à la coque
Foie de boeuf aux fines herbes
Viande froide
Fromage de gruyère

He says of that last engagement, 'Military historians have described this Battle of Servigny and its consequences. All I have to say is that shells came down like rain and it was the last time I went out of Metz until the end of the siege.'[15] Back in the town, rationing had been imposed. One order, however, calling in all milking cows for the use of the army, was quickly reversed when the cry went up that the milk must go to the women and children.

On 2 September Napoleon III, Marshal MacMahon and 83,000 French troops capitulated at Sedan. Those beleaguered in Metz heard the news on 7 September, and also that the Prussians were closing in on Paris. The same day a balloon post was started out of Metz. Auguste attributes the idea to a Captain Rossel. Letters were written and addressed on tiny pieces of paper, each the shape and size of a cigarette paper. These were bundled and labelled to the effect: 'Please will the person who finds this packet take it to the nearest post office.' Each packet was attached to a small balloon and released to travel with the wind. Many got through.

The next day, the commanding officer issued an order that each cavalry regiment must provide forty horses for slaughter to feed the army. Those losing their mounts were given infantry rifles. The remaining beef was reserved for the sick and wounded.

On 11 September, M. Debaino, a civilian interpreter with Headquarters who had diplomatic status, was sent off to seek news. He presented himself at a Prussian advance post where he was arrested and taken to Ars-sur-Moselle. The Hessian officers there allowed him no external contacts and sent him back with the blackest possible picture of conditions in France.[16] He did learn, however, that the Emperor had been formally deposed in his absence, and that the Third Republic had been declared in Paris.

By the 18th, rations in Metz were thin. Auguste was still able to produce his *pièces de resistance* using his allowance of horsemeat.[17] They were *pot au feu* or *braisé*, 'enriched' with macaroni and a range of dried vegetables – lentils, haricots and a purée of peas. The animals butchered were always those in the poorest condition, and the meat was not of the best. He always took the precaution of blanching it, which he said removed the bitter taste.

Deep now into his reserves, he was still keeping up a good standard at table but with a careful eye to the future. At dinner there was always a soup, a second course and a roast – apart from his horsemeat rations he could call on the inmates of his farmyard at the bottom of the garden. Then followed a salad, fruit and finally coffee and cognac. 'Nothing Sardanapalian, but it seemed good at the time.'[18]

Lunch he nearly always produced from the leftovers from dinner of the previous evening. 'Certainly,' he says, 'I reached heights never before attained when it came to using up scraps. My colleagues were amazed.' He went on, 'As for ourselves – Bouniol, Fagette, his assistant and me – we lunched much as the officers, for example, on superb *gratins* of poultry scraps with chopped macaroni bound with a few spoonfuls of *béchamel*. One day there was great jubilation among us select few when I managed with great difficulty and at high price to acquire some little pike fished from the Moselle. I made a fish stew.'[19]

Fresh vegetables were rarities, and by 20 September potatoes had disappeared altogether – although some appeared later, dug at night by troops from under the noses of the enemy in their forward positions. Auguste had a stock of turnips which he used in many ways – but none better, he said, than with a duck from his farmyard. Some of his hens laid regularly, and he used eggs to make the Sunday delicacy, *à la coque* or poached, and served either on a bed of endive or on minced horse meat leftovers with a tarragon sauce. Early in October, the cavalry's horses were still providing a reasonable meat ration but there was not much to go with it, either for the troops or the civilians of Metz. Auguste's chief complaint was that there was now no salt left. He blamed the high incidence of dysentery in the town on the bad rye bread, black and heavy, and on horsemeat, both cooked without salt.

The siege was by no means a static affair. Engagements with the enemy continued in which the French had some successes. Once a surprise artillery bombardment of a farm used by the Prussians was followed up by the French infantry who took seven hundred prisoners. They could have captured cannon, too, but they had no harnesses with which to tow them off. However, with the defeat of the main French army, relief of Metz was an impossibility. Auguste killed his last piglet on 20 October and the town was almost out of food. The end was near. It came on 27 October. The Prussians marched in on the 28th, the soldiers of the French Army of the Rhine became prisoners of war and Auguste had to throw his Prussian carbine into the Moselle.

Right up to the last day, Auguste struggled to keep up his culinary standards. He still managed to produce entremets. One, which he called *Riz à la Lorraine*, he made with rice cooked in goat's milk. He layered this in a timbale with his precious jam, the *Confiture de mirabelles de Metz*, topped it with a compôte of apple sprinkled with crushed military biscuit, and crisped it in the oven. He served it laced with kirsch.[20] He seemed to have an inexhaustible supply of wines and spirits, but on the last day his food reserves were down to:

> One chicken
> One pot of beef extract
> One tin of tunny fish
> One goat

He sold the goat.[21]

Interlude 3

Lobster Tales

'Tis the voice of the lobster; I heard him declare,
"You have baked me too brown, I must sugar my hair".'

Lewis Carroll

By the time Auguste got into the culinary business, eating out at restaurants had long been a sophisticated entertainment, and in his earliest years in cook's whites he was preparing complex dishes for *gourmands*. One of his early creations was to become a restaurant speciality and have a profound effect on his career. The dish was *Langouste niçoise*, which he made first at Chez Philippe in Nice.[1] When later he moved to the Restaurant Favre, Chez Philippe continued to feature the dish. Auguste also promoted it at the Favre but, in deference to Chez Philippe, renamed it *Langouste provençale*.[2] He often referred to it later in life as 'my first *chef d'oeuvre*'.[3] It finds no place, however, under either name in his famous cook books.

He took the dish with him to his first job in Paris at the Petit Moulin Rouge, where it was again adopted as a speciality of the restaurant. But first it had to be promoted to the lobster class, better suited to the upper-crust clientele of the Petit Moulin: a name suggesting a country recipe would not have been suitable for a dish intended for royal tables. Escoffier changed it to *Homard à l'américaine*, although he would sometimes include *langoustes* early in a menu, for example as *Petites langoustes à l'américaine*.

The French *homard* is the true lobster (*homaridae*). The *langouste* is the

spiny lobster, crawfish or sea crayfish (*palinuridae*). Both have five pairs of
legs. The true lobster has claws on the first three pairs. The two at the front
are asymmetric and much enlarged, the main weapons of this 'knight in
armour' of the seas – one, the massive hammer claw, is used to hold prey
to be cut up by the other, the razor sharp shear claw. The dark pigment in
the shell of the lobster is a compound of red carotinoid, as found in carrots,
and a protein. Boiling releases the carotinoid from the protein to show as
the familiar lobster red. Lobsters live on the sea bottom, but they can swim
– using the tail and small swimming legs along the abdomen – backwards.
Young lobsters are eaten by dogfish, cod and other predators, but the larger
ones only have man as an enemy – except when they moult, when they are
easy prey. They take their sex missionary style and, not that there is necessarily a connection, they can live for fifty years and attain a weight of 40lbs.

The name *Homard à l'américaine* was not new, and many people laid
claim to originating it and the dish. Pierre Fraisse, for example, chef-pro-
prietor of the Restaurant Noël Peters in Paris in the 1870s, tells of a lobster
dish he once concocted in desperation for some Americans who turned up
late for dinner when he had little left to give them. When they asked the
name of the dish, since they were Americans and he had in fact run the
Café Américain in Chicago, he replied, *Homard à l'américaine*. It is possible
that he had merely prepared the lobster dish in his usual manner since he
was born in Sète in the Languedoc where *Langouste à la sètoise* bears a
striking resemblance to *Homard à l'américaine*.

Philéas Gilbert was on Auguste's side: he denied other's claims to priority.[4]
The Restaurant Bonnefoy, he wrote, had certainly served the dish before
1870 as *Homard Bonnefoy*. But, he pointed out, the dish was in any case a
transformation of Auguste Escoffier's earlier *Langouste niçoise* – his recipe
was published in 1867 by Jules Gouffé.[5]

Escoffier does not himself claim the *à l'américaine* tag as his own, but he
has something to say on the subject: his hand-written recipe has survived.[6] He wrote:

> There is no well-established formula for lobster cooked *à l'américaine*. The method
> of preparation varies from place to place, but here is the simplest one, which I
> think the best and particularly easy to prepare.
>
> The first essential is to have a live lobster. For four people, choose one 1 to 2kg.
> Kill it by plunging it into boiling water for a few minutes, or asphyxiate it by
> shutting it in a hot oven for two minutes.
>
> Remove the large claws and crack them to extract the meat.
>
> Cut the body in two along its length; dispose of the sac found at the top of the
> head, which usually contains gravel.
>
> Put aside on a plate the intestines, the green part to the side of the sac.

Divide each half of the lobster into three and season the pieces with salt and freshly milled pepper.

Heat in a sauté pan 4 spoonfuls of olive oil and two of butter. Put in the pieces of lobster and sauté them until the flesh is well sealed and the shell has turned red. Add 2 finely chopped shallots, a few spoonfuls of good Armagnac and 2 decilitres of white wine; reduce the volume to half. Add 4 or 5 medium-sized tomatoes, peeled, seeds removed, and chopped; mash a large pinch of chopped parsley with a piece of garlic the size of a pea and add – alternatively add a pinch of chopped tarragon. Finish with 4 spoonfuls of meat jelly. Cover the pan and cook for 18 to 20 minutes at low heat.

Meanwhile, mix the green intestines that were put aside with 4 spoonfuls of butter, the juice of half a lemon, and a dash of red wine.

When serving, arrange the lobster pieces on a plate with the shells beneath and pour the sauce over.

Homard à l'américaine is still prepared like this. Different chefs have their slight idiosyncratic variations – some even declare the lobster should be cut up while alive – but their dishes are usually recognisably similar to Escoffier's simplified version. The recipe has survived more than a century – in which time we have advanced, if that is the word, from horse and buggy to spaceships – indication enough of the greatness of a dish good enough to launch Escoffier on his unparalleled career.

A long period in Auguste's career was spent in England at the Savoy and later the Carlton Hotels. Since during this time a high proportion of his customers were Americans, it was reasonable that he should include in his repertoire Lobster Newberg, or Newburg, as it was and still is alternatively spelt – and even New-Burg in the first English edition of Escoffier's *Le Guide Culinaire*. For the American customers from the East Coast it was a dish from home. Its first public appearance was probably in the early 1890s in New York's Delmonico restaurant – which had a French chef. It was at first called Lobster Wenberg in honour of a Mr Ben Wenberg who had popularised cooking at the table in a chafing dish. He was a customer, and a rich one.

It turned out that Mr Wenberg did not feel honoured by this dedication: perhaps he didn't like his lobster cooked that way. To avoid offence, two letters in the name were interchanged to arrive at the renowned but impersonal Newberg.[7] An alternative version of the story is that the name was changed when Mr Wenberg was disgraced. Whatever the reason, the name was changed.

The original sauce, made with Madeira wine and cream thickened with egg yolks, was in the French style. Escoffier's adaptation was to enrich it and to give it a finer flavour. He has left us one recipe starting with a live lobster and another for a lobster that has been boiled. This gives us a choice according to availability – it isn't easy to buy live ones inland, and they do draw attention to themselves in the bus. It also panders to the squeamish who prefer to think of lobsters as decorative inanimate objects in plastic vermilion, rather than squirming, black, claw-clacking creatures they have to dispatch in some alarming fashion.

Escoffier would normally have bought live lobsters, and his recipes imply that your dish will taste better if the animal is killed immediately before it is cooked – you can certainly tell the difference between one that has died in your honour and one that has spent months in a freezing lobster mortuary. In his day, before universal refrigeration, he probably felt it safer to know how long the animal had been dead. There are still restaurants where the lobster is brought out squirming on a plate, too weak now to stretch the rubber bands on its claws. Does anyone want such spurious proof that their lobster is to be killed specially for them? Usually, men smile with cold teeth and nod their acceptance while women shudder and turn away.

You might find it difficult to detect a difference in a dish of this sort whether you started with a live lobster, one killed for you that morning, or one from the supermarket – which buys frozen farmed lobsters in bulk and arranges them in neat rows on the cold slab, cooked, blushing red, and as appealing as puppies in a window.

This is Escoffier's recipe using cooked lobster:

Homard à la Newburg

1 Lobster (2–2½lb.)

Court bouillon

Salt, pepper	½ pint Madeira wine
½ pint cream	3 egg yolks
2½ oz butter	

Cook the lobster in *court bouillon* for 20–25min. Remove the meat from the tail, discarding the membrane underneath, and cut into even slices. Arrange in a well-buttered sauté pan, add a little salt and pepper and heat through, turning once.

Add the Madeira and reduce by about two thirds.

Just before serving, add cream and egg yolks mixed. Draw the pan to the side of the stove and dot on butter a little at a time. As the yolks cook, the sauce will thicken. Serve at once in a hot dish.

The butter dotted on at the end is to add a glaze to the sauce and it adds gloss to the taste if it is not mixed in. There seems little reason to take extravagance to the extreme of throwing the claws away. Unless, like Escoffier, you have other uses for them, it would not be disloyal to the Master to crack the shells, extract the meat, slice it and include it with the tail meat in the sauté.

Modern cooks have their own ideas on how to adapt the recipe to suit themselves, current fashions and the materials available. One modernisation of the original changes little, but includes the claw meat. It suggests using dry Sercial Madeira rather than one of the sweeter wines grown at lower levels on the island.[8]

On the plate, rice is an excellent non-detracting accompaniment, but in the glass you can extend extravagance to vintage champagne or a fine white burgundy. Think what a wine even just a little on the better side of middle-of-the-road would have cost had you gone out for the meal. The recipe does need more attention than one might give to grilling a steak. It calls for some extravagance and care in making the sauce, but in the end it is a dish fit for any table and sheer delight to eat.

An American has commented on French adaptations of Lobster Newburg – note his spelling – an 'indigenous American dish'.[9] Quoting (in 1956) a current French cookbook, he says, 'You start by boiling a lobster in consommé and you then dress it with a sauce velouté enriched with curry powder. Finally, and this is really beyond credence, you are exhorted to throw "a glass of burning whiskey" on the remains of the unfortunate crustacean, which you finally entomb in a curried rice.' He doesn't name the book or its author.

It has been said, but not too loudly, that to dress up a lobster in these ways is to lose its essential delicate flavour. The outspoken Edouard de Pomiane says distinctly that the taste of *homard à l'américaine* is a 'gastronomic cacophony'.[10] In putting forward a recipe for the dish he says the sauce is too highly spiced and too rich in tomato and brandy.[11] He says, however, that one can eat the dish from time to time – which, after all, is all most of us would do anyway – 'but just take the right medicines afterwards to avoid getting gout'.

Other advice is that small English Channel lobsters weighing around half a pound each – *demoiselles de Cherbourg* – are best cooked *à la nage*, in highly seasoned wine and sea-water *court bouillon*, and served, still warm, with melted butter.[12] Large lobsters, the rule goes on, should be served either *á l'américaine* or Thermidor. Then there are those who say that, unless you are fond of well-vulcanised rubber, lobster should only be cooked in *court bouillon*. *Chacun à son gout*.

The Thermidor process for the lobster was probably named by the Café de Paris around the middle of the nineteenth century. The word, from the

Greek, adds up to 'gift of warmth'. It first appeared in France in 1793 as the name of the eleventh month of the new Revolutionary calendar (19 July to 17 August on ours), when it is warm in France.

There are plenty of proposals for the origin of the dish, for example that an army chef invented it for Napoleon who named it Thermidor because of its mustard content. It would be difficult in this case to account for the fifty years it took to appear in public. Nevertheless, Napoleon's mess could easily have been the origin of the dish under a different name. Certainly, the recipe for such a dish appeared in England in 1804 as Dr Hunter's Stuffed Lobster (none of your pretentious French names in those days):

> Boil the lobster (live) for 15 minutes, cool, split in half lengthways and remove claws. Extract the meat – less stomach and intestines – from the shell and cut into half-inch cubes. Make a cream sauce from 1 tbsp each of butter and flour with 1-cup half-and-half cream and milk. Add half a tsp. anise extract. Season and add lobster meat.
>
> Smooth the mixture into the half shells, sprinkle with bread-crumbs, dot with butter, and grill to a delicate brown.[13]

As fast as one establishes a priority, however, someone will find an earlier example. A quick look back to the first century for instance shows the Romans making a credible ancestor of the Thermidor:

> Brown a chopped spring-onion. Add pepper, lovage, caraway, cumin, Jericho date, honey, vinegar, wine, liquamen, olive oil, defrutum, mustard. Serve with boiled sea crayfish.[14]

Some plump for the Restaurant Thermidor in Paris as the origin of the name – but the dish appeared decades before the restaurant. It is more likely that Tony Girod, the chef at the Café de Paris, dedicated the dish to an important customer, Victorien Sardou, who wrote the play *Thermidor*. Tony Girod gave the recipe to Prosper Montagné for his encyclopedia of food, wine and cooking.[15]

Escoffier states his version of *Homard Thermidor* in simple terms:

> Split the lobster in half lengthways, season and gently grill, then remove the flesh from the shell and cut into thick slices on the slant.
>
> Place some *sauce crème* finished with a little English mustard in the bottom of the two half shells, replace the slices of lobster neatly on top and coat with the sauce. Glaze lightly in a hot oven or under the salamander.[16]

Escoffier's *sauce crème* is a slight reduction of Béchamel sauce with cream and a little lemon juice.[17] His formula follows Tony Girod's original except for replacing chervil and tarragon with thyme and nutmeg in the Béchamel.

Modern chefs still make the dish this way but some apply the label to preparations far removed from the original. It can be found degraded with mushrooms and paprika, Vermouth, and Parmesan and no mustard – nor even anise. The 'Thermidor' often seems a pose and the lobster a superfluous afterthought.

4

Prisoner's Dilemma

'Horsemeat is delicious when one is in the
right circumstances to appreciate it.'

Auguste Escoffier

There is no doubt the Prussian victory had a deep and lasting effect on
Escoffier, but he kept his faith in France. On patriotism and heroism his
language might seem to us overblown, Kiplingesque:

> Refute on all occasions those who scorn our national honour, and feel at the
> bottom of your hearts the imperishable hope, the absolute certainty that we shall
> one day again be conquerors. Our beloved France is still what it was over centuries
> past and will raise again the heroes and military geniuses who will achieve great
> victories under our flag.[1]

But this was not just the emotional reaction of a young man at the moment
of defeat. He was writing in maturity nearly a quarter of a century after the
war. Similarly he minced no words when it came to placing the blame for
the surrender of the Rhine Army: 'The army at Metz was capable of the
greatest deeds since it had ... a corps of officers of established bravery and
soldiers ready to make the ultimate sacrifice. Bazaine didn't know how or
didn't want to use them ...' Auguste goes on to say that the Council of
War, which had merely imprisoned this 'traitor to his country', had treated
him with extraordinary leniency. If, instead of generals, the Council had
been made up of NCOs or ordinary soldiers Bazaine had commanded, the
verdict would have been different: 'military degradation, followed by a dozen
bullets from a firing squad'. As it turned out, on 10 December 1873, the
court militarily degraded Bazaine and sentenced him to death. Marshal
MacMahon, then President of the Republic, commuted the sentence to
twenty years imprisonment. Bazaine escaped after a few months. He died
abroad in poverty fourteen years later.

When the news of capitulation was received in Metz on 27 October,
feelings ran high among the defenders who had suffered the siege so resol-
utely – in only three months the enemy had overrun France. They blamed
Bazaine. One officer, Captain Yung, galloped off on his horse in a great rage

to tell the commanders of the regiments of the line and to exhort them not to give up their arms. He was too late. He returned to Headquarters in the early hours of the morning covered in mud in such a suicidal state of mind that his colleagues thought it best to relieve him of his arms. Yung remained in his room in a state of collapse for three days, and Auguste was told to look after him while the evacuation of the French troops went on. Jérémie Bouniol stayed too.

There was some gain from the delay: the two men were able to make their own way to the station at Metz to take the train for Mayence (Mainz) in Germany. Unlike their comrades who went off earlier, they didn't have to walk shamefully in a long column of prisoners of war between rows of armed Prussians lining the route. The reason for their relative freedom was that the terms of the capitulation allowed the French officers to keep their servants and to be responsible to the Prussians for them. Auguste was still to be in the service of Colonel d'Andlau while Jérémie Bouniol was assigned elsewhere. Headquarters staff had taken on soldiers as secretaries at the beginning of the war. These were educated young men mostly, as Auguste put it, 'from very great families'. Since in captivity these embryo aristocrats would have been treated as common soldiers, they were given the acting rank of lieutenant. They were then entitled to a servant and Bouniol became one of these. This seemed quite a proper arrangement to Auguste – things were different then.

Auguste and Jérémie Bouniol were to rejoin their officers in Mayence. Their friend Fagette was accompanying a Colonel Levral to Hamburg. The train had steam up and departed as soon as they were aboard. It was the last one to leave Metz with prisoners. They were off into exile. Auguste says:

> We travelled through the desolate countryside under sombre autumn skies absorbed in our thoughts. We recalled with bitterness the trip from Paris to Metz only a few months before when we were so cheerful and full of hope, with no suspicion of the series of disasters that was to follow.[2]

The first stop was Nancy. There the platforms were guarded by Prussians – not to prevent the escape of prisoners, but to protect them. There had been ugly scenes when previous convoys of prisoners had gone through. As it was, a 'stupidly ferocious and dissolute French mob ... threw stones at the train, shouting, "Down with the cowards! Death to Bazaine! Long live the Prussians!"' Auguste goes on, 'The women in this ragged crowd were more savage than the men'. 'Cowards?' he queried, '. . . these men who had fought so bravely ... and who had wept when forced to give up their weapons?'[3] The Prussian soldiers made some attempt to control the mob but they were clearly delighted with events. 'What more could they have desired' thought Auguste, 'than to see French soldiers being insulted in France by the ... French?'

They arrived at Mayence the next day, at midnight. The Prussians had not provided them with food on the journey, but they had been free to buy what they wanted at the stations. At Mayence, Auguste and Jérémie again found themselves free to go into town. The hotels were full to overflowing, but they were pleased to find a corner of a stable in one of them where they could spend the rest of the night.[4] They could, of course, have taken the opportunity to slip quietly away. What wouldn't prisoners of the Germans in more recent wars, digging escape tunnels with their fingernails, have given for such an opportunity? Auguste and his friend, however, had the worry that the officers responsible for them might then have been shot by the Prussians.

First thing in the morning they were out around the town making the most of their liberty. Auguste tried to find out how prisoners were being treated in the town, but was frustrated by his lack of German. 'I had to express myself to the Teutons with gestures', he says. He did better when he had bought a phrase book. He found that their own officers had already left Mayence for Hamburg. Colonel d'Andlau's batman had stayed on with the colonel's two horses, one of which he had sold to buy fodder for the other and food for himself. There was nothing for it, they would have to find a job of some sort. Auguste was concerned for Jérémie, who was at the end of his tether. He had to find him a job. 'His moans were heartrending', says Auguste. Eventually he found a *pâtissier* on Ludovic Strasse who would take them on – he was no lover of the French but doubtless recognised they were in no position to bargain over wages. The snag was they had to get a permit from the military commander to work in the town. Auguste expected no difficulty, but he was wrong. They got as far as the commander's guardroom and were promptly escorted between two large Prussian soldiers in spiked helmets, not to the great man's presence but to the citadel. There they were confined with 250 other prisoners in some discomfort and with very little food.[5]

Three days of this and they were transferred to a tented prisoner-of-war camp outside the town. The first person Auguste met in the camp was the drum major of the Turcos he had last seen leaving the Bonaparte Barracks in Paris exhorting his companions to take a good look at the gates they might never see again. The bandsman was a permit-holder and was just going into town where he worked. Auguste persuaded him to explain to the *pâtissier* why he and Jérémie Bouniol had not returned, and to go and see the military commander on Jérémie's behalf. Three days later Jérémie was making gingerbread in the establishment on Ludovic Strasse.

At the camp there was one meal a day, potato soup, and bread was made once a fortnight – each loaf had the date it was made baked on it The soup might have some scraps of beef added or some old ham with rancid fat, lentils, split peas or haricots. It was all prepared without care or cleanliness – 'it was not rare to find fat, white worms in this frightful stew'. Twenty-four prisoners peeled more than 500 kilos of potatoes each Saturday. They threw these into a large beer cask and their job was done. The Prussian cooks threw in a few buckets of water. Auguste says: 'You can guess how well the potatoes were washed.'[6]

The soup was passable at the beginning of the week, when the potatoes from the top of the cask were used. By Friday the potatoes sitting in stagnant dirty water for a week were rotten and only severe hunger held back physical revulsion. The meal was delivered to half the prisoners in the morning and to the rest in the afternoon.[7] The peculiarity of the system was that the order was reversed each week so that those who had had their soup at eight thirty in the morning would have to wait until nine in the evening of the following day for their next ration; more than thirty-six hours without food.

On one such evening, Auguste recalls, raucous trumpet had sounded to announce the arrival of the soup trolley with its armed guards – the trolley, he says, was like those used then to collect the greasy dish-water from the restaurants in Paris. Each section of prisoners had to send up a man with one mess tin to collect the ration for them all. It was raining and one 'poor devil' slipped in the mud. His team, with 'frightful maledictions, energetic swearing and furious vociferation', scrabbled around in the mire for the few solids from the spilt soup. Then, risking the guns of the guards, they made a mass attack on the soup trolley scraping at the walls of its cask with their hands to recover the last residues of food.

Auguste marvelled at the tenacity of these prisoners, battle-fatigued survivors of the butchery of Gravelotte, Saint-Privat and Serviguy, and of the privations of Metz under siege. Some succumbed. They could count the dead from the salvos of musketry fired as each corpse was committed to its foreign grave in the cemetery nearby. Auguste makes little of his own discomforts, although he mentions that he shared the hardships of his companions. There was always food to be had for those with money, but he leaves no doubt that those prisoners dependent on the camp food suffered terribly at first.

There was some improvement later as more people obtained permits to work in town, and as various forms of self-help were developed in the camp. The town workers brought in supplies (including alcohol) for sale to prisoners with money, while prisoners made their own soup from filched potatoes and scraps, and generally, with ingenuity, improved their lot. There was also organised work that took prisoners out of the camp. Auguste was involved at one stage in unloading boats on the Rhine.[8] The cargoes were mostly of timber for building huts to replace the tents they lived in. He also took part in construction work. Another routine task was for a team of four men to fetch water morning and evening to augment the camp supply. The water pump was on the road into town. Once when Auguste was on this duty, another member of the team, Lecoq, with whom Auguste was friendly, told him how by an incredible bit of luck he had been saved from the firing squad.

Lecoq had been one of a team of *franc-tireurs* under the command of a captain. They had been trapped in a farm building by the Prussians. The snipers had soon run out of ammunition and with no further hope of escape had surrendered. They were immediately lined up for mass execution. As the firing squad raised their carbines a German general came by who recognised the captain as a friend from Biarritz, where they had both holidayed. The general countermanded the execution order and the snipers were sent into captivity as ordinary prisoners of war.[9]

Auguste says, 'I liked Lecoq and we became friends'. The day Lecoq told his story was an important one for Auguste. While getting Jérémie Bouniol fixed up with work in town, Auguste had not been idle on his own behalf. He had written several letters to people of influence. Among them were the managers of the famous Kursaal in nearby Wiesbaden, MM. Jung and Traut. They were waiting to see him when he got back from his water-pump fatigue with Lecoq. They had the necessary authorisation papers for Auguste to go to work at the Kursaal. Armed with these, he could leave without escort as soon as he wanted.

'My kitbag was soon ready,' he says, 'and an hour later I left this place of misery and went into town, where, after visiting Bouniol, I took the train for Wiesbaden.' Wiesbaden was a popular spa resort and Auguste refers to the Kursaal as 'an establishment of great importance'. It was, however, in some decline since the banning of public gambling in Germany two years earlier, and there was no vacancy in the kitchens. Jung and Traut were French from Alsace and, in offering a non-existent job, they sought only to do what they could for a French prisoner in Germany. There was not much for him to do, but he helped around the kitchen, befriended by the *rôtisseur* he knew as Pierre, a Frenchman too old for military service.

It happened that Auguste was not left in this comparative idleness for more than a few days. The Prussians brought Marshal MacMahon to Wiesbaden as an internee along with the staff of his military headquarters. MacMahon was installed with his family in a villa on Sonnenberg Strasse. He had his own *chef de cuisine*, Jules Servis. Another villa, a hundred metres along the road, was assigned to his senior military staff, the Duke, d'Harcourt, the Marquis d'Abzac and others. When they asked M. Traut if he could provide a *chef de cuisine*, Auguste got the job.

A little later, the Count de Beaumont, the brother-in-law of MacMahon, arrived with his family. He also asked the Kursaal if they could provide a cook for his household. Auguste suggested Jérémie Bouniol, who, he said, 'was going grey making gingerbread in Mayence'. Bouniol arrived. 'It was a great reunion for us,' Auguste said, 'sheltered thereafter from the invective of German NCOs and far from the camp of misery where so many of our comrades were still in abject boredom.'

The kitchen arrangements at what Auguste still referred to as 'The Head-quarters' were quite good and provisions were in abundance and of good quality and variety. He said:

> I could have produced *la belle cuisine*, but in the circumstances the officers decided to confine themselves to plain fare. Lunch was eggs or fish followed by some meat with vegetables, an entremets or a dessert and finally coffee. Dinner was soup, fish of some sort, a roast joint of beef or mutton, with salad and vegetables, entremets and dessert, coffee.[10]

Venison, hare, partridge, and grouse were in abundance and Auguste found it difficult to restrain his enthusiasm to 'vary and extend my work', as he put it. He did sometimes let go a little: when fish was not available he would serve roast poultry or game.

Auguste admits with typical litotes that life in Wiesbaden 'would not have been too disagreeable' had it not been for the unhappy circumstances that had brought them there. As in Mayence, the locals were not actively friendly, but nor did they make it too obvious that their guests were in fact prisoners. Their captors were also courteous. The only formalities were a muster for a roll call twice a week – which Auguste was usually excused – and a seven o'clock evening curfew.[11]

Christmas came. The Terrible Year was nearly over, but 'blood still flowed at the gates of Paris and thousands of French prisoners of war wasted their lives in squalid camps all over Germany'.[12] Auguste, comfortably placed, had twinges of guilt when he thought of his less fortunate compatriots. As *chef de cuisine* to MacMahon's Headquarters, he had no difficulty getting a permit to take the train on Christmas Eve to visit his old companions in the camp at Mayence. 'I shall never forget the enthusiasm with which they welcomed me', he says, 'demanding news as though I had just come from their various villages.' Eventually they got down to the food and wine Auguste had brought. A camp bed was used as a table, lit with a single candle; they squatted on their heels around it. 'It was half-past nine when

I regretfully had to leave my unhappy comrades', he says. 'I felt as a matter of duty I should have spent Christmas night with them in the cheerless camp.'

After an armistice on 28 January 1871, a preliminary peace treaty was ratified on 1 March. Adolphe Thiers, head of the French provisional government in Versailles, appealed to Bismarck to release prisoners of war so that he could form an army to suppress the Commune in Paris and, when the peace treaty was signed on 14 March, French officers in Mayence were notified that they were free to leave for France. Other ranks had to wait a while, but one of the Headquarters generals got a pass for Auguste to go to Paris, provided he paid his own fare. The condition gave him little bother and he bought his ticket that day. He travelled with his civilian friend Pierre from the Kursaal, who wanted to return to France. They went first to Metz, where August called on the Beaubourg family and other friends in the town, and then on to Paris and 'liberty with unlimited horizons'.

Interlude 4

Solea Solea and Other Flatfish

'The sole is quite a clever fish
The way it fits an oval dish
With bones removed along the edges
Leaving room to put the veggies.'

Kenneth James

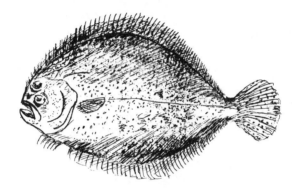

Solea solea is the common sole we call the Dover sole to distinguish it from the other hundred species in the family *Soleidae*. It is caught in the inshore waters of the eastern Atlantic and the Mediterranean, and is considered the best of the lot to eat. Like other bottom-feeding flatfish, it wears both its eyes on the same side of the body and so can use both while lying in the mud awaiting prey. It isn't born that way: on metamorphosis the starboard eye of the young fish migrates through the head to appear above the other one. Lying flat, the eyes are normally on the right of the mouth seen from the tail end.

The sole was the subject of one of Auguste Escoffier's first published recipes.[1] The dish was an extreme example of his dictum, 'Faites simple':

Filets de Sole à la Orly

Take fillets of sole, dip them in fresh milk and roll them in flour. Skewer them end to end in pairs and fry. Serve on a napkin with a separate *saucière* of tomato sauce.

Elizabeth Cleland had advised that in England a century and a quarter earlier, although not with the Orly fashion of a separate boat of sauce:

Flea them and drudge them with Flour, and get a Pan almost full of clarified Butter, or good Dripping of Beef, when it is boiling hot, put in the Soals and fry them a good Brown on both Sides; drain them very well from the Fat, put crisped Parsley and slices of Orange over them.[2]

In May 1878, a few years before releasing the secret of his fried sole, Auguste made his first trip to Normandy. He was on a course of army training. He says: 'I belonged to the Class of 1866, the last to have done seven years active service and the first to form part of the Territorial Army after *les désastres de l'Année Terrible.*' He spent a fortnight going through all the phases of military instruction from the simplest drills to battalion manoeuvres. Sunday was free, and he with some of his comrades decided to go out for the day.

One of his companions, the son of a local farmer, knew the district well. They made their way to a well-known auberge on the outskirts of Caen. Writing about this trip more than forty years later, Auguste didn't remember the name of the hostelry but he had a note of the recipe for the *Sole à la crème* they had enjoyed there:

Having cleaned the sole, put it in a well-buttered dish (using fine Normandy butter), sprinkle with a few spoonfuls of dry cider and a little lemon juice. Season with pepper and salt and a small spoonful of finely chopped onion.

Put in the oven, or just on the fire – in the latter case the dish must be covered.

After three or four minutes cooking, add for each sole a half glass of fresh cream and finish cooking. If cooked in the oven, the sole must be basted from time to time.[3]

He says he thought that in some way this dish was the ancestor of 'our excellent *Sole à la Normande* without the garnishings'. He admits it would have been improved with the addition of a few dozen fresh mussels.

Others dispute Auguste's theory of origin. '*Sole à la Normande* is nothing but a *matelote Normande* with less fish variety', says Jules Gouffé.[4] Most say it was invented in 1837 by Langlais, chef at Le Rocher de Cancale in Paris, where it was enjoyed by men as famous as Balzac, Dumas père, and Victor Hugo. Brillat-Savarin also came in every week, but he went for *Turbot à la broche.* Gouffé admits that he favours Langlais as the one who produced the dish as he knew it. He is not sure that Langlais wasn't at Le Cadran Bleu at the time. Yet Gouffé is wrong. Carême produced a more complicated version very early in the century and Langlais merely simplified it,[5] replacing carp roes with trussed crayfish.[6] Alternatively, it has been claimed that it was created by Philippe in his restaurant in rue Montorgueil in Paris.[7] Tracing the origin of a recipe is like tracing the origin of man back through a hierarchy of primates with tails, when you've only got the modern versions and a few old bones to look at: all the contenders for ancestorship have been changing all the time from their own antecedents.

Whatever the primeval ancestor of the splendid *Sole à la Normande*, and it might well have been something like Auguste's *à la crème*, it is now no more *à la Normande* than King Harold. Just look at the recipe. Auguste's recipe, as he published it early in the twentieth century,[8] follows closely the substance of a description in broader form in the *Pall Mall Gazette* late in the nineteenth. A woman wrote the article but, a sign of those times, she is unnamed. The text is a love poem and the reader is given the choice of stopping before things get too complicated or going on to an intricate Paradise:

> Take your sole – from the waters of Dieppe would you have the best – and place it, with endearing, lover-like caress, in a pretty earthenware dish, with butter for only companion.
>
> At the same time, in sympathetic saucepan, lay mussels to the number of two dozen, opened and well cleaned, as a matter of course; and let each rejoice in the society of a stimulating mushroom; when almost done, but not quite, make of them a garland round the expectant sole; cover their too seductive beauty with a rich white sauce; rekindle their passion in the oven for a few minutes; and serve immediately and hot. Joy is the result; pure, uncontaminated joy.
>
> If this be too simple for your taste, then court elaboration and more complex sensation after this fashion: from the first, unite the sole to two of its most devoted admirers, the oyster and the mussel – twelve, say, of each – and let thyme and fragrant herbs and onion and white wine and truffles be close witnesses of their union. Seize the sole when it is yet but half cooked; stretch it out gently in another dish, to which oysters and mussels must follow in hot, precipitate flight.
>
> And now the veiling sauce, again white, must have calf's kidney and salt pork for foundation, and the first gravy of the fish for fragrance and seasoning. Mushrooms and lemon in slices may be added to the garniture.
>
> And if at the first mouthful you do not thrill with rapture, the Thames will prove scarce deep and muddy enough to hide your shame.[9]

Truffles? White wine? Normandy? And where's the cider or the Calvados? Meat sauce with fish? That's sheer Paris.

During the First World War, when sole was so difficult to come by, Auguste discovered *la petite limande*. The little dab he considered made a fine substitute for sole. He would cook them very simply using the fillets floured, dipped in beaten egg and rolled in freshly prepared breadcrumbs. He would have cooked them in butter if it had been available, but he was reduced to using cocoa butter with such poultry fat as he was able to save.[10]

Another sole substitute he writes about was hypothetical and merely his idea of how a realistic fake could be concocted:

> Take the breasts of two young pullets and pound them flat. Moisten half a cup of white bread crumbs with fresh cream, add the white of one egg and a pinch of salt, mix and pour over the chicken. Pound again for a few seconds and then put the flattened breasts on a floured board, roll them up into the form of a cigar and flatten each of them into the shape of a fillet of sole. The 'fillets' are then brushed with beaten egg and sprinkled both sides with very fine breadcrumbs patted-in with the flat of a knife.
>
> Cook in a pan with clarified butter to a golden colour both sides. Serve very hot, lightly covered with anchovy butter and a twitch of red pepper.[11]

To elevate this to a royal dish, top with thin slices of truffle warmed in the clarified butter to which a little chicken fat has been added. The dish may then be presented, according to Auguste, as *Filets de sole Monseigneur*. There is no evidence that Auguste ever perpetrated this hoax, but many a hostess must have been presented with the problem of how to answer a guest savouring her chicken and asking 'And what is this lovely fish, my dear?'

Auguste's fondness for the sole is expressed in his having left us 180 sole recipes in one of his books first published in 1902 and another eighty or so, which only partially overlap, in another published in 1934. After another half century, there are 332 recipes for sole in an English version of *Le Répertoire de la Cuisine*, a dictionary of recipes dedicated by the author and translator 'to the Master of Modern Cookery, Auguste Escoffier'.[12]

One of the recipes is *Sole Escoffier*, which was one published by M. Morin in 1895 as *Timbale de filets de sole Escoffier*.[13] Made in a dome-shaped mould, the dish comprises a crayfish mousse covered with discs in aspic cut from paupiettes of sole stuffed with a fish forcemeat. In some, the stuffing is coloured red with lobster butter, and others are black with chopped truffles. The paupiettes are made by covering sole fillets with the coloured forcemeat and rolling them up and poaching them.

Plaice, *Pleuronectes platessa*, Auguste dismisses as seldom used in the 'classical kitchen'. It does nothing for a sauce; its flavour is so delicate as to be non-existent. It is best deep fried, he says, thus consigning it to the fish and chip shop.

The monster of the flatfish we eat is the halibut (*Hippoglossus hippoglossus*). It was the fish that was to be seen displayed as huge cuts on the fishmonger's slab, when there were such things – and you could see the blood. It can grow in the North Atlantic up to seven feet long and weigh over 700 pounds. It is getting scarce and was in fact one of the first fish to be subject to fishing quotas. It is not a fish Auguste favoured much and certainly it has nothing of the delicacy of the sole or the turbot, *Scophthalmus maximus*, and its close relatives.

Turbot is a fish whose lordly leer is so twisted it could bite its eyes, a fish so special that its devotees reserve a particular utensil for it, the *turbotière*. Talleyrand, Charles-Maurice de Talleyrand-Périgord, diplomat and gastronome, who when Foreign Minister of France at the beginning of the nineteenth century employed the great Carême as his chef, regarded the turbot as the king of fish. He was once given by M. Chevet, the renowned caterer of the Palais Royal, two exceptionally large turbots for a small but important dinner he was giving. Talleyrand's problem was that the fish were sensational not just for their giant size but for the fact there were two of them. It would be ostentatious to bring on the two for a dinner party of just twelve people. But, he had an idea. Only one fish was brought in. The doors were flung wide and, with great ceremony, two footmen entered bearing high between them an enormous silver tray on which reposed one great turbot, beautifully garnished. The guests scarcely had time to express admiration when one of the footmen slipped and the great fish crashed to the floor. 'Bring in another', Talleyrand ordered quietly, and went back to his conversation.

Auguste was certainly in favour of the turbot, but preferred something smaller than Talleyrand's great beasts. Most of his recipes are for young or chicken turbot, *turbotin*, 'among the most delicate and nicest of fish', he says.[14] Young or old, he preferred the fish to be boiled in salted milk and water. Actually, just brought to the boil and then taken to the side of the fire to keep close to the boil until cooking is complete. To avoid distortion of the fish during cooking, and to ease serving, gash the fish down the backbone at the thickest part of the back, break the bone in two or three places, and ease the fillets a little off the bone. Serve with fresh-cooked, boiled, floury potatoes. If anyone insists, he says, *turbotin* may be cooked like *sole*: grilled, *à la Meunière*, fried or *au gratin*, or braised like salmon or trout.

5

Rat au Vin

'History, has no comparable example of such greatness.
Its martyrs are enshrined forever in the great heart of the
working class.'

Karl Marx, on the Paris Commune

1 September 1870. Defeat was in the air in Paris. Napoleon III and the main French army had surrendered to the Prussians at Sedan. With the bulk of the Army of the Rhine bottled up in Metz, there was now little to stop the Prussian advance on the capital.

Paris deposed the Emperor in his absence, exiled Empress Eugénie, declared the Third Republic and prepared for the worst. Retreating troops were surging in to swell the garrison. Cavalry were stamping the boulevards, camping where they could and hanging their washing on the railings. Foreigners, merchants and aristocrats were making their way out of the city with their moneybags, while others stayed and sung the *Marseillaise* at every opportunity. Houses outside the walls were knocked down for materials to strengthen fortifications. Peasants crowded in from the country for protection, some with a sheep or two or a cow and a handcart of meagre possessions. Wagons and vans streamed in with provisions ordered in haste to arrive before the gates were closed. The boom of cannon grew daily more intense. By mid-September, Paris was under siege. On the 23rd, Gambetta left in a balloon to make a desperate move to raise armies to renew effort against the enemy.

At Voisin's, Bellanger, the restaurant's manager, brother of the original Bellanger (or Bellenger) who sold the restaurant just before the war to M. Braquessac, had stocked his cellars to the ceiling with everything he could get in the food line, including live rabbits and poultry in cages, and even tanks of fish. By December these luxuries had disappeared and horsemeat was getting scarce. Rats were on sale in the markets at one franc each, or one franc fifty for a big one.

One dinner menu at Voisin's was:

Purée de lentilles
Sardines à l'huile

Vol-au-vent
Selle d'espagneul
Haricots blancs et rouges
Oranges

The saddle of spaniel was not too popular with the clients, but at least it was a distraction from the more mysterious vol-au-vent.[1]

The zoo in the Jardin des Plantes had to dispose of the animals that it could no longer feed, and Bellanger joined Lesserteur of Restaurant Foyot in buying various exotic meats. He was soon featuring *La trompe d'éléphant, sauce chasseur* as a popular speciality, while Lesserteur became famous for his bear steaks.[2]

Christmas Day 1870, the ninety-ninth day of the siege, Bellanger offered a splendid menu:

Beurre, radis, sardines
Tête d'âne farcie
Purée de haricots rouges aux croutons
Consommé d'éléphant
Goujons frits
Le chameau rôti à l'Anglaise
Le civet de kangourou
Côtes d'ours rôties sauce poivrade
Cuissot de loup, sauce chevreuil
Le chat flanqué de rats
Salade de cresson
La terrine d'antelope aux truffes
Cèpes à la Bordelaise
Petits pois au beurre
Gâteau de riz aux confiture
Fromage de Gruyère
Vins: Xérès
Latour Blanche 1861
Château Palmer 1864 – Mouton Rothschild 1846
Romanée Conti 1858
Bollinger frappé
Grand Porto 1827
Café et Liqueurs[3]

Even in time of plenty, where would a balanced menu of such variety be found? Apart from the fish and the cheese there was donkey, elephant, camel – there's a certain appeal to camel, English style – and kangaroo, bear, wolf and roe deer, the humble cat delicately embellished with rats, and antelope with truffles no less. And those wines! Most people could not, of course, afford such luxuries and many were dying of malnutrition, food poisoning and pneumonia. It had to end.

Peace when it came to Paris had limited popularity. The Prussians had their triumphal march through l'Arc de Triomphe at the end of February and then, in accordance with the peace agreement, left Paris to the French. This left the Parisians to indulge in a favourite pastime, a revolutionary movement.

On 16 March 1871, just as the Republican Paris Commune was about to declare itself, Auguste and his friend Pierre, the *rôtisseur* from Wiesbaden, arrived in the City. They didn't like what they saw. They had walked several kilometres in the freezing rain from Pantin. The trains were manned by Prussians and were not allowed to enter the city. This was a circumstance such as cab-drivers the world over pray for, and Auguste and his friend were not willing, or perhaps able, to pay the extortionate price demanded by a coachmen for a cab from the nearest permitted station.

When they got to the Pont de Flandre over the Seine, empty cabs on their way back to Paris from the station caught up with them. They were the ones who had failed to pick up passengers. The friends signalled the very cab they had refused earlier and, with some satisfaction, rode the rest of the way to the Champs Elysées for the normal fare. They parted there and Auguste went home to his flat on rue Boissy-d'Anglas, which he found intact. He tidied himself and went out again immediately to look up old friends. He found only dejection and a longing by Parisians to emerge from the long nightmare and return to the old ways. 'A vain hope', he thought.[4]

Two days later Paris was in the hands of the Communards and some of Auguste's army friends, involved in early clashes, had been shot or thrown into prison. 'On this awful day,' Auguste says, 'you could see regular soldiers siding with the rioters and, inspired by the Central Committee, murdering two of their own generals.' It was then that prisoners of war back from Germany had to take up arms again 'to fight not the invading foreigner but Frenchmen, or so called Frenchmen, rioters and organisers of the formidable insurrection that terrorised Paris for two months.' Auguste says nothing of his adventures in the early days of the Commune, except that Jérémie Bouniol, released from Mayence, had been able to rejoin him. They were still in the army but had not been caught up in the fighting. On 6 April, however, large posters announced that all able-bodied men between eighteen and forty had to take up arms in defence of the Commune.

Auguste says, 'I had no intention of becoming a soldier of the insurrection. My duty was to rejoin my own unit as quickly as possible.'

He realised he would have to leave Paris at once since preparations were being made to prevent the departure of anybody of military age except foreigners with passports. 'I ran immediately to la Gare Saint-Lazare', he wrote, 'but exit was already barred there. I went then to la Gare du Nord where I was thankful to catch the last train to leave Paris freely.' He made a large detour and reported to Army Headquarters in Versailles where he was posted to Marshal MacMahon's own kitchen. The Marshal still had his *chef de cuisine*, Jules Servis, who had been with him in Mayence. Auguste worked under him.

By the end of May, Marshal MacMahon had crushed the Paris Commune in a bloodbath unparalleled in French history. More than twenty thousand Communards were killed in the street fighting or were summarily executed. Thousands more were deported to penal colonies. It was the end of what Karl Marx later claimed was the first Socialist government in history, 'the first great uprising of the proletariat'. The Commune made Marx an international figure.

When it was over Marshal MacMahon and his household moved to Paris. During this period, Auguste was able to attend the reopening of the Petit Moulin Rouge where Rahaut was still to be in charge of the kitchens. Auguste stayed with MacMahon until mid-August. He was then posted to a new regiment, the 17th Provisionals, accommodated in the Bank and the Louvre. The regiment was commanded by Colonel Comte de Waldner and Auguste joined his household staff as *chef de cuisine* – with Jérémie Bouniol to help.

This was a relaxed period for Auguste, particularly when the Comte moved to Ville-d'Avray in the country, near Porte-Blanche. 'I was able to put my leisure to profit,' he says, 'in studying, quite at ease, the reproduction in wax of natural flowers.' The Waldner family encouraged Auguste in this hobby, as well as in his cooking, and life was pleasant. When he had been with the Comte for a year he began to recognise that this calm and leisurely existence was not for him much longer. 'I needed a much wider field of activity if I was to get anywhere,' he said, 'and I discussed the matter with the colonel.' As a result of this discussion, Auguste found himself with six months demobilisation leave starting in November 1872. He went back home to Villeneuve-Loubet.

It was a time of some indecision for Auguste. At the opening of the Petit Moulin Rouge for the summer season, which he had attended, he had been welcomed and knew that he could take up his job there again. He knew too that to go far in his profession he had to return to Paris. The difficulty was that Rahaut was still *chef de cuisine* at the Moulin. Auguste felt that, having been in charge of kitchens in the army and in large private households, it would be a step backwards now to take a subordinate position. The problem was resolved in a few days.

The story of Auguste's experiences in the Franco-Prussian War and its immediate aftermath comes mostly from his own accounts written and published a quarter of a century later. It may be telling us more of the middle-aged man, the writer, than of the young man he is remembering. He writes as a man of ambition now attracting public attention, and we must wonder whether what we read into his writing is any more than the image of himself he wants to project. He tells his tale with meticulous modesty. There is no personal puff, and the flags hoist are those of a patriot. There is nothing of his own heroics. There is much of his admiration for the heroism of others in the service of France. He complains of the privation and discomfort of others but is poker-faced on his own hardships.

One thing is certain: the story says something of the man at the time he was writing it. And the time of its writing is important. At the end of the nineteenth century his style and attitude is what was then expected of him: he waves flags and keeps a stiff (if French) upper lip. Through it all comes the strong message of his concern for others, and it isn't just for what he can gain from them. He is often helped by those he works for, but that is because he has gained their respect with his conscientious and effective efforts on their behalf. He is solicitous of colleagues and acquaintances while clearly expecting nothing but friendship from them. He also has a keen eye for trouble to be avoided. He is in fact a survivor. No less certain is the fact that he is a winner. He is good at his job, he is optimistic and self-confident – and he has luck. All this helps, but what always puts him ahead is persistent drive and opportunism.

Interlude 5

Take Six Eggs

'Yet, who can help loving the land that has taught us
six hundred and eighty-five ways to dress eggs.'

Thomas Moore, *The Fudge Family in Paris*

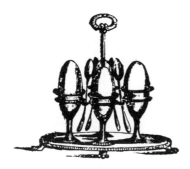

Doubtless man has always eaten eggs, and his primate ancestors probably ate wild ones before they got the taste for meat. In early recorded history there is little detail to be found of egg dishes as such. They were too usual. But the use of them in cooking is mentioned very early.

Before 1000 BC the nomadic Hebrews were using eggs to thicken sauces, and Apicius in Rome, in about 14 AD, gave a recipe for a white sauce using them. The sauce was based on liquamen – made from fermented, salted fish – to which were added crushed pepper and pine kernels, chicken stock and milk, and then eggs to thicken the mixture.

In the Christian era, eggs soon became the customary food on which to end the Lenten fast. This led to the convention of the gift of eggs at Easter, which, from the thirteenth century, were usually coloured with vegetable dyes.

With eggs associated with life's beginnings, it was natural that myth and legend grew around them: they were used in love philtres; they were symbols of good luck and of fertility – a bride in seventeenth-century France would break one for both reasons on entering her new home; they were also considred to be 'unlucky, particularly if taken in or out of the house after dark; they were associated with witchcraft – witches wrote their spells on eggshells.

The Romans always destroyed eggshells so that spells could not be cast. They took the habit with them around their vast empire, and it persisted in recent times in such far-flung outposts as Britain even after the reason had been forgotten – people having eaten their boiled egg would invert the empty shell in the egg cup and break it with their spoon. It might just be, of course, that the habit persisted because children thought it fun to invert their empty shells to pretend they hadn't yet eaten the contents.

In France, until the middle of the seventeenth century, eggs were just a minor part of the crude medieval-style cuisine that persisted there. It was La Varenne and his seventeenth-century cookbook that brought the humble egg from obscurity. He gave sixty recipes for egg dishes, and egg production became a growth industry.

When we say egg, unless we happen to be gynaecologists, we mean a chicken's egg. If we meant plover's egg or caviar we would say so. Nowadays we are encouraged, on the one hand, to eat eggs because of their nutritive value, to 'go to work on an egg'. On the other hand, we are discouraged by the spectres of artery-clogging cholesterol and salmonella. Despite such uncertainty, we each eat twice as many eggs as people did a century ago – about six a week each, including those used in general cooking and those we don't know about in the processed-food packets. That's a rate a bit higher than a single commercial hen can produce at her peak, sitting in line at her work station with nothing else to do. Allowing then for a six-month pre-lay period and for those before and beyond their peak, we have to feed about twice as many of them as we do of ourselves.

Auguste Escoffier, charged with feeding his army officers in the field, put a lot of store by eggs. With no access to commercial egg supply, he still managed to provide eggs at about the rate we now enjoy. He had no need to stimulate appetites, and eggs were pleasant to eat as they were, so he didn't fuss with them. They were a scarce and valuable commodity and he kept them for special occasions – perhaps before a battle or to celebrate the return from one. Then he would serve them just as boiled eggs, *à la coque*. Only on Sundays did he allow the artist chef to emerge. He would create a simple dish; poach the eggs, for example, to join other ingredients and a dressing. He carried his appreciation of eggs with him into the luxury hotels of his later life. They might be simple food, but not beneath his dignity.

Nor were eggs to be considered just a quick, scratch meal. They often are, although not perhaps taken to such an extreme as by Piero di Cosimo. He was a recluse and an obsessional painter who ate only hard-boiled eggs so as not to waste 'psychic energy' feeding himself. He boiled them forty at a time.

In the cookbook Auguste wrote thirty years or so after the Franco-Prussian

War he declared: 'Of all the products put into requisition by the art of cookery, not one is so fruitful of variety, so universally liked, and so complete in itself as the egg.'[1] He then spent a couple of pages on the detail of how to boil or poach one – which takes the punch from the tyro's declaration 'I can't even cook an egg'.

Auguste's view that eggs are worth taking a lot of trouble over is reflected in modern times: 'Egg dishes have a kind of elegance,' says Elizabeth David, 'a freshness, an allure, which sets them quite apart from any other kind of food, so that it becomes a great pleasure to be able to cook them properly and to serve them in just the right condition.'[2]

Auguste was aware of the claim made with dubious precision early in the nineteenth century that French cooks had the choice of 685 ways of serving eggs.[3] Nevertheless, when he came to publishing recipes, he exercised restraint saying he would give recipes only of those in current use.[4] So he records no more than 370. One of these had its origins as one of the Sunday treats he produced during the siege of Metz, but with chicken replacing minced horsemeat leftovers:

Oeufs Bignon

Finely mince 4 oz. raw chicken breast-meat and mix in the white of an egg. Season with salt and a little nutmeg and mix in 4 oz. double cream. Pipe this mixture, using a large star, as three connecting rings in a buttered dish. Cook in a moderate oven. In each circle place a poached or soft-boiled egg coated with tarragon-flavoured velouté. Decorate each egg with a fan of blanched tarragon leaves.

If Auguste wanted to titillate someone's appetite he was most likely to give him or her eggs, probably scrambled. He says, 'This dish is undoubtedly the finest of all egg preparations, provided the eggs be not overcooked, and they be kept soft and creamy'. He gives precise instructions:

For six eggs, slightly heat one ounce of butter in a thick-bottomed sauté-pan. Add the eggs, beaten moderately, together with a large pinch of salt and a little pepper; place the pan on a moderate fire, and stir constantly with a wooden spoon, taking care to avoid anything in the way of sudden, fierce heat, which, by instantaneously solidifying the egg-molecules, would cause lumps to form in the mass – a thing which, above all, should be guarded against.

When, by cooking, the eggs have acquired the proper consistence, and are smooth and creamy, take the sauté-pan off the fire, and finish the preparation by means of one and one half oz. of butter (divided into small quantities) and three tablespoonfuls of cream. Only whisk the eggs when absolutely necessary.[5]

No magic; we just do as we always do, not paying much attention to the 'molecules' but avoiding the lumps. No mention of the secret process he withheld from Sarah Bernhardt – who said he made the best scrambled eggs in the world – namely, stirring with a crushed garlic clove on the point of the knife.

But scrambling an egg, or boiling or poaching, frying or baking it, is usually only the basic process in the preparation of an egg dish. Each calls on the imagination for the choice of companion ingredients, garnishes and seasoning to take us beyond even the three hundred odd combinations that Auguste gives us. With such variety, and averaging our six eggs a week, we shouldn't get bored with eggs in a lifetime.

6

A Goal Achieved

'Tis a common proof,
Lowliness is young ambition's ladder,
Whereto the climber-upward turns his face ...'

Shakespeare, *Julius Caesar*

In November 1872, Auguste was at home in Villeneuve-Loubet on his final leave from the army. His ambition to reach the heights in the culinary world had not been changed by his experience of war and he could again start to plan his way ahead. There were decisions to be taken, of course, on how to get back into the swim, but it would not have been in character for Auguste to ponder them long. His old job at the Petit Moulin Rouge was there for the taking, but he was sure his aim should be higher. Paris it had to be, but the time was not right. There would be little on offer in the capital until its season started in the spring.

The Côte d'Azur's winter season was well advanced so there would be few vacancies there either. He moved fast. He was well known in culinary circles in Nice and it was not difficult for him to ensure that news got around that he was back. In a few days he was offered the post of *chef de cuisine* at the Hôtel du Luxembourg. He took the job having negotiated a place for Bouniol alongside him.[1] It was a short interlude, but a time of rehabilitation for him. This was not so much to heal the abrasions of war; his periods serving the MacMahon and the Waldner households had done that. It was more to accustom himself again to the demanding disciplines of the commercial kitchen, a larger staff, more complex buying, a greater variety of dishes, and the fickle whims of many customers.

After Christmas the news came: Ulysse Rahaut was leaving the Petit Moulin to run his own restaurant. Auguste was offered the vacated post of *chef de cuisine* at the famous Parisian restaurant. He lost no time in accepting.

Auguste returned to Paris in the spring of 1873 to take over the kitchen of the Petit Moulin Rouge.[2] He knew his inheritance from Ulysse Rahaut well, the noise and heat of the kitchen, the chaotic working arrangements and the crude behaviour of the staff. He also knew the workers were used to the rule of a bully, with orders from Rahaut reinforced by blows and coarse shouted invective. Auguste had promised himself while suffering as a raw apprentice in his uncle's restaurant that he would improve working conditions when he ran his own kitchen. He may well have rehearsed changes in his previous management roles but kitchen reform was his priority when he took over at the Moulin.

The first impact on the staff was his management style – quiet, controlled and incisive. His first staff change, while perhaps the simplest, was eventually effective. He changed the title of the man who shouted the waiters' orders to the kitchen from 'barker', *aboyeur*, to 'spokesman', *annonceur*, a term from the theatre. The *annonceur* was forbidden to shout – so shouting around the kitchen had to stop to hear the orders. 'The rush hour in the kitchen is not the time for a rush of words', Auguste told his staff.[3]

This move did not at first solve the problems of bad temper and uncouth behaviour, since it did not attack the basic cause. The coal or charcoal fires glowing red hot for the spit-roasting made the kitchens intensely hot. Cooks sweated profusely. The smoke and fumes from the fires also parched their throats. Constant drinking was essential, and beer swilled for twelve or fourteen hours of the normal working day would soon turn the most angelic cook into a vulgar drunkard.

Auguste banned alcohol in the kitchen and, taking medical advice, made barley water available at all times. There was a dramatic improvement, but he kept a careful eye. 'Should one of the kitchen staff allow himself any excessive liberty of speech', said one of his staff in later years, 'Escoffier would beckon to him and say, "Here, you are expected to be polite. Any other behaviour is contrary to our practice".'[4]

He followed his own rules meticulously and was polite at all times to his staff and colleagues. There was a sign he made when he was losing his temper, perhaps with a recalcitrant cook: he pulled at an ear lobe with thumb and finger while rubbing his cheek, a habit from childhood.[5] He would then say, 'I am going out for a while, I can feel myself getting angry'. He would return after a while and deal firmly but calmly with the cook.

His new post allowed him to have closer contact with clients of the restaurant, 'princes, dukes, the highest personalities in Society and in politics and the financial giants'.[6] He could study their tastes and desires and learn to please them. This he did and started on his way to fame. Many of the pre-war clients returned to the restaurant. Not the least of these was Marshal MacMahon, or to give him his full title, Marie-Edmé-Patrice-Maurice,

Comte de MacMahon, Duc de Magenta. He replaced Adolphe Thiers as President of the Republic on 24 May 1873.

Elisabeth the flower seller was also back. Proof of Auguste's regard for her was that she graced his private roll of honour with a dish to her name: *Le petit poulet de printemps Elisabeth la belle bouquetière*. The 'gracious Blanche d'Antigny', as Auguste calls her, had also taken over her terrain again and rated an Escoffier dish of her own when she was fêted by Prince Galitzin. It was no mean menu that included it:

> *Caviar frais*
> *Blinis*
> *Consommé Rossolnick*
> *Bouchées Moscovites*
> *Mousselines d'éperlans aux crevettes roses*
> *Selle d'agneau de Béhague poêlée*
> *Petits pois à la Française*
> *Pommes noisettes*
> *Canetons de Rouen à la Rouennaise*
> *accompagnés d'une fine gelée au Frontignan*
> *et de coeurs de romaines à l'orange*
> *Soufflé au fromage Périgourdine*
> *Coupe d'Antigny*
> *Gaufrettes Bretonnes*
> *Café mode Turque*
> *Fine vieille Champagne*
> *Grande Chartreuse*
> *Vin: Steinberger Auslese 1859*
> *Mouton Rothschild mise du Château*
> *Champagne (servi frais)*
> *Veuve Clicquot, gout français*

The dinner was for six, served in a reserved salon 'deliciously decorated with roses'.[7]

A problem Auguste had in Paris was in the use of garlic. Coming from the south it didn't make sense to him to cook without it, but he now met a distinct prejudice. He writes of an incident at the Petit Moulin.[8] Among the most faithful of the Moulin's clients was a certain prince, whom he doesn't name, 'who dined every Wednesday in company with a charming young lady. The menu varied little; it was nearly always soup, a lobster or crayfish in a *court bouillon* served hot with a butter fondu or a mayonnaise, an entrée of chicken or game, a roast saddle of lamb, a vegetable, an entremets and fruit. The saddle of lamb was never left off the menu.' 'One evening,' he says, 'I took it upon myself to serve the roast with a *sauce tomate à la mode provençale*. The Prince and his charming companion were so pleased with this sauce they ordered it each time they came.'

> Six or eight months later the Prince said he'd been unable to get the sauce at home or anywhere else and asked me for the recipe. I told him what it was immediately, since it was so simple, but, when I mentioned adding a little garlic, his graceful young lady sprung to her feet, furious, as though an electric spring had suddenly been released.
>
> What, monsieur, you have given me garlic to eat for more than six months? Garlic! *Quelle horreur!*
>
> But, Madame, I thought you liked the *sauce provençale*.
>
> I detest garlic. And I just can't believe it would be served in a first-class restaurant like this. Garlic!

The Prince calmed her down, and Auguste argued the case for garlic and eventually won her round. 'Thanks to the sauce,' he says, 'the lovely young lady finished by smiling broadly so that I was able to admire the beautiful pearls she kept in the wonderful jewel box between her rose-red lips.'

Auguste bemoaned the fact that many times later he had to stand in defence of garlic, but recognised that, while he found it inexplicable, the bias against the bulb is of long standing. He relates that in Ancient Greece, the Temple of Cybele was closed to anyone who had taken garlic. Much later, King Alphonse of Castille set up the *Ordre de la Bande*, the members of which were forbidden garlic or onions 'under pain of expulsion from the Court'. Auguste goes on to say: 'It would be an error and a heresy to deprive ourselves of a condiment so necessary in cooking simply because ancient prejudice had rendered it suspect. If we were to rebaptise it with a different and pleasant name the prettiest girls in France would go mad over it.'

His viewpoint is one that would still be argued about today, for and against. But garlic has always had its adherents. Variously, apart from appreciating its culinary benefit, people have favoured the use of garlic in love potions, and as a medicine so potent as almost to guarantee survival for a century or more. Mythical benefits, perhaps, but not without some basis. This bulbous perennial of the lily family, a native of Asia, grows wild in Italy and southern France, but has been spread by man around the world. It contains an antibiotic, allium, and it has antiseptic properties. It is also an expectorant and an intestinal antispasmodic. All to some extent on the good side, but they were not matters uppermost in the mind of Auguste's dental paragon. There were other things that mattered to her than the taste of a sauce. Garlic insidiously perfumes the body, which is scarcely a property to be sought in a love potion: friends are likely just to turn away rather than tell you that your allure has taken a knock.

Auguste organised his life carefully to take full advantage of the spare time he now allowed himself to indulge his passion for the theatre and his hobby of making wax flowers. These two interests in fact came together in this period in a remarkable way. At 5 Rue Bayard, just round the corner from the Moulin, was the studio of the artist Gustave Doré – best known in England perhaps for his illustrations of *Paradise Lost* and *Don Quixote*. He frequently had lunch in the Moulin and Auguste got to know him well. Apart from his painting, Doré was a sculptor,[9] and it was not long before he was teaching Auguste some of the rudiments of sculpture and advising him in his work on wax flowers.

Then Sarah Bernhardt entered the scene, Sarah, aged twenty-nine, an actress already well on her way to international fame – she was accepted as *sociétaire* by the Comédie-Française the following year. Sarah was a beautiful eccentric, of ever-changing lovers, who slept in an open silk-lined coffin and whose friends had to restrain her from having a tiger's tail surgically grafted on the base of her spine. Sarah Bernhardt, 'the quasi-divinity,' says her biographer, 'inspiring awe-struck reverence' in her audiences.[10]

She had the part of an artist's model in a play but no experience on which to base the character. Her lover at the time, Georges Clairin, suggested to his friend Gustave Doré that he gave her some instruction and practice. She started regular visits to the studio in rue Bayard and invariably stayed to dinner in the evening, a dinner sent in from the Moulin. 'Knowing Doré's tastes,' Auguste says:

> I got a lot of pleasure from the careful preparation of these little suppers. I knew too a dish Sarah doted on, a *Timbale de ris-de-veau aux nouilles fraîches* served with a *Purée de foie gras* embellished with thinly sliced truffles. I prepared this for her myself on several occasions.[11]

Auguste knew and greatly admired Sarah Bernhardt as an actress. He had seen her in all her plays and often across the dining room. Now, meeting her in person, inevitably he was captivated. He was twenty-seven. He says that it was to the famous *timbale* that he owed what was to become a lifelong friendship.

Auguste often refers to Sarah's passion for a dish of some sort and this is surprising. He would have called her a gourmet except there was no feminine form of the word in French – women were not then supposed to be concerned with such matters. In fact Sarah ate little; she was anorexic, pathologically thin to the point of emaciation. She was probably in love with the idea of fine food, however, especially that prepared with her in mind.

They had much in common to talk about in those early days. Auguste knew her plays well and could talk of her performances, but their recent war experiences would have been a major subject of conversation. They had both coped with providing for others under siege conditions, Auguste in Metz, Sarah in Paris, where she had set up, provisioned and run a military hospital. Like Auguste she had stockpiled food while it could still be obtained, even to the extent of keeping flocks of geese and chickens in her apartment. Sarah had become ill in July 1870, coughing blood. Her doctor, pronouncing her condition grave, had sent her on the cure to a spa near Bordeaux. When Paris was threatened she cast off her illness and returned there at once and got permission to set up her hospital at the Odéon.

Another event Auguste recalled was in July 1874 when a government messenger brought him a card from Léon Gambetta reserving a private salon for 7.30 in the evening for himself and two guests for dinner.[12] The card specified that the menu was to include a *Selle d'agneau Béhague* and a *Poularde en gelée à l'estragon*. The wines would be chosen on arrival. One of the guests was Albert Edward, the Prince of Wales, and the other 'a foreign diplomat'. Auguste's menu for them, featuring yet again his Béhague saddle of lamb, was:

Melon Cantaloup
Porto blanc
Consommé Royal
Paillettes diablées
Fillets de sole aux laitances à la Meunière
Selle d'agneau de Béhague poêlée
Haricots verts à l'Anglaise
Pommes noisettes à la crème
Poularde en gelée à l'estragon
Salade d'asperges
Soufflé d'écrevisses Rothschild
Biscuit glacé Tortoni
Gaufrettes Normandes
Les plus belles pêches de Montreuil
Amandes vertes
Café Moka à la Française
Grande fine Champagne
Liqueur des Chartreux
Vins choisis: Chablis

Col d'Estournel, étampé 1864
Veuve Clicquot 1864 [13]

Gambetta and the Prince of Wales met several times in this way. Auguste comments that the friendship and community of thought between Gambetta and the Prince were well known. Both were epicures, but he was sure the dinners were for serious political purposes and not merely for the joys of the table.

Writing many years later, he considered that the meetings were the start of the process leading by 1904 to the Entente Cordiale between Great Britain and France, ending the long period of enmity between the two countries.[14] There is little doubt that the pro-French tendencies of the Prince of Wales, later King Edward VII, eased the path towards this Anglo-French agreement and to the alliance of the two countries in the 1914–18 war. The other side of the coin was that Albert Edward's roving diplomacy around Europe was seen by the Germans as aimed at securing agreements effectively encircling them. This suspicion perhaps added to tensions that precipitated the war. Be that as it may, the dinners at the Moulin were appreciated by the Prince, and he became aware of Auguste Escoffier as their originator. It was the start of his patronage. He favoured establishments where Auguste was subsequently to be found; and where the Prince went, much of upper-crust British, and indeed European, Society followed.

During this period in Paris, Auguste had the time to work on a problem close to his heart, that of food preserving. His field experience with the army during the war with the Prussians had given him a new insight into the value of tinned foods.[15] How often had his jealously guarded tins provided meals when supply lines were blocked. How often had the tin of sardines secreted in his pack saved him from personal privation. He was sure a lot more could be done with preserves to ease the lot of the soldier in the field. He saw too the commercial potential not only for supplies to the services but also for the civilian kitchen.

His first experiments, late in 1874, were with the preservation of tomatoes. He wrote later:

> At this time it was customary, during the tomato season, to preserve tomato purée in champagne bottles which were then sterilised. The purée could, however, only be used for sauces. It occurred to me that one might go further in introducing a product which could replace fresh tomatoes at any season.[16]

His experiments were to his own 'complete satisfaction', and he contacted food manufacturers to interest them in commercial production: Maison Caressa in Nice and Maison Gilbert of Lambesc, Bouches-du-Rhône. Despite repeated overtures he was unable to interest them. Discouraged, that was the end of Auguste's ambitions in tinned tomatoes as a business venture for many years to come. He did, however, preserve tomatoes for use in his own kitchens and continued his interest in the subject.

Auguste's commercial appetite took him further afield. He bought a grocery shop in Cannes sometime between 1876 and 1879 – the earlier date fits his other movements more easily. It was the type of shop selling southern fruits, olive oil, various pastas and so on, that was known as an Italian warehouse. It was called Le Faisan Doré. He built a restaurant on the side of it to function only in the winter season.

Cannes, thirty-two kilometres south west along the coast from Nice, started its career as an international resort of the French Riviera in 1834. It was the year Lord Brougham, the British Lord Chancellor, built a villa there. It was then a fishing village separated from the sea front by the reeds, *cannes*, which gave the village its name. Brougham, when he was not working for the freedom of the press or of slaves, lending weight to the foundation of London University, designing a one-horse carriage that bears his name, and involving himself in much else of note, spent his spare time in Cannes. Many followed his lead, helped by the growing railway network. Cannes soon outgrew its village status. By the time Auguste arrived it was a flourishing town, a privileged resort for the rich of many countries.

Auguste says nothing of his reasons for going to Cannes. Perhaps none is needed. As a matter of routine he had spent his winter seasons in Nice and any chance acquaintance could have mentioned the opportunity to buy a business in prospering Cannes nearby. Perhaps we are seeing something of an internal urge towards commercial venture. Whatever his reasons for the Cannes episode, there was an event during his time there that most men would have thought momentous. Auguste affords it little comment.

Interlude 6

Four and Twenty Blackbirds

'When I demanded of my friend
what viands he preferred,
He quoth: "A large cold bottle,
and a small hot bird".'

Eugene Field

We naturally err on the side of caution in the food we eat. Naturally, because evolutionary selection has eliminated most tendencies to recklessness. We don't have to have reasons for avoiding certain foods and, indeed, the rationale is not always clear. It's obvious why we shun poisonous berries, but not why we eat rabbit and not cat, both of which we first met in anthropomorphic cuddliness when we were children. Is it that the carnivore has a bad taste?

But eating habits are not universal. In the West we don't eat dogs, but in South-East Asia there are no strays. The Aztecs gave up eating dogs when the Spanish *Conquistadores* brought in cattle; so, again, perhaps it's a matter of what tastes good. But then horse tastes all right but is avoided in Britain – originally, perhaps, not just because they were loveable, but rather that we would have been eating our working capital. We export old ones for others to eat.

Customs change with time, too. We used to eat little birds in Britain. We still do occasionally, but at one time no little bird was safe around the place. Take this fourteenth-century pie:

Having lined the pie mould with pastry, put three young, boned partridges in the centre and ring them with six boned and stuffed quail. Around these arrange twelve boned larks. Sprinkle in some bacon diced small, some sour grapes and a little salt. Fill up the pie with boned thrushes and other small birds. Top the pie and bake in a slow oven for several hours. The bones are used with other game available to make a stock to pour in the pie when it comes from the oven.

It was towards the end of the reign of Elizabeth I that baking four and twenty blackbirds in a pie was all the rage. The general idea probably came from the Romans, or so Petronius Arbiter's first-century *Satyricon* suggests. Lampooning Roman excesses, he has the wealthy Trimalchio, with tasteless affectation of culture, serve a great dinner. The menu includes various monstrosities such as hare dressed with wings as Pegasus, and pork cut to look like fish and various birds. The star attraction is a wild sow with its belly stuffed with live thrushes.

We got the pie idea from later Italians. The process was given in *Epulario: or The Italian Banquet*:

To Make Pies
that the
Birds May Be Alive in Them,
and Fly Out When it is Cut Up[1]

The live birds were of course not baked in the pie. A large pie dish full of rye flour was covered with a pastry lid and a hole pushed through it. When this was baked and the rye emptied out there was a 'pocket', left below the crust.[2] A separate small pie was made just the size to plug the hole in the crust. When time came to serve, the blackbirds were put live into the large pie dish and the hole closed with the little pie. At the table the large crust was cut and the birds flew out. The idea was supposed to be that the birds' flapping put out the candles and caused 'a diverting Hurley-Burley among the Guests in the Dark'.[3] Order restored, the little pie was served. Wasn't that a dainty dish to set before the king? The released birds are reported to have taken revenge – but on the wrong person. While the king was counting his money and the queen eating some bread and honey – to make up for the small meal – the maid got her nose pecked off in the garden.

It wasn't only birds that suffered undignified incarceration. A seventeenth-century English cook, Robert May, having learned about eating frogs from the French, published a recipe in 1660 for a frog pie.[4] When the pie was cut, live frogs would leap out 'and cause the ladies to squeak and hop about'.

Early man probably ate little birds as soon as he found ways of catching them, and they are mentioned as food in the earliest records in clay and stone, on papyrus and parchment. The early Egyptians are recorded as feeding carefully and eating only light meals – doubtless they felt that their little aprons would look silly overhanging a protuberant pot. But they are known to have included many varieties of little birds in their diet, and they would chew them up raw. Around Rome by the first century AD the very popular lark – which the slaves found a toothsome morsel when they had served their masters with the tongues – had become a rare bird.

The Romans tended to have specific dishes for their larger birds – crane, ostrich, pigeon, duck and so on. They would use smaller birds indiscriminately in various dishes. A glance at their dressings shows why selectivity was superfluous. One for general use was:

Sauce for Various Birds

Pepper, grilled cumin, lovage, mint, stoned raisins or damsons, honey, myrtle wine, vinegar, liquamen and oil. Heat up and stir with celery and savory.

If the bird was 'high', mustard was included. The best liquamen (or garum) was made from the entrails of tunny fish with its gills, juices and blood, salted and left for a couple of months in a jar. When the jar was then pierced the liquamen flowed out.[5] Liquamen was used with everything, rather as we use salt. With all that as a sauce it wouldn't be easy to taste the difference between a lark and a bunting. And yet, they were fussy about the type of bird. They bred thrushes for the table in aviaries, feeding them on wheat flour, millet and figs, and made fine distinctions – they considered fieldfares the best of the thrush family for this purpose.

China by the eleventh century was a rich country and traded with the world. The Chinese were fond of little birds. They preserved sparrows in rice wine and served them roasted over embers, accompanied by a stir-fry we would recognise today – the wok had arrived by then. They also acquired a taste for a soup made from the nests of one of the many species of swiftlets, *Collocalia fucifaga*, which lived in millions in the caves of South-East Asia. The birds made cup-shaped nests almost entirely from concentric layers of a mucilaginous secretion from their salivary glands. The nests were constructed adhering to the cave wall.

In Escoffier's time, the Manila-Yellow bird's nest was most prized by gourmets. White nests from Borneo and Indochina were used for savoury dishes while those from Thailand were favoured for sweet. Less favoured was the black nest harvested from cliffs on the seashore, particularly since it usually incorporated feathers and debris from the sea: it was built by the petrel from part-digested seaweed. Escoffier served the soup only from high-quality nests as an exotic luxury under the inaccurate name of *Consommé aux nids d'hirondelle* – swiftlets do look a bit like swallows.[6] The dish was a favourite of Edward Prince of Wales, and Auguste often included it in menus for him. He also served it at a dinner in 1903 for Monsieur Loubet, President of the French Republic, at the Carlton Hotel Restaurant, London.

Another little bird included in the President's menu, and one that Auguste often featured along with bird's nest soup in his richer menus, was the ortolan bunting, *Emberiza hortulana*. Ortolan were found across Europe and Asia in summer and collected in large flocks in autumn for migration to the Middle East and North Africa. They were then at their fattest and were trapped and netted. In south-west France the birds were caged and fattened up on millet for about six weeks and then given a precious death by drowning in brandy.

Auguste wrote of *l'ortolan* in one of his earliest published articles: 'The bunting is smaller than a lark but plump and with multicoloured plumage. Its beak and legs tend to red ... The flesh is tender, delicate and succulent and the taste is exquisite.'[7] Fifteen years later he was less enthusiastic. He wrote in 1902 that bunting could be classed with other luxury dishes because they are very expensive, but they do not provide a dish of true gastronomic excellence.[8] He added that neither foie gras nor truffle should be used with buntings since the subtle flavour and aroma of the birds would be masked. The bird is best roasted, he advised, and should not be boned out. But he was not dogmatic, and he broke these rules in his various recipes. One was:

Ortolans en Caisse

Stuff the buntings with a hazelnut-sized piece of foie gras; wrap each in a square of muslin and poach them for 5–6 minutes in a good strong stock.

When cooked, drain well, remove the muslin and place each bird in a porcelain or paper case half filled with a fine salpicon of foie gras and truffle. Coat the buntings with a little well-reduced game fumet.

This derived from a method used in south-west France where each bird was actually cooked (without foie gras) in a corrugated paper case on the hotplate. To eat, pop the whole bird in the mouth and chew it up with a bite from toast fried in goose fat and spread with Roquefort cheese.

Ortolan buntings were plentiful in south and eastern England a hundred years ago and were popular for the table. They were usually cooked on the spit or on the hooks of the game oven, although many French cooks preferred methods which better retained the birds' succulent fat. By the time the ortolan had become scarce in Britain in the 1920s the fashion for them was dying out.

There are more than five hundred species of wild birds in Britain and they, their eggs and nests are now all legally protected. Licences may be granted to kill or take birds for special purposes and there are some general exceptions: open seasons are specified for some twenty wild game birds, but birds classified as pests can be killed at any time by authorised persons.[9]

Among the pests is the rook. Older people in country districts these days remember rook pie as a delicious dish their grandmothers made for Sunday lunch. The secret is to remove the backbone before cooking, since it is bitter. The birds are skinned rather than plucked. Auguste makes no mention of the rook but it was cooked commercially in his day. It was usual to use only fledglings and to discard everything except the breasts. The feral pigeon is also among the pests, but finds favour with Auguste. He is emphatic, however, that only birds less than a year old, *pigeonneaux*, be used in cookery. He published more than thirty recipes.

As for game birds, at President Loubet's dinner buntings were served as a garnish to quail in *Caille escortée d'ortolans*. The quail was one of Auguste's favourite small game birds and few of his important menus would be without it in the season. He normally used only the breasts – during his quarter-century long career in London he had the quail legs from his kitchens saved to be collected daily by nuns, Les Petites Soeurs des Pauvres, as special treats for their charges. You can still get quail of course, but you'll have to do without the escort of ortolans, birds that are fully protected both in Britain and in France.

The grouse Auguste considered to be one of the finest game birds, but he classified it with such as the capercaillie, which he treated as too exotic for other than occasional attention. For grouse, he does little more than recommend that it be prepared *à la broche, en Salmis, en Chaud-froid, en Soufflé, Mousselines*, or *à la crème*. He also warns us not to serve the legs of the roasted bird since they taste of pine. 'Cooked in other ways the legs should first be removed'.

Of the other game birds still available to us, pheasant is followed by partridge at the top of Auguste's list. Again he insists on young birds – older ones are fit only for forcemeat or fumets. He gives us the hint that the tip of the last large wing feather of the pheasant is pointed on the young bird and rounded on the old. Woodcock and snipe then follow quail and the various, now illegal, little birds. Of these, the thrush was a popular game bird in France and tinned *paté de grive* is still a fast line in the *supermarchés*. A thrush dish Auguste often featured was *Grive au nid* – he made a similar dish with blackbird or quail.

The birds are boned and formed into spheres around a gratin stuffing, each tied in muslin to keep the shape, and poached in stock. Each sphere is then set on a large artichoke bottom cooked in butter, and surrounded with tiny egg-shapes formed from forcemeat. The construction is coated with a little demi-glace and glazed in the oven. An imitation nest is then made around each artichoke bottom using a very fine piping of chestnut purée. The gratin stuffing is made with the livers, augmented with chicken livers, lightly fried in chopped pork fat with shallots and mushrooms – or better, truffles. Auguste would have pounded and sieved this, but the food processor makes an easier job of it. Quail done in this fashion are not only decorative and amusing but also delicious to eat. Auguste served the dish with an actual bird's head placed on the spherical bodies. A little modelling with forcemeat might be preferred.

Auguste tells a story concerning one of his recipes (still given in the latest printing of *Le Guide*) for serving larks.[10] He went on a shooting trip with some friends in the Basse-Alpes in 1873. One of the party had a great-uncle, le père Philippe, who farmed in the region and had invited them to stay. Auguste says: 'We were welcomed with open arms, our good host putting his house and his cellar at our disposition.' They went to bed that night promising that the following evening they would come back laden with 'victims they were expecting to come upon in the deep forest'. They started out early the next morning. It was very cold and game was not in evidence. They dragged on unhappily the whole morning without success. At midday, they emerged from the forest and there was a whole flock of larks. They set about them with such fury that they soon had them nearly all in their game bags. That was the start of it. Soon they had partridges along with the larks and were overjoyed at not having to go back empty-handed to le père Philippe's farm.

That evening they took their places at a great long table in front of the bright fire burning in the 'patriarchal fireplace'. They were ready to do justice to the wonderful meal they were sure le père Philippe would produce. To their surprise, after *La soupe provençale*, they were served a plate of large baked potatoes as the main dish. They all looked at their friend wondering why his uncle was suddenly treating them this way after the unbounded hospitality he had shown them the previous day. The friend calmly took one of the potatoes and opened it. A wonderfully delicate aroma arose which, as Auguste says, 'totally aroused their gastronomic awareness'. They were pleasantly surprised to see that their potatoes had been transformed into succulent *petites timbales d'alouettes*.

Auguste gives the recipe in *Le Guide* more or less in its original country form:

> A slice, to form a lid, is taken off each Dutch potato which is hollowed out and half cooked in the oven. The boned larks are quickly coloured in hot butter with a little diced pork. They are then shut into their potato coffins with the pork, and their cooking completed under hot cinders.

He also gives an up-market version:

The larks are stuffed with a gratin forcemeat of foie gras and truffles, and cooked under cover with butter in the oven. The potato pulp is removed from the cinder-cooked potatoes, fried in butter and returned to the cases. They are served with the lark lying in state on top, draped with a little Sauce Chateaubriand – a reduction of veal stock with white wine, mushrooms and shallots, spiced with thyme, bay leaf and tarragon – and finished with Maître d'Hôtel butter.

7

César Ritz

'Where Ritz goes, I go.'

Albert Edward, Prince of Wales

Auguste Escoffier was four years old when César Ritz, who was to be inseparably linked with him, was born in Niederwald, a small village clinging to a hillside high in Switzerland's Rhône Valley where, even today, the only stone building is the little church; the rest are of weather-blackened timber. There are no shops, just peasant houses and a bar. By the time he was five years old César had decided that he hated the cows his father took him to watch over every day in the field above the house, the one highest on the hill. His mother listened patiently while her husband, Anton, ranted in the Valaisan dialect, their only language, that the boy would never make a farmer, that it just wasn't in him. César was her thirteenth child and she had learned tolerance in dealing with children, and tact in manipulating her husband. She reminded him that not all his family had been farmers.[1] They should send César to school in Sion, the capital of the canton, as soon as he was old enough, to learn to be something other than a peasant.

César spent three years at the school, boarding out with a blacksmith's family. He was not a good pupil, but he did learn to speak French and some German. It was a scant education but much better than most lads from a Swiss mountain village could then expected. He showed no ambition and had no idea what he wanted to do in life. His father, in some desperation, arranged with a Monsieur Escher of the Hôtel des Trois Couronnes et Poste in Brig to take the boy on as an apprentice wine-waiter. The fee of 300 francs probably made a large hole in Anton's life-savings. If César was aware of this, the knowledge was no spur to his activity. After a year, Monsieur Escher threw him out. He told him: 'You'll never make anything of yourself in the hotel business. It takes a special knack, a special flair, and it's only right I should tell you the truth: you haven't got it.' It was the glimpse of the hard real world César needed. Faced with the alternatives of returning to Niederwald and its cows or fending for himself, he chose to search for a job.

He was not long finding a place: the Jesuit seminary in Brig took him on as assistant waiter in the refectory. This time, determined to succeed, he worked diligently and tried at all times to please, but after a few months he was dismissed because he had not shown himself to be sufficiently devout. The monks, however, were in need of a *sacristain*, a sexton, and he was given the job. He spent the next few months as chapel-bell ringer and general factotum to the monks, until he was attracted to Paris by the advent of the Paris Exhibition. In Paris, he took a job as waiter in the small Hôtel de la Fidélité and found himself lumbered with menial tasks – polishing boots, scrubbing floors and carrying bags. Undaunted he got down to work, determined now to advance himself.

César was entranced with the wealth and beauty of Paris and his aim was to make money, enough to become part of the leisured life of the city. Handsome in his one good suit, elegant and easy mannered, he was now unrecognisable as the humble peasant from remote Niederwald. Valaisan dialect rusty from disuse, his French was good and his German improving. He also had a smattering of several other languages, spoken haltingly and with an accent, but attractively so. He pressed as close as he could afford to the high life he envied. Indeed, he got rather too close to a charming young Russian baroness and had to leave the Fidélité in a hurry.

He found a lowly job in a small wine-bar serving lowly customers. Then followed another, as a waiter in a *prix-fixe* establishment serving cheap lunches. He was soon out of there, sacked for breaking too much crockery in his attempts to be the fastest server. His next job was up a notch, as assistant-waiter in a slightly better class restaurant on the Rue Saint-Honoré. He got on well in the job and with the proprietor who, during the next two years, elevated him to waiter, headwaiter and then restaurant manager.

Young César's smouldering ambition was fanned into flames when he met a waiter from Voisin's, a restaurant, on the Rue Saint-Honoré, probably of the highest reputation in Paris. The waiter told him of the sumptuous food and wines served at Voisin's, of the statesmen, the generals, the poets who dined there, painting a picture of excellence and splendour beyond César's imagination. He was incensed with the need to gain such heights above mediocrity. Monsieur Bellenger, the owner of Voisin's, with little enthusiasm, offered him a job as an assistant waiter. César, at the age of nineteen, so as to achieve his high ambitions, started again at the bottom but in a high place.

The onset of the Franco-Prussian War found César still a junior waiter and Voisin's business rapidly disappearing. His one idea now was to raise enough money to go to Switzerland and get on with his career. He went down market to a café, the Château d'Eau, but with its clientele of prostitutes it was too far down. 'C'était un vrai marché de bêtes humaines', he said. He moved to the Brasserie Netzer on the Champs Elysées and did well for tips – serving beer. Finally, he had saved enough, got his passport and left Netzer's to get a train to Switzerland. It was the day the Commune pulled down the column commemorating *La Grande Armée* of Napoleon Bonaparte in the Place Vendôme.

Toppling statues in the Place Vendôme was becoming a sport of the Parisians. They had last pulled down the Bourbon, Louis XIV, on his horse during the Revolution. His fine white marble plinth became a convenient bier for the corpses of local dignitaries. In 1810, Napoleon had been set on top of a 140-foot circular column spiralled around with a fine bas-relief made in bronze from cannon he had captured at Austerlitz. Royalists destroyed the statue in 1814, but left the column. César, in 1871, enjoyed the spectacle of this great monument crashing to the ground, but with no premonition of the significant parts Place Vendôme and *la Colonne* would play in his future.

It was two days before he was able to get a train out of Paris. As he left on 21 May, the army of the government of Versailles, under the command of Marshal MacMahon, was advancing into the city. It was the beginning of 'Bloody Week'.

After the war Paris quickly repaired the ravages of bombardment and insurrection. In 1872, nevertheless, scars remained: there were still blackened ruins where there had been fine houses, burnt-out government buildings were still being rebuilt and the large plinth in the Place Vendôme, supporting nothing, a monument only to rebellion. César Ritz meanwhile was back from Switzerland and established at the luxurious Hôtel Splendide in Paris as floor-waiter. The hotel manager, Ehrensberger, was quick to recognise César's exceptional capacity for work, his tact in dealing with clients and, above all, his burning ambition. He was very soon promoted to *maître d'hôtel.*

There were other changes. There was no royal pageantry to draw crowds to the park – Napoleon III, the exiled Emperor, and the Empress Eugénie were living a private life in rural Chislehurst in England. But, the Republic was not without its beauties and excitement. The boulevards resounded again to the clatter of horses' hooves and the rumble of carriages taking fashionable, well-dressed people to fashionable places. Under the steadying hand of Thiers, the Third Republic's first President, the economy was beginning to flourish and Paris was striving, to some effect, to regain its place as the luxury capital of the world. Foreign wealth was flooding into the capital, money brought in by the new American millionaires wishing to emulate the old from titled Europe.

César was where he wanted to be, among the rich and the beautiful. He would first charm, with flattering attention and impeccable manners, perhaps a countess, and then persuade a meat-packer from Chicago to drink a Chateau-Lafitte 1848 with his dinner: 'It is the surest antidote to the doubtless poisonous waters of the Seine, sir.' All the time, he was making friends in high places and taking careful note of what such people wanted of a hotel, of what would bring them back time after time. He knew now where his future lay. He was sure that the key to his success was to be found with the famous clients he was impressing. When the social centre moved from Paris to Vienna with the advent of the World Exhibition there in 1873, César, now aged twenty-three, moved there too and quickly found work as a waiter in the Restaurant les Trois Frères Provençaux. He soon found that the mighty, there for the exhibition, were attracted to the nearby Imperial Pavilion rather than the Trois Frères, but fortune smiled on him: the Imperial was often overwhelmed with 'the crush of noble and princely visitors' and César was one of the waiters the manager of the Trois Frères would lend to help out.

Many of the German elite were there, the German Emperor, Wilhelm I, still sprightly at seventy-six, and Bismarck the architect and builder of the new Germany, now a world power. Albert Edward the Prince of Wales was also there, irritated perhaps at taking second place in precedence to his brother-in-law, Crown Prince Frederick of Germany. There were also the Kings of Italy and Belgium, and the Tsar of Russia. There were many more from the great families of Europe, to say nothing of millionaires from America. From among them, Austria's Emperor Franz Joseph selected his guests for dinner. And what dinners they were, where hawks and doves perched together in temporary peace. All were there for César to study, to learn their tastes in food and wine, music and entertainment. And, there were the women. It was not all work for this ambitious young man. He found time to be fascinated by a beautiful young Bohemian girl who was not slow in bestowing her favours.

At the end of the Exhibition he was ready to leave Vienna for the next stage of his career. He felt ready for big things; he had finished with being a mere waiter, or even *maître d'hôtel*. He was taken on as restaurant manager of the Grand Hôtel in Nice. The city was now the centre of fashion on the Riviera, crowded 'with a throng of gentlemen, whiskered and silk-hatted, and of ladies with trailing skirts and tilted sunshades'.

Still he needed to wander, following international Society, hungry for the chance that would set him on the high road to success. He changed location with each summer and winter season: the Hôtel Rigi-Kulm on a mountain top in Switzerland, the Grand Hôtel in Locarno on the shores of Lago

Maggiore, the Hôtel de Nice and later the Hôtel Victoria in San Remo on the Ligurian coast.

During the winter of 1876–7, which César Ritz spent at the Victoria in San Remo, he was visited by Colonel Pfyffer d'Altishofen. Pfyffer had built the Grand Hôtel National in Lucerne, considered to be the most luxurious hotel in Switzerland, perhaps in the world. He had intended his hotel to be a 'great private palace, such as an Italian gentleman might have, and where he would delight to receive a selected list of guests'. It had not worked out that way. Due to bad management, and to his own ignorance of running such a business, it had gone rapidly downhill. He needed an experienced manager to restore its fortunes. He offered César the job. César accepted the challenge immediately and Pfyffer said, 'I like a man who knows his own mind and can make quick decisions'.

The job turned out to be much to César's liking and he worked tirelessly to put the business on an even keel. He also started on a process of modernising the once luxurious but now faded and old-fashioned hotel. One of his early innovations was the installation of modern gas-lamps throughout – lamps with Bunsen burners and incandescent mantles, which replaced gas jets and oil lamps. He recalled later that guests of the hotel had been known by the staff as 'one-lamp clients, two- or three-lamp, according to what they paid or their social standing – some were rated only as candles'.

A major weakness was the cooking. The chef was competent if uninspired in the kitchen and careless in his buying. Moreover, he was difficult to work with. César was accustomed to dealing with such people and, by the end of the summer season, the chef was taking his marketing duties seriously. He was even managing to be a bit creative in the kitchen. The hotel began to draw important customers.

The Lucerne hotel closed for the winter and it was a time of relative relaxation for César. He took a job in Menton on the Riviera – a resort made popular by Queen Victoria – at the Hotel des Iles Britanniques, owned by the Rosnoblets, fugitives from German-occupied Alsace.

César was not aware of the importance of this winter job to his future career. Nor did he realise at the time that he had met his future wife there. He was only too aware that Mme 'Tony' Rosnoblet had designs on him as a husband for her daughter Louise. He had no time for such matters; he had a career to carve out.

They were visited that winter by Mme Rosnoblet's sister, Alexandrine Jungbluth, with her niece Marie-Louise Beck. Xavier and Alexandrine Jung- bluth owned the Grand Hôtel in Monte Carlo. Two things happened that were to matter to César later: Alexandrine Jungbluth was constantly making broad hints that César would be much better off working for her rather than for her sister; and César was somewhat dismissive of the thirteen-year-old Marie. Later she said of him, 'he was terribly elegant, I thought, with his brown side-whiskers and his beautifully tailored clothes. But he was old – he must have been twenty-seven at least – and I paid as little attention to him as he did to me'.

César was not sorry to leave Menton to go back to Pfyffer at the National in Lucerne for the summer of 1878. The scarcely veiled attempts by Alexandrine to lure him away from her sister Tony's employ, and Tony's blatant efforts to ensnare him in marriage, were embarrassing.

He liked working with Pfyffer, who was pleased with his manager's success in snatching the National from the brink of failure and gave him complete freedom of action. César was content to stay with the hotel for the summer seasons. He was, however, still restless and sought to vary his winter jobs. That winter he went to Enghien-les-Bains to manage the Hôtel Bellevue. His comment was that the proprietor was so stingy that everything in the hotel was too small – beds, bedclothes, water jugs and even the pots under the beds.

At the end of the summer season of 1879, César Ritz felt he had to make a move towards realising his dream of owning and managing his own business. He took an opportunity to lease for the winter the buffet of the Jardin d'Acclimatation in the Bois de Boulogne, where he had fifty waiters in his employ. The venture was a success.

Back at the National in Lucerne for the following summer, he was still thrilled with the excitement of his winter gamble when he was offered a partnership in a leased hotel, Les Roches Noires, in Trouville, Normandy. He accepted and, almost without warning, left Lucerne for the new undertaking.

César had learned at the National the importance of the cuisine in the success of a hotel, but there he had found the chef difficult to work with. It was different at the new place. He enjoyed very much the rapport he was able to establish with the chef, Jean Giroix, and together they planned excellent food for a discerning clientele. For César it was a great experience, but an expensive one; his partner had managed to run the season at a loss, and César realised he had lost most of his savings in the project. He also realised that in future he would have to be more careful in his choice of partners. His immediate problem was where to go for the summer season. Having walked out on Colonel Pfyffer, at the height of the season in Lucerne, he could scarcely expect to be welcomed back. But, in fact, he was.

During the summer of 1881, back at the National, he received a letter from Alexandrine Jungbluth offering him the position of general manager of the Grand Hôtel, Monte Carlo. He accepted without hesitation and poached the chef Jean Giroix from Les Roches Noires to take with him. Under César's control, the old-fashioned and rather dowdy Grand Hôtel was successful and attracted a new and elegant clientele. The 'triumphant event for Ritz and for the hotel', was when in 1881 the Prince of Wales sent a telegram reserving rooms. César Ritz was well pleased that he now had the opportunity to acquire a royal following, especially that of Prince Albert Edward: where he went, world society would follow. But there was a snag; there was no royal suite. There was not even an apartment with a private bath available. With twenty-four hours to go, César set in hand a suitable conversion and stood by encouraging the builders, plumbers and upholsterers until, in the last hour, it was done. Bathed and frock-coated he went to meet the royal party at the station.

Immediately the Grand was the rage. The highest society flocked there and profits boomed – for a time. The first set-back came with the French financial crisis of 1882–83. Millionaires left IOUs instead of cheques and deposited heirlooms as security – or just went off without their luggage.

The hotel managed to survive the period, but then, in common with all other hotels in the area, it was punished by the cholera epidemic of 1883–84. At the first death from the disease there was a panic-stricken rush away from the eastern Riviera. Hotels emptied. Those who stayed breathed the fumes from sulphur bonfires lit to sterilise the air, and took laudanum to stave off the disease. The medicine probably did little to reduce the chance of infection but, since its main ingredient was opium, it may have made the fumes less irksome. More important, it did a lot to subdue horror and fear induced by the constant stream of hearses, the misery of the bereaved and the empty houses. People carried the drug around in little bottles and took frequent sips – many of those who didn't die of cholera must have become opium addicts.

Trade on the Riviera wasn't helped by the publicity given the disease by that delightful best seller, *A Manual of Conversation in Six Languages: English, German, French, Italian, Spanish and Russian*, published in Leipzig, which found its way across the world. It was the seventh edition of the handbook, which in its first impression fifty years earlier had warned the world of the danger to postillions from lightning strike.

This time the book said:

'Are you going to Nice, Sir?'

'I am, Sir.'

'Are you not afraid of the cholera-morbus?'

'I need not fear it, Sir, because I have what may be called a wet nature.'

Despite these difficulties César steered the hotel through and it throve again.

In 1883 Marie-Louise Beck, the little girl César had met and ignored when he was working in her aunt's hotel in Menton, finished her schooling at a convent in Nice. She was sixteen. She went to live with her mother in Monte Carlo, in her 'old-fashioned and unpretentious Hôtel de Monte Carlo'. It had originally been the home of François Blanc, who had made a commercial success of the Casino and put Monte Carlo on the map.

A new problem arose for the Grand in 1884. Their chef, Jean Giroix, was induced by an absurdly high salary to join the competition, the Casino's Hôtel de Paris. César was not stumped. He knew that Giroix had been taught all he knew by the *chef de cuisine* of the Petit Moulin Rouge in Paris. If Giroix was good, his master must be superb. The master's name was Auguste Escoffier, and César Ritz sent for him.[2]

Interlude 7

What Goes with a Trou Normand?

'Tripe's good meat if it be well wiped.'

John Ray, 1670

Auguste, as an army reservist on annual military training in Normandy in 1878, lunched one day at an auberge near Caen with some comrades. Their first course had been *Sole à la crème* and the next would have been *Poulet à la crème*, another speciality of the region. Not wishing to have two cream dishes in one meal, but still hungry after their long walk during the morning, they ordered yet another speciality, *Tripes à la mode de Caen*.

Tripe? The lining of the rumen and stomach proper of an ox. Its recorded history as a food goes back a long way. The Ancient Greeks thought highly of it, and Homer thought it food for the gods. In the eleventh century it was already a speciality of Normandy, then called Neustria, and William the Conqueror is reported to have enjoyed tripe with Neustrian apple juice to drink with it. Rabelais, in the sixteenth century, tells of the drastic effects on Gargamelle of a great meal of tripe just before giving birth to the giant Gargantua.[1] He wrote of it then as a coarse dish. He was conveying an atmosphere of gourmandising, set for effect against the growing refinement under Florentine influence of the cuisine in Lyon, where he lived. Refinement applied to tripe awaited Benoît, a Norman, antedating Carême as one of the great chefs of France, to whom *Tripes à la mode de Caen* probably owes its origins.

Tripe is not much in favour in Britain today. It was once difficult – it had to be cleaned up before use. Soft, slimy rubber to the touch, it looked for all the world like an old cellular blanket ready for the wash. In fact the clothes-washing tub or 'copper' was often taken into service for the laundering operation on tripe, using salt or baking powder rather than soap. There were several treatments with boiling water in which, each time the water had cooled enough, the tripe was scraped, scoured with a large scrubbing brush, thrashed and pummelled. Then, over a period of twelve hours or so, the suffering tripe was left in cold water which was changed three or four times. Nothing looked less like food than the clean ivory plastic that emerged after these treatments ready for cooking. These days, the butcher (if you can find one) does all this preparation and the tripe is sold clean and parboiled. It is as well to ask him how much more cooking it will need.

There are many ways of cooking the prepared tripe. There are some ascribed to nations. *Gras-double de boeuf à l'espagnol* is one – *gras-double* is the selected best of the tripe, usually of the non-cellular part from the rumen. The cooked tripe is grilled after marinating in olive oil. The Poles are accredited with a tripe *pot-au-feu*, and with a fry-up in thin strips. The Portuguese have tripe stewed in a tomato sauce. And there is of course the tripe and onions of Old England, a milky stew made by our grandmothers or great-grandmothers – it seemed good in the old days, but it can be much improved using a good beef stock and Béchamel. A celebrated regional dish in France is *Gras-double à la Lyonnaise* for which the cooked tripe is shallow fried with onions. But the romantic one is *Tripes à la mode de Caen*.

Writing about his Normandy trip, Auguste gives the recipe for the famous Caen tripe.[2] It is indeed an heroic dish. He takes the whole tripe of an ox, long soaked in cold running water then blanched. This is cut into two-inch squares – it takes a little time. These, along with the ox's four feet – meat off the bone and the bones cracked open – are put into a casserole. Classically, a special large earthenware pot is used, the shape of a slightly squashed orange, with a small top opening and lid. Added to the pot are onions stuck with cloves, carrots, salt, pepper and a huge *bouquet garni* of leeks, parsley stalks, thyme and bay leaf. All this is covered with thick slices of beef fat and drowned in cider, well laced with Calvados. The casserole is roofed with flour and water dough to seal the lid on the casserole. Cooking is at a low even temperature for twelve hours or so. We are warned not to use calves' feet – not enough jelly, and they cook too soon. The cider should first be tested – in a cooking pot – some types go black on heating. We must not search for ostentatious elegance in presentation; serve very hot in earthenware dishes.

Is it worth the trouble? The trouble is that it is not easy to achieve good results. For one thing, the dish is one that seems to work only when prepared on this large scale. Len Deighton shoots from the hip: 'There is a great mystique surrounding this dish, but the only secret of *Tripes à la mode de Caen* is the long slow cooking.'[3] He doesn't deny, however, that it is good to eat, especially, he says, with cider to drink – in Normandy they don't stop to drink with it, but the *trou Normand*, a large slug of Calvados, to follow is regarded as essential to stimulate digestion.

To the home cook, Escoffier says, 'this fare is best left to the specialists'.[4] These are really only to be found in France where the dish can be bought from the *boucher* or *charcutier* in a sealed casserole – in various sizes to suit two to eight people – cooked and ready to warm up and eat. It can be a rewarding purchase to bring back from a holiday. *Tripes à la mode de Caen* properly made is a mile away from tripe and onions.

1. Auguste Escoffier.

2. Escoffier in about 1873.

3. Delphine Escoffier, née Daffis.

4. César and Marie Ritz in 1888.

5. The Savoy Kitchens in about 1900. (*Savoy Group*)

6. The Savoy Restaurant in about 1900. (*Savoy Group*)

7. Edward, Prince of Wales, the future King Edward VII.

8. Sarah Bernhardt, 1899.

9. Escoffier with his wife Delphine and four grandchildren.

8

Marriage

'She whom I love is hard to catch and conquer.
Hard, but O the glory of the winning were she won.'

George Meredith

At the age of thirty-two Auguste had learned a great deal about women –
at least as restaurant clients. He saw them as sensitively discerning at table
and the real judges of his art. The view beyond was hazy, although there
were bright lights – individual women whose achievements shone through
the mist. These were mostly the stars of theatre and opera, the great writers
and artists, but there were others. He understood achievement in men; that
was what men were for. But there was something special about clever,
ambitious women with drive. He held them in awe, but among them he
sought his friendships and liaisons. He knew that when he married it would
have to be to such a woman. To Auguste, marriage was a state a man would
enter as a matter of course. It was the proper thing to do, to marry and
start a family. He had never doubted that he would do this once he had
established himself in his career. Now was the time.

A pastime Auguste enjoyed was billiards, and in 1878 he was playing the
game regularly with a friend, Paul Daffis. When Daffis lost he complained
that Auguste had an unfair advantage since he didn't have to bend over to
sight the cue. Actually, they were fairly evenly matched, although Daffis
could usually win if he put his mind to it. One day Auguste said to him:
'Today I shall win.' 'What will you bet?' asked Daffis. 'Whatever you want,
against the hand of your daughter in marriage', was the reply. They played,
and Auguste won – perhaps because Daffis thought Auguste a good catch
for his daughter.

His Faisan Doré in Cannes must have been going well – he was not only
contemplating marriage but also leaving his substantial job at the Petit
Moulin Rouge. He reports simply:

On the 15 August 1878, I finally left the dear old Moulin Rouge and on 28 August
I married Mlle Delphine Daffis, eldest daughter of Paul Daffis, a publisher well

known to book collectors, keeper of the Elzevierian collection. Our union gave us two sons and a daughter: Paul, Daniel and Germaine.

That is all he has to say on the subject. He doesn't even mention that Delphine was herself literary and had already gained a reputation for her poetry. He implied, later, that he and Delphine had little, if anything, of a honeymoon. He says: 'The first days of September we went to Cannes to reopen the Faisan Doré.' Married on 28 August they could easily have travelled to Cannes and squeezed in a long weekend before opening the restaurant on Monday, 3 September. But such personal details he never wrote about.

Scarcely two months after Auguste's marriage, Delphine's father, Paul Daffis, died suddenly. He left a widow and two small daughters, the eldest three years old. Four months later the two little girls contracted diphtheria and both were dead in a week. Auguste says that, 'following these dramatic circumstances', he gave up the business in Cannes and returned to Paris with Delphine. Obviously Delphine would have wanted to go back to Paris at such a time. What is not so obvious is why Auguste had to give up his business, leaving himself jobless, even if he had to accompany her for a while. As luck would have it, he met someone from Maison Chevet, the renowned restaurant and catering establishment in the Palais Royal in Paris, who offered to put him forward for the job of general manager that was vacant. He was offered the position. It was not a job he would normally have sought but, 'not wishing to remain inactive', as he puts it, he accepted.

Paris was recovering some of its pre-war beauty. Electric lights were replacing gas lamps on the Place de la Concorde, trees planted to replace those cut down for fuel during the siege would soon be shading the streets, and the column of the *Grande Armée* stood again on its massive pedestal in the Place Vendôme. The management task Auguste had undertaken was no light one. As well as the restaurant, there was the catering side of the business to handle, and it was complex – Chevet catered for large government banquets and private dinners in town, country and abroad. Auguste mentions the difficulty of organising a dinner in England where several hours crossing the Channel in bad weather could have 'regrettable consequences'.

'For various reasons,' he says later, 'I remained in sole charge of the business for only eight months'.[1] He wasn't sacked, but apparently he was not good at general management. He was offered a job closer to the kitchen. By this time Delphine was pregnant and it was no time for him to be taking risks: he stayed on with M. Chevet in his lowlier capacity. He emphasises that he 'remained on the most friendly terms with M. Chevet'.

Paul, Auguste's son and heir, was born in 1880, although Auguste doesn't mention the fact in his writings. He records only one happy event in this period, a village fête.[2] It was organised by a Madame Adam and featured an *al fresco* luncheon on tables under the trees in the grounds of her house at Gif, and a dinner at night in the light of flares. An orchestra accompanying singers from the Opéra enriched the atmosphere. All this was to thank some 150 artists who had each given one of their works for sale at auction to provide funds for the victims of disastrous floods in Alsace. Mme Adam spent her winters in Cannes and had been a customer of Auguste's at the Faisan Doré, where they had often chatted. Knowing him, she had given him the responsibility for producing and serving these large meals.

He leaves that story hanging and an impression that there was not much of interest to recall from his Chevet days. He did, however, find time for outside interests. He exhibited some of his splendid wax flowers at the Culinary Exhibition held at Le Skating, Rue Blanche, December 1882. His showpiece was a model of a sailing ship with its pedestal decorated with wax flowers.

During 1883, he also founded, in conjunction with a journalist, Maurice Dancourt, a review, *L'Art Culinaire*, to which he subsequently contributed for many years.

Auguste left the Maison Chevet in the spring of 1884 to go to Le Casino in Boulogne-sur-Mer. The establishment was a complex including, as well as its gaming rooms, a theatre and a dance hall with an excellent orchestra. A new building, the Café-Restaurant, had been added and was leased by MM. Pellé and Adolphe of the Café de l'Opéra. They engaged Auguste as *chef de cuisine*. The Café de l'Opéra on Boulevard Haussmann in Paris was a restaurant of high repute. Auguste thought how fortunate the holiday makers in Boulogne were to be able to enjoy the equivalent of the famous restaurant with the added advantage of a fine view out over the Channel 'as far as the coast of England'.

The opening of the new restaurant was marked by a three day fête with a succession of shows given by 'the best artistes from Paris'. Auguste particularly noted the dance, *genre Folies-Bergères*, performed by pretty girls scantily dressed as what he calls shrimp fisherwomen.[3] Auguste had to organise the banquet for the opening but he also managed to join in. He sat at the table with the journalists invited to publicise the occasion but found they were interested only in tasting successive dishes. They were also of the opinion that 'tasting a *premier cru* wine was infinitely preferable to all the discussion in the world, be it in French or Chinese'.

As far as Auguste's career was concerned, the six years from 1878 to 1884 were retrograde. There had been excitement when he started out with his own business in Cannes and it apparently went well enough for him to feel he could leave the Petit Moulin and embark on marriage and a family. But it hadn't worked out for him. It may even have been that his leaving the Moulin was not in fact from choice. The restaurant was probably already going downhill. Certainly, two years later it had failed and was under the auctioneer's hammer. Seeing what was coming, Auguste may have felt it was time to leave, even if the management had not by then decided they could no longer afford his services.

There can be little doubt, however, of his enthusiasm for his new life. Since the days of his apprenticeship, he had wanted to run his own business. Even if his leaving the Moulin had not been voluntary he would have been confident about his immediate future. His Faisan Doré he believed was already doing well, and he would certainly be able to find employment for the summer season in Cannes or nearby; he had never had difficulty finding work. His confidence was expressed by his plunge into marriage.

What went wrong? He says he gave up his business following the tragedies in Delphine's family, not because of them. Perhaps it was simply that the business had failed. Whatever the reason, he left one general management job only to take on another with Maison Chevet, in which he did not do well.

Such evidence suggests that Auguste was not at his best in general management, but when he joined Le Café-Restaurant du Casino in Boulogne he was on safer ground, back in the kitchen where he excelled. He assures us it was a high-class establishment – for Boulogne. And, since he was in charge, it gained a cuisine up to Parisian standards. He was, however, a step or two down from the heights he had previously attained in Paris.

In August 1884, at the end of his summer season in Boulogne, Auguste was invited by M. Paillard to join him at Maison Maire in Paris. The restaurant was well placed on the corner of the Boulevards Saint-Denis and de Strasbourg. It counted among its customers Albert Edward, the Prince of Wales; Tawfiq Pasha, the Khedive of Egypt; Carlos, later King of Portugal; and various Russian dukes. Now at last he was back in his element and his elation is evident in his writing. He tells of the fame of Restaurant Maire for its cellar and its cuisine, of the faithful who kept coming back for the *Canard au sang*, the *Bécasse flambée*, the *Perdreaux en cocotte parfumés de mousserons frais et de truffes*, the *Langouste à la crème* and the 'unforgettable *Pomme Maire*'.[4]

Auguste stayed only two months with M. Paillard. In October the most significant event in his whole career occurred. At the invitation of César Ritz, Auguste left the Restaurant Maire to manage the kitchens of the Grand Hôtel de Monte Carlo. César's offer must have been an exceptionally good one and his approach persuasive to tempt Auguste from the capital where he had been sure his future lay. Like most people in the hotel business in France, he would have heard of Ritz, but hoteliers of note came and went and Ritz was not yet clearly in a different class.

Interlude 8

Faites vos Jeux

'Whether you play *rouge* or *noir* it's always Blanc that wins.'

Said of François Blanc – perhaps by himself

At the eastern end of the Riviera – not yet called the Côte d'Azur – was Monaco, ruled by princes of the Grimaldi dynasty since 1297, the oldest sovereign family in Europe. In 1854 Prince Honoré-Charles was regent for his father Florestan, who preferred to live in Paris. Charles's full title started with Prince de Monaco, Duc de Valentinois and continued through twenty-one more styles to finish with Grandee of Spain – but he was close to bankruptcy. The politics of France and Sardinia had crossed to scissor away at his tiny empire, and the bulk of his income. He was left with a principality, mostly rock, about the size of Hyde Park in London, with a tiny work-shy population too poor to tax adequately.

Prince Charles's mother, Princess Caroline, suggested he should issue a concession for a gambling casino along the lines of those run so profitably by various spa towns in Germany. He should not be too blatant about it: to avoid criticism, it should be just a part of the entertainment to go with a health centre. And so, since sea bathing was the new health-promoting fashion, Charles allowed a company to be formed in 1855 to set up a gaming facility with the name *Société des Bains de Mer*. The Princess's idea was a good one: where there was high-class gambling, nicely presented, the rich were bound to go – if it was not too much trouble to get there. Getting to Monaco was not easy. The journey from Nice was a four-hour bone-rattling trip in an eleven-seater omnibus on awful roads – if the two ageing horses were well enough that day for the punishing trip. The alternative was to go by sea in the *Palmaria*, an old steamer that would sometimes, unaccountably, stay in harbour for weeks on end. Then, somehow, you had to get back to Nice the same day, since there was nowhere to stay. Perhaps such snags were not apparent to Prince Florestan far away in the capital. Encouraged by his wife Caroline, he signed the concessionary order in April 1856. He died a few weeks later leaving Honoré-Charles to find the money to reign in his own right as Charles III.

Monaco soon had a casino. It was the only one in southern Europe, and there were indeed gamblers, just a few, inveterate enough to suffer the various discomforts to satisfy their urges. The casino, a converted villa, and an undercapitalised, drab affair, was able to go along quietly for seven years under several succeeding *concessionaires*, but it contributed negligibly to the prince's coffers. The *Société des Bains de Mer*, despite its name, never featured any bathing facilities.

Then François Blanc, who had made a huge success of a casino in Homburg – dubbed Rouletteburg – came to Monaco. The Prince in desperation sent for him. Now it was a different story. First, Blanc formed a new company, *Le Société des Bains de Mer et Cercle des Etrangers* — and this time he did something about the bathing facilities. His reputation ensured success in placing shares and he put an ambitious programme in hand immediately. This included rebuilding the casino and adding a luxurious hotel, the Hôtel de Paris. He also built himself a fine villa and set a fashion. By 1866 there was a new town. Prince Charles agreed it could be named after him, Monte Carlo. Blanc wrote in his diary:

> the large house of sin, blazing with gas lamps by night … flaming and shining by the shore like Pandemonium, or the habitation of some romantic witch. The place, in truth, resembles the gardens of Alcina or any other magician's trap for catching souls, which poets have devised … Play was going forward like a business. Roulette and rouge-et-noir tables were crowded. Little could be heard but the monotonous voices of the croupiers, the rattle of gold under the wooden shovels, and the clinking of the ball that spun round for roulette.[1]

He was ready, and Monte Carlo was ready, for the railway to be extended from Nice. Many from across the world would then make the fifteen minute trip to the gaming tables and the town would boom.[2] So Monte Carlo made itself ready for Ritz and Escoffier.

9

Climbing

'Nice – really nice – people know how to dine
as they know how to dress or bow.'

Auguste Escoffier

When Auguste Escoffier and César Ritz joined forces at the Grand Hôtel
Monte Carlo, Auguste was thirty-eight and César four years younger. Looking back over their lives it was as though they had each been through a
period of training to suit them for their future together. From their triumphs
and failures they had each discovered their strengths and what they lacked
in themselves in order to realise their dreams. Not the least of their needs
was for each other, which they quickly saw.

César, who wanted nothing more than to run his own great hotel, had
learned that comfort and luxury would only draw discerning clients if
accompanied by a superb cuisine; success came through the kitchens and
the man that ran them. It was essential too that an hotelier and his *chef de
cuisine* work in close harmony – but he had not previously found that easy
to achieve.

Auguste also wanted to run his own business, to be free to work in his
own way to exploit the culinary talent he was confident he had. He had not
lost the urge for independence, but he realised that a flair for creative cooking
was not enough. It had to be done in an establishment attracting a clientele
able to appreciate and afford the luxury of the best cooking. He had learned
the difficulty of managing such a business himself. But what was the alternative? It seemed to him that capable managers were so confident in
themselves they needed other people only to do their bidding. That killed
independence and creativity.

César soon recognised Auguste's qualities. In the brief notes César left,
he wrote, 'Monsieur Escoffier is undoubtedly the finest chef in the
world.[1] He is far in advance of all the other chefs I have ever met.'[2] He also
admired the artist in Auguste and his meticulous attention to detail. He
enjoyed discussing with him matters of décor, table setting, service style and
even staff management beyond the kitchens. César was delighted too that

his new *directeur de cuisine* clearly understood the need for collaboration between kitchen and general management – so many chefs wanted only to rule their own roost without concern for what supported it.

Auguste for his part was greatly impressed by César, obviously an exceptional hotelier, willing to discuss his plans in detail and accept suggestions enthusiastically – and then leave him free to manage his own side of the business in his own way. He was impressed too with César's sensitivity in culinary matters and always valued the hotelier's opinion on a new sauce or a special dish. From the start, the new partnership went well; they were amicably disposed to each other, and complementary in their approaches to the running of the hotel. It was a true synergy: together their performance was greater than the sum of their separate contributions. The rate of their climb to their summit of fame accelerated.

When Auguste arrived in Monte Carlo in 1884 it was thriving around its casino. The railway was running de luxe trains to the Riviera: the Orient Express, which had made its first run the previous year, and the Paris to Istanbul and the Nord and the Sud expresses. Restaurant cars had just been added to them all. Monte Carlo could now be visited comfortably and was an accepted part of the holiday coast. It drew the rich, the noble and the royal in gambling mood – or most of them. An exception was Queen Victoria. On a visit to the town from Menton, she gave the casino her seal of disapproval by returning the flowers sent by the directors – but, if anything, this was favourable publicity.

François Blanc had been dead seven years, but the gaming tables continued to provide Prince Charles with adequate funds. He was now, however, almost totally blind and unable to appreciate the splendour of the renovated casino and its fine new theatre. It was the centrepiece of a resort with a great future. For César and Auguste, Monte Carlo was an exciting place in which to mould a fine future for themselves.

Auguste, who had done so much during his time with the Petit Moulin Rouge in Paris to improve the working conditions and efficiency of the kitchen, could now, at the Grand Hôtel with its enlightened management, spread his influence beyond the bounds of his immediate area of control. He particularly wanted to reduce the complexity of meals and so permit, he was sure, greater attention to the quality of individual dishes, and enhance enjoyment of them.

The French style of presentation of a meal derived from the system pioneered by the great chef Marie-Antoine Carême (1784–1833). Carême, abandoned as a boy in the streets of Paris by his father who was too poor to keep him, became known as the Architect of French Cuisine – he was essentially the originator of *haute cuisine*. Before his time, a French meal had been a hotchpotch of a large number of complicated dishes, with attention only to coarse flavours and little to general appearance. Carême planned his meals in fine detail, simplifying dishes and attending closely to their composition for the balance of flavours and the harmony of colours and textures. He then arranged a large variety of them on tables as magnificent three-dimensional structures. Some dishes were on plinths, mounted works of art, while others were incorporated in *pièces montées* – set-pieces with models of classic temples, rotundas and bridges all rendered in pernickety detail in marzipan, carved pork fat, pastry or plaster, elaborated with spun sugar and fruits. These architectural table exhibitions were flamboyant in the extreme. Carême's view was: 'A well-displayed meal is improved a hundred per cent in my eyes.'

In *his* eyes perhaps, but his spectacular shows did little to enhance the chances of getting a good meal. By the time the edifice had awaited the guests and they had finished admiring it, what should have been hot was cold. Then, seated at the table, which was usually very large, each guest could only be sure of eating what was within reach – it was not good manners to pass dishes. At very grand affairs a flunkey behind each of the guests to attend to their wishes reduced the difficulty. A couple of generations later, *service à la Française* was still in Carême's style with only slight modification. The static display was paramount, but the meal was now usually divided into three sections, all the dishes in each section being exhibited at once. The sections were not courses as we know them – the first, for example, might comprise all the soups and the various roast meats, poultry and game.

Auguste was originally a staunch supporter of the display system, although he wanted to continue the simplification of dishes started by Carême. Auguste's catch-phrase was indeed '*faites simple*'. This, to a Frenchman, would imply getting rid of all inessential elaboration while, as Elizabeth David has observed, 'not skimping on quality of work or basic ingredients, throwing together a dish anyhow and hoping for the best'.[3] For Auguste, simplification meant careful refinement.

His '*faites simple*' extended to reducing the number of dishes offered, but he was not at first inclined to do away with intricate display. He changed his mind eventually but only after the persuasive efforts of several friends. The first of these was a young man who would later be reckoned among the great French chefs, one of his staff at the Grand Hotel, Prosper Montagné. Montagné, aged twenty, was convinced that all *pièces montées* and any decoration extraneous to the food should be discarded. He put his views to Auguste, who was unimpressed. That could have been the end of the matter except that another friend, Philéas Gilbert, himself an eminent chef, persuaded Auguste that Montagné was talking sense.

Auguste changed and, like most converts to anything, became an enthusiast. Merely to dispense with complicated decoration in display was no longer enough for him. In his view the client's desires were the first priority; he should be given individual attention. He was influenced in this, as in many other culinary matters, by his friend and mentor, the great chef Félix Urbain-Dubois, who, as early as 1860, had started the move away from *service à la Française*.[4] He favoured Russian-style table service, serving single dishes in courses, much as we do today.[5]

Auguste in abandoning grandiloquent display could introduce *service à la Russe*. He could at the same time – such was César's confidence in Auguste's judgement beyond his kitchen domain – make further changes to the dining table, realising a youthful dream. He introduced square plates, 'silver plate to hold the heat', similar to the pewter plates his uncle had bought a quarter of a century before for his restaurant in Nice.[6]

He then introduced a totally new mode of serving a meal in the restaurant of the Grand at Monte Carlo. The new style – simplified dishes in a much-reduced menu, served in courses, *à la Russe* – was to spread eventually across the world. He had sparked off a culinary revolution, even if the world didn't take to the square silver plates.

Consider the transformation. A meal served by Carême at an important dinner might display as many as 150 different dishes. Such elaboration was not necessarily for some wild foreign banquet: he served such a meal for forty people in England, at a luncheon for the Prince Regent at the Royal Pavilion in Brighton.

How did they choose from so many dishes? Even now, with menus small enough to justify their name, it can be a mind-numbing experience picking a meal before the waiter comes back for the fourth time. In Carême's day, it was perhaps just as well that choice was limited by the length of your arms – little consolation perhaps when the dish you craved was on pharaoh's barge three metres away on the other side of the table.

Compare all this with a menu designed by Auguste for the Prince of Wales – again the ubiquitous Albert Edward – at one of the dinners he gave at the Grand:

Caviar frais
Blinis au sarrazin
Velouté d'écrevisse au beurre d'Isigny
Nostèles à l'anglaise
Selle d'agneau de lait de Pauillac

Petits pois frais du pays
Pomme de terre Rosette
Perdreaux cocotte Périgourdine
Salade de laitues rouges
Coeurs d'artichaux à la moelle et parmesan
Mousse à la vanille
accompagnée de cerises Jubilé[7]
Friandise de Monte Carlo
Café mode Turque
Grande fine Champagne 1860
Chartreuse du Couvent
Champagne brut Lafite, 1874
Porto vieux

Essentially eight dishes, no choice to make – except perhaps between yes and no – served separately to each person as an individual.

At the Hôtel de Monte Carlo, young Marie-Louise Beck was learning the hotel business – it was expected of her, 'as daughter of the house and as a member of a hotel-owning family'. The training was to stand her in good stead. In visits to her aunt, Alexandrine Jungbluth, at the Grand Hôtel she inevitably met César Ritz again. This time he noticed her and, gradually, they became friends.

Marie recalled:

I learned to tease him gently for his little vanities. He was painfully convinced, for instance, that he had 'peasant hands and feet' – a fault noticeable only to himself. But because of this conviction of his he sometimes would have his shoes made a half-size too small, suffering consequent agonies; and, as to his hands, he spent as much time on their care as any vain woman could ... But I admired him for something more than physical charm and elegance. There was his remarkable courage and capability. Though sometimes his courage failed him, and then I learned to laugh him out of his periods of black depression, which would descend as a consequence of some trifling set-back.[8]

Marie also remembered a particular picnic, a foray with several friends, on donkey-back, into the hills above Monte Carlo. César, who was in the party, remarked that the ribbon on her hat matched the colour of her eyes. It was from that moment, Marie thought, that César's friendly attention resolved gradually and almost imperceptibly into courtship.

At the end of the winter season in Monte Carlo, César returned to the National in Lucerne for the summer season accompanied by Auguste, who was to take over the kitchens. The Swiss hotel was already going well, but

César knew the kitchens to be an area of uncertainty: the chef still tended to be hostile and unreliable. He threw out the kitchen staff, and Auguste brought his whole team with him. Auguste was immediately impressed with the National. He says of it:

> It was an old-style establishment but, by virtue of the improvements and modernisation initiated by César Ritz, it had maintained its high prestige and world-wide reputation as a sumptuous hotel. It was built on the shore of Lac des Quatre Cantons [Vierwaldstäter See] with a superb view – the mountains of the Righi to the left and the Pilatus to the right and, in front, the lake with its smart pleasure boats, reflecting in its depths a line of snow-covered peaks. At daybreak, you could fling wide the windows without being overlooked, and enjoy the sunrise and the perfume of the wild flowers from the surrounding mountains.[9]

César and Auguste divided their time thereafter between the Grand in Monte Carlo and the Grand National in Lucerne. Years later César said, 'The National only became a great hotel when Escoffier took over the management of the kitchens'.[10]

The many festivities César organised at the National became famous. He had new ideas continuously and was ingenious in carrying them out – and particularly resourceful when something went wrong. There was for example the moonlight boating party that had been arranged by mistake at the time of a new moon. He had a huge white paper moon erected on the prow of the boat and illuminated with a lantern from behind.

One event César often described in later years was to celebrate the betrothal in 1885 of Princess Caroline de Bourbon to a Polish Count, André Zamoyski. It was a superb affair. Auguste produced a fabulous banquet in the ballroom, a fitting prelude to the climax of the evening outside. César had arranged illuminated fountains around the lake shores, and for fifty sailing boats on the water displaying coloured flares and setting off Bengal lights and Roman candles. A larger boat sailed past carrying an enormous lantern of a thousand candles – its illuminated parchment shade was painted with the arms of the Bourbon and the Zamoyski families. Then, on the tops of the snow-covered peaks around the lake, huge bonfires flamed out. The party went on all night.

The point of his often told story seemed to be that he could start by alluding to another Count Zamoyski. 'Count Jean Zamoyski,' he would say, 'the one that published his measurements – you know …'[11] Count Jean was an eccentric who always travelled around with his four cats. His marriage was not a happy one and the countess successfully sued for annulment on the grounds that Jean was not the man she had thought he was when she married him. The count had four famous doctors examine him, take measurements, and then widely publicised their detailed reports.

It was in this period that Auguste and César learned the effectiveness of sumptuous treatment in attracting high society. The process fed on itself. The hotel did so well that 'Colonel Pfyffer could afford to indulge his manager and foster his brilliant imagination by even more generous expenditure on lavish spectacle. Ten thousand candles would be needed for illumination? Good, good. A better orchestra needed? Then get one, get one. Exotic flowers would lend enchantment to the ballroom? Then send to Naples for them.' Auguste was similarly indulged. He wanted for nothing in his kitchens, whether staff or equipment, and he could buy the best ingredients for his increasingly imaginative dishes. For Auguste and César the years spent at the Grand and the Grand National were triumphant, but they were only a dress rehearsal for an even greater show to come and, stars that they were already, they were still learning.

Auguste looked back with some pride on his culinary creations of those days, mostly connected with someone of note.[12] He quotes:

> La timbale Grimaldi
> Poularde au ravioli à la Garibaldi
> Les suprêmes de perdreaux Marquise
> Les cailles Richelieu
> Les cailles Carmen
> Les cailles du Chevalier Lombard
> La poularde Yodelling Patti

Such dishes could be served at both the hotels since the clientele varied little between them, and those named went to each hotel in its season. In fact his pride seems related as much to his association with the person named as to his creation of the dish. He named dishes in that period for many high-placed people, including the Empress Eugénie, Prince Fouad (later Fouad I of Egypt), the Maharajah of Baroda, the Earl of Derby, Joseph Chamberlain (recently resigned from Gladstone's cabinet) and, inevitably, the Prince of Wales. Such people were a part of the following of Auguste and César, the fuel that fired their continuing success. They were people seen subsequently wherever the Master Chef and Grand Hotelier provided board and lodging.

One habitual visitor to the Grand who didn't get a dish to his name was eventually to affect their lives more than most. He was a theatrical impresario named Richard D'Oyly Carte. He was famed mostly for his presentation of the Gilbert and Sullivan comic operas in London's Savoy Theatre, which he had built for the purpose. From the start he enthused over Auguste's cuisine: 'There's not a hotel in London', he said to César, 'where you can get a decent meal – much less one where you can dine like a god, as one does here.' [13] He would go on to recommend the opportunities for a superior hotelier in London. 'You'd make money hand over fist'.

On his tour of the United States with his theatre company, D'Oyly Carte had been impressed with the comfort and quality of service in the hotels and wanted very much to do something even better in England. A site was available next to his Savoy Theatre: a hotel there would be somewhere for his leading actors, and for rich and fashionable audiences to stay and to eat. He saw César Ritz as the man capable of organising and running such a hotel. He missed no opportunities on his many visits to the Grand to attempt to influence César on the subject – it was as though he needed enthusiastic support from him as the spur to set him off on his ambitious project.

César was not impressed and certainly had no wish to go to England. He had heard too much from his English clients of the trades unions, licensing laws, early closing, Sunday closing, and expensive alcohol licences difficult to obtain. And, what was more, no one dined in public restaurants: women wouldn't be seen in one and men had their clubs.

Similarly in France, women were not supposed to appreciate good food, at least not where it showed. But respectable women were beginning to be seen dining in public and César encouraged the tendency with his welcoming charm, as did Auguste with culinary flattery. Many a famous lady dining in the Grand or the National, whether an actress, a duchess, a dancer, an opera singer or a princess, was likely to find listed on her menu card a dish adorned with her name.

Auguste also made a point of visiting the tables of important women to discuss their meal. In the winter of 1885 one such woman was the beautiful Hungarian dancer Katinka, mistress of the Russian Prince Kotchoubey and perhaps the most fashionable demi-mondaine in Europe at the time.

One story is of the doctor who attended her at the Grand for a minor ailment and who fell instantly in love with her. He poisoned himself when she spurned his orchids and refused his attentions. Among his effects was found a series of photographs of Katinka provocatively posed in varying degrees of undress. (Marie discovered later that César had one of these photographs – had his approaches, in contrast, not been spurned?) Auguste's visits to the prince's table after dinner were more than routine. Katinka liked to talk to him about the dishes of her own country and gave him the recipes of some, which he often used. One little foible she confessed to him was one with which many a visitor to France today would have sympathy: she liked her *écrevisses* peeled. She didn't like shelling them and getting her hands covered in sauce.

In the next menu for Katinka and the prince the shrimps were shelled and Auguste had included another dish, quail with foie gras, prepared by a method she had described to him. The menu was:

Caviar gris de Sterlet
Blinis Moscovite
Vodka
Velouté léger de poulet
Paillettes aux amandes grillées
Mousse de merlan aux écrevisses, 'Le Rêve de Katinka'
Selle d'agneau de Pauillac poêlée
Petits pois frais à l'Anglaise
Pommes Rosette
Cailles à la Hongroise*
Asperges de serre au beurre fondu
Soufflé au parmesan à la Périgourdine
Fraises au Curaçao
Fleurettes Chantilly
Sablés Viennois
Café Mode Orientale
Vieille Fine Champagne
Grande Chartreuse

*Cailles pochées dans un fond de veau brun, servies
froides dans leur gelée, accompagnées d'un foie gras,
préparé d'après la recette donnée par Katinka

Merlan for the fish course? A common touch? Auguste wondered whether eyebrows would be raised on his choice of whiting, but he protested that the fish had delicate white flesh, friable, light and not gummy. It rested lightly in the stomach and was excellent for convalescents. It deserved higher esteem. 'If whiting had a pompous name', he said, 'such as "Star of the Sea" it would be proclaimed the King of Fish.'

Katinka, the Prince and their two Russian guests were well pleased with their meal, and the next day Katinka sought out Auguste to thank him. She said the Prince would be wanting the same menu for some more guests but, she confided, he was very fond of frogs' legs. It would be a nice surprise for him if some plump *cuisses de grenouilles* could join the *écrevisses*. It was the sort of tip that delighted Auguste, and the surprise he later arranged was well received by the Prince.[14]

By now, Auguste was inured to hard work over long hours and, in those early years with César Ritz, there was no let up. Released from the need to plot, wheedle and persuade in order to pursue his ideas, his enthusiasms allowed him no respite. His whole waking day was taken up planning his meals, marketing and supervising the kitchens. Any time he could find, he liked to talk to the diners, learning their likes and dislikes to note methodically for future reference. Then at night, when the kitchen staff had cleaned up and departed, he would try out his latest ideas for new dishes or methods of preparation and, before bed, read of the work of others in the culinary field. As relaxation he would read books on the history of France.

Tucked into this routine, he also pursued a growing passion for writing. He still contributed regularly to the periodical, *L'Art Culinaire* he had helped launch, and he was researching a book, a culinary guide. Many years later he wrote about it to his friend and fellow chef, Paul Thalamas:

> When in 1881 to 1888 I directed the kitchens of the Grand Hôtel and restaurant at Monte Carlo, Monsieur Urbain-Dubois, retired from active life, came to spend the winter in Nice, and nearly every week visited Messieurs Noël and Pattard, proprietors of the Grand Hôtel. Knowing M. Dubois quite intimately over a number of years, it was rare that he came to Monte Carlo without bringing some new recipes to try, recipes for his new cookbook, *Cuisine d'Aujourd'hui.*
>
> During this period, I told him about my idea to write a little pocket dictionary, an *aide-mémoire* for the use of the kitchen people and the waiters in restaurants, so that arguments would no longer occur between the two sides as to the name and composition of dishes. It would also permit kitchen staff to know the make up of garnishes and for waiters to be able to respond to clients' questions. All this would facilitate service and good relations between dining room and kitchen. Monsieur Dubois, who was interested very much in my idea because of his new book, was in favour.[15]

Félix Urbain-Dubois, himself an accomplished writer and an eminent chef, not only encouraged Auguste in this work but also contributed a number of his own recipes to Auguste's wealth of material. Auguste was not able to finish the book before he left the Monte Carlo and Lucerne hotels.

It has been reported, without obvious source, that Auguste did not finish the book because he was uncertain of his ability to write well enough. This opinion has become apparent fact by repetition, but it seems unlikely to have been so: Auguste was not given to self-doubt. Eugéne Herbodeau, who knew Auguste well in his later years, does not take this view. He says that Auguste had amassed a great quantity of notes but, 'the prospect of editing his material alarmed him'.[16] That was probably nearer the truth. During the 1880s Auguste wrote many articles, particularly for *L'Art Culinaire*, and was well used to his work being accepted for publication. But putting together a book is no light undertaking to be squeezed into the odd minutes of a busy working life. There was just not the time to write the book then, but he continued the work as time permitted.

Like most creators, Auguste had an insatiable curiosity in the subject of his creativity. He always wanted to see how others cooked, and what specialities were appreciated outside his own sphere of activity. Somehow he managed in this period to find the time to travel around on his researches. In October 1885, about to enter his fortieth year, Auguste visited Bresse and the surrounding country in the *département* of Ain, which he found 'interesting in all respects and especially the local commercial activity in the raising and distribution of poultry'.[17] He went to see Monsieur Edouard, a large-scale poultry farmer near Châtillon. M. Edouard was also at the time the mayor of Châtillon. Having given Auguste full information on the raising of poultry, he invited him to lunch. In his description of his visit Auguste pays scant attention to Edouard himself, but he is voluble in praise of his wife.' He wrote:

> Let me pay homage, to the courtesy and charming kindness of Mme Edouard, who was justly proud of her culinary talents, and very happy to find the occasion to get them appreciated; she had all the best qualities of a French housewife. Having presented us with a nicely dressed hors-d'oeuvre, she prepared for us a delicious *omelette au petit lard* cooked exactly to a golden brown; then a *Poularde à la crème* embellished with chicken kidneys and shrimp tails.

The meal went on with spit-roast young partridges accompanied with spinach sautéed in butter and finally with an abundance of local fruits. Auguste remarked that the products of M. Edouard's cellar matched well Mme Edouard's very delicate dishes. It was a dinner exquisite in all respects – and the food was all a product of the farm. Mme Edouard gave him the recipe for the delicious *Volaille aux écrevisses*, which, he said, led to him 'creating a mass of preparations and of new combinations with which our menus are so enriched'.

There is no indication that Auguste took Delphine on his trips. Understandable on this occasion, perhaps, since she had just produced their second child, Daniel. Paul was now five years old. Auguste seems in fact to have regarded such journeys as a necessary part of his job, excursions to gain experience of regional food production and cooking. He was certainly dedicated to his work and it is easy to see him as very serious-minded and humourless. But he was a man of his time. His essential formality carried on through to his writing. As for humour, there are hints to be found: on a trip in 1885, this time to the Auvergne, he was taken to the Plateau de Mirabeau, named after Mirabeau-Tonneau, a famous gourmand who lived there. Auguste reports nothing of food or cooking this time, but perhaps exposes something of a humorous streak. 'One of my memories,' he wrote, 'is of the young shepherd lad who acted as my guide amusing himself and his friends by shouting as loudly as he could: "Have you had a good dinner,

Mirabeau?" A marvellous echo then repeated the last syllables several times, to the delight of the young peasants.'

He was later told the story of a local dignitary who

> envious of this incomparable echo, decided to create one in the grounds of his château. He ordered one of his valets to take up his post behind a hedge to be the 'echo' every day after dinner, and to repeat eight or ten times the phrases he heard shouted. Then he invited in some neighbours, including Mirabeau himself. After a sumptuous dinner, he took them out to admire the astonishing power of his 'echo'. With his hands as a megaphone he shouted as loudly as he could: 'Echo, are you there?' 'Immediately, in even louder voice, the echo replied: 'Yes, I've been here for two hours.'

The story would scarcely qualify as schoolboy humour today, but Auguste thought it worth publishing. It might just have been *Punch*-worthy in Victorian England.

The year 1887 was eventful and one of considerable change for the Escoffier and Ritz partnership. The Grand Hôtel was now a recognised winter ren-dezvous for the High Society of many countries. Not all clients were of the Idle Rich. There were the workers too – sugar and steel magnates, mining millionaires and bankers. They all came to increase their wealth on the green baize of the casino, or to enjoy watching others losing theirs. But the comfort and superb service administered by César, and Auguste's incomparable cuisine, were clearly attractions too, since so many followed them to the National in Lucerne in the summer – there, the only green baize was the cellarman's apron.

Other visitors were the stars of the theatre and opera world, among them the De Reszke brothers, Coquelin, Adelina Patti and Sarah Bernhardt. They came to perform, and to be seen by the right people; they also liked to eat well and in comfort. Auguste continued to indulge his passion for the theatre and, in particular, missed none of Sarah Bernhardt's plays, invariably hurrying back to the hotel to oversee the preparation of her supper. 1887 was also the year of the earthquakes. There were numerous shocks over a period of six weeks and some internal walls collapsed in the Grand. Stories were told of panic-stricken ladies, past the first flush of youth, in full screaming flight down the stairs, jewels in one hand and nightdress in the other. One positive outcome was that César was able to overcome the reluctance of the Jungbluths to spend money on the structure. In addition to the work enforced by the earth's stirrings, they authorised rebuilding and redecoration long overdue. Less welcome was the fact that hotels emptied, just as they had in the cholera epidemic a few years earlier. It was this exodus that probably triggered the Jungbluths, who were getting on in years, to sell the renovated Grand Hôtel and retire. César had no wish to stay with the new owners.[18]

Meanwhile, at Lucerne, Alphonse and Hans Pfyffer had taken over the National from their father and considered they had no need of a manager. César, therefore, was without a job for winter or summer. But this was no worry to him; he was now well known as a successful hotelier. A telegram or two would have brought employers to his door. But he was no longer after jobs.

With convenient timing, the Restaurant de la Conversation in Baden-Baden came on the market and, backed by an influential friend, Herr Otto Kah, César bought it. At the same time the Hôtel de Provence in Cannes became available and, scraping together every last franc, and again with Kah's backing, César bought that too. He had then the two seasons of the year covered, but his work cut out to modernise two establishments and build them up to his own high standards. Several of the staff of the Grand and the National moved with César, including Agostini, the cashier who had been with him for the whole of his time at the two hotels. But Auguste stayed on – the Master Chef was more than César could now afford.

Auguste and César were separated, but in their time together at the Grand they had created a 'new style' hotel, echoed in the National in Lucerne. They had introduced the *service à la Russe* and the *à la carte* menu to the restaurant, and an imaginative cuisine served with an efficiency not found elsewhere. They had dressed the waiters in white ties and aprons, the headwaiters in black ties, and themselves in morning coats – familiar now, but astonishing then. Auguste himself is often pictured in a *toque blanche* and kitchen whites, but mostly he dressed like a banker; he was to be seen, even in the kitchen, in his frock coat, striped trousers and carefully knotted cravat.

Together they had charmed the ladies into the public dining room and exploited their tastes, more refined and less conventional than those of their menfolk. Part of the charm had been in the dining room decor, the exquisite serving dishes to suit the exquisite food, and the highest quality tableware – little problem at the National where Pfyffer had been open-handed, but achieved at the Grand despite the parsimony of the Jungbluths. They had not had freedom of action to provide the extremes of comfort and gracious living they believed should be found in a great establishment, but there is no doubt that together in Monte Carlo and Lucerne they had shaped forerunners of the modern top-class international hotel.

Interlude 9

The Strand

'Give us the luxuries of life and we
will dispense with its necessities.'

Oliver Wendell Holmes

In the thirteenth century, the King of England, Henry III – who built
Westminster Abbey around the shrine of Edward the Confessor – presented
Count Peter of Savoy with a site on the north bank of the Thames between
London and Westminster. The Count built a fine palace on it. When he died,
he left it to the Hospice of the Great St Bernard in Savoy. Henry's wife,
Queen Eleanor, bought back the estate for her son Edmund Crouchback,
Earl of Lancaster. The site is today still part of the Duchy of Lancaster.

The estate has had a chequered career. The palace was ransacked in 1381
by Wat Tyler's rebels and then, so the story goes, razed leaving thirty-two
of the assailants, who were busy guzzling the wines in the cellars, entombed

alive. The place was then left as a ruin for more than a century, rebuilt as a pauper's hospital, scrapped and re-established. Jesuits under James II built a school there but were thrown out by William of Orange. With increasingly disreputable uses, the buildings declined until they were finally demolished in the early nineteenth century to clear the approach to Waterloo Bridge. The remaining site was derelict apart from encroaching coal wharves.

Richard D'Oyly Carte did well financially in his staging of Gilbert and Sullivan light operas and with the proceeds built a theatre on the site. He opened it in 1881 as the Savoy Theatre, perpetuating the ancient name. It was said to be the first public building in the world to be lit by electricity – with gas jets ready in case the engine in the basement should fail. He then set out to erect next to it, in collaboration with Gilbert and Sullivan, 'the most perfect hotel in the world'. He was encouraged in this by his wife, Helen. She had been D'Oyly Carte's secretary before they married, a well-educated and talented actress who had been a keen observer of American de luxe hotels and brought modernity to the design of his new hotel. She eventually became his business manager.

Building started in 1884, and the Savoy Hotel Company was incorporated on 28 May 1889, with a share capital of £200,000.[1] To acquire the new hotel and Beaufort House, the adjoining building facing the Strand, D'Oyly Carte drew together a powerful board, including the Lord Chamberlain, the Earl of Lathom, and Hwfa Williams of the Marlborough House set, led by the Prince of Wales. They were large shareholders, but clearly that was not the only reason they had been brought in as directors.

On 6 August 1889 D'Oyly Carte opened the Savoy, his dream hotel, with a flourish of publicity unprecedented for such an event. It was indeed the most advanced hotel of its day. An impressive feature was its sixty-seven spacious bathrooms in marble – the builder, Mr Holloway, was reputed to have asked whether the guests were expected to be amphibians. It was usual at the time for a hotel to have perhaps three or four bathrooms for several hundred guests. Most of them were expected to use the flat bath to be found under the bed. It would be pulled out onto a blanket to have hot and cold water poured in from two large pitchers. The carriage entrance was into a courtyard with a central fountain, but the approach was steep and carriages were liable to slither down out of control in icy weather. A less hazardous entrance from the Strand was later devised.

The hotel made its own electricity with a power plant in the basement, and had its own artesian well for water. There were six hydraulic lifts: four were service lifts but the others were for the guests and advertised as 'two of the largest "ascending rooms" ever seen in Europe'.[2] A sales brochure claimed:

The hotel is designed to embrace suites of rooms, each suite compact, comfortable and complete in itself. A suite comprises a private sitting room, or rooms, one or more private bedrooms, a private bathroom, lavatory etc. Each set is thus a little home in itself. Those nearest the sky are just as spacious and lofty as those on the ground floor. That is why the charge is the same for a set just under the roof.[3]

D'Oyly Carte had timed the Grand Opening for the London season and to follow immediately on the wedding of Princess Louise and the Duke of Fife on 27 July. Foreign royalty were in London in force for the event: the Shah of Persia, the German Emperor, the King of Greece and many others from the courts of the world. Several board members were well enough connected to guide such eminent people to the Savoy, knowing that where they went international society would flock.

10

The Savoy

'Je compris qu'il y avait en Angleterre une
clientèle prête à payer n'importe quel prix
pour avoir ce qu'il y avait de mieux.'

César Ritz

After César left Monte Carlo in 1887, Auguste wintered as usual at the Grand. He was also welcomed for the summer by the Pfyffer brothers, Alphonse and Hans, now running the Grand Hôtel National in Lucerne. He missed, of course, the satisfying life he had enjoyed in rapport with César Ritz and looked forward to rejoining him in due course in his new ventures.

César Ritz at thirty-seven, now owning two substantial establishments, had become his own man again. He felt able to make a formal proposal to Marie. She wrote: 'César always swore he had known his own mind long before this, but had waited for two things: for me to be of age, and for his affairs to shape up so that he could ask me to be the wife of an independent man and not merely of my aunt's employee.'[1] They married in Cannes on 17 January 1888, left the Hôtel de Provence in the hands of the workmen, and went to Baden-Baden for their honeymoon. They had an apartment over their Restaurant de la Conversation which they were about to reopen. It was not long before César Ritz's following, an appreciable span of international high society, found its way to the restaurant – the old Kaiser Wilhelm was there the first night. Success was immediate; César and Otto Kah, his backer, were soon making a good deal of money.

Marie and César moved in March back to their Hôtel de Provence in Cannes. Within a few days they went to Paris, where César had some business. Marie was to shop – and daringly bought a 'mannish' tailor-made suit with a short skirt which, she said, 'almost showed my ankles'. It was an exciting time in the capital. Never a dull moment in French politics, the Third Republic had nearly fallen to the Boulangistes – and would have done so had not General Georges Boulanger on the crucial evening preferred the soft bed of his mistress, Marguerite, Vicomtesse de Bonnemain, to the discomforts of a *coup d'état*. César and Marie arrived in Paris as Boulanger was about to slip away into exile. Nor was Marguerite the only mistress in high places exciting the Parisian gossip circuit. The Austrian court was not keen on their Crown Prince Rudolf's extra-marital association with Baroness Mary Vetsera. He shot himself and her – appropriately, at the shooting lodge in Meyerling – although the buzz was that somebody else with political motives had dispatched them *in flagrante delicto*.

Then there was the Centennial Exposition due to open in May. Gustave Eiffel's 300-metre tower of wrought-iron latticework, the tallest building in the world at the time, was already illuminated in readiness. César was much impressed by the tower. He thought it the crowning achievement of the century and forecast that soon all buildings would have iron frames.[2] Through friends, César had a preview of many of the exhibits. He remarked on the new 'talking machine' which he thought 'might well get somewhere'.

They were back in Cannes in time to open the Hôtel de Provence at Easter. The Prince of Wales was close to being the first to book in, accompanied by Princess Alexandra and their five children. But they were preceded by an army of 'elderly English spinsters and their knitting', who crowded the lounge, giving it, César felt, quite the wrong image. Ever resourceful, and with great tact, he invented on the spot a special 'ladies' withdrawing room' where, he suggested, they were much less likely to be annoyed by 'unwanted overtures on the part of "foreigners"'.

With his two enterprises running successfully, César was ready for further excitement. He took on the lease of the new Hôtel Minerva, a little gem in Baden-Baden on the banks of the River Oos. He left Marie in charge of the Provence while he saw to the launching of his new enterprise – Marie was glad of her early training with her mother in the Hôtel de Monte Carlo.

The big adventure for César, however, had modest beginnings at the Restaurant de la Conversation. It all started at a party that César arranged for Prince Radziwill, equerry to the Kaiser. César turned the whole restaurant into a woodland scene. He turfed the floor, hung the walls with roses, and populated the room with potted trees. A fine orchestra at one end of the room accompanied a fountain feeding a small fishpond. The centrepiece was a huge circular dining table specially built around a giant fern borrowed from Baden-Baden's horticultural gardens. The critical figure was Richard D'Oyly Carte, who was taking the cure in Baden-Baden at the time. The crucial moment was when he saw César's arrangement for the party. He said, quite simply, 'This is the sort of thing I'd like to do at my new hotel in London'. He went on to tell César of his dream hotel, the Savoy, nearing completion between the Strand and the Thames Embankment in London.

César Ritz felt a sense of excitement as the plan of the great new venture unfolded. It was a theme dear to him, a de luxe hotel built to be the most comfortable in the world, sparing no expense to incorporate all modern conveniences on a lavish scale. Wonderful. Wonderful – anywhere but England. He would not be drawn, but the seed of his future had started to germinate. And so, as it was to turn out, had that of Auguste Escoffier.

Richard D'Oyly Carte was persistent. He was determined to get Ritz at least to the opening of the hotel, perhaps to give the impression that he was involved in the organisation: it was likely then that Ritz would draw with him some of his huge following of influential people. His great hope, however, was that César would be so impressed that he would want to stay. César was well aware of D'Oyly Carte's motive. He said to Marie: 'He wants the clientèle I can give him.'[3]

The Savoy Hotel Company then offered César a large fee to attend the opening and to spend a few days at the hotel – the sum was reputed to be about the same as D'Oyly Carte himself drew from the company as an annual salary. César accepted. Auguste was not alarmed when César went off to London in August 1889 for the opening of the Savoy Hotel. He knew César was not contemplating a move there; they had similar views on England and its dour way of life.

César Ritz was given a royal welcome when he arrived at the Savoy at the beginning of August. A fine suite of rooms had been reserved for him, and the staff treated him with the greatest respect. Richard D'Oyly Carte arranged for him to meet and talk to the directors and to examine all the facilities in detail. He was encouraged to ask questions and to make suggestions.

César was back in Cannes in less than a fortnight and, according to Marie, 'in a fever of excitement'.[4] He told her of the riches of the British Empire pouring into the lap of London. Never had he imagined such wealth. The richest people in the world were there, so many beautiful women, so many diamonds. He showed her newspaper cuttings glowing in their praise of the opening of the Savoy. He told her in great detail of the luxurious setting and of the modern equipment. 'But, Mimi,' he said, 'it will fail.' His main criticism was of the staff, particularly the senior managers, who knew nothing of running a hotel and had no commercial experience: they had mostly been drawn from positions in private houses. He said: 'The staff is quite good and could be whipped into shape. The cuisine is uninteresting. It should be much better. But the management and the organisation will have to be improved or the thing will not be successful.'

Three or four months after the opening of the Savoy, the board realised that not only had the early promise not been sustained, but that actual failure of the business was not unlikely. They knew why. The manager,

Hardwicke, had neither the ability nor the necessary flair for organisation at the required levels of excellence. Auguste said later that Hardwicke was a charming man but knew nothing about running a hotel and did not seek the advice of those who did.

D'Oyly Carte longed to get César Ritz to do the job but felt there was now no chance of this. Ritz had been very positive in his refusal, even after the obvious success of the opening; he was not prepared to give up the care of his own establishments. The board decided that Hardwicke would have to go. They soon had several people in view to replace him and even got as far as choosing their man. It was the actress Lily Langtry, a friend of the D'Oyly Cartes as well as a regular customer of the hotel, who put up the objection to their final selection, Romano. 'He's a man's man,' she said, 'but Ritz will attract the ladies.' In January 1890, D'Oyly Carte determined to have one more go at Ritz, and telegrams began to fly between London and Cannes.[5]

César had been impressed with London and the Savoy but he could not easily overcome his strong desire to run his own business. His present establishments were doing well and he had before him a vision of a growing hotel empire. But in the end he accepted the job, as Marie Ritz said 'at his own price'. The price was not only a princely salary but also six months free each year to look after his own affairs. César set about gathering a team to take with him to London. First and foremost had to be Escoffier.

César visited Auguste at the Grand in Monte Carlo and told him of his decision to go to London. He said, 'I am counting on your support in this affair, Auguste. I want you to take on the organisation and management of the kitchens.'[6] Auguste was keen to rejoin César, but less than enthusiastic about going to England. There was now more to his reluctance than his view of the English way of life. He had agreed with Delphine that it was time to settle down with a stable base and he was in the process of buying a family house, the Villa Fernand in Monte Carlo. He agreed, however, to spend a few months at the Savoy to reorganise the kitchens along the lines he had developed at the Grand, and to train staff in the exacting discipline for servicing an *à la carte* menu. César had to be content with this and went off to gather the rest of his team and to arrange for the management of his own establishments in his absence. Auguste contacted the Pfyffers at the National and they agreed that he could skip the summer season with them. He intended returning to Monte Carlo at the beginning of the next winter season and then to resume his double act between the Grand and the National.

César's contract was signed in January 1890 and, by the end of March, César had agreed with D'Oyly Carte on those of the Savoy staff who would no longer be needed, and he had commissioned their replacements. In addition to Escoffier, there was Monsieur Echenard, a Master of Wine, a friend of many years standing of both César and Auguste. He had for the past few years managed the Midland Hotel in London and was now to be César's chief assistant on the management side. Second to him was William Autour, who had been managing César's Hôtel Minerva and Hôtel de Provence. Henry Elles was to be restaurant manager, François Rainjoux *maître d'hôtel*, and Agostini, César's loyal and trustworthy shadow, head cashier.

It was in the 1890s in England that the half of the adult population who had previously only exerted its power from behind the scenes began to come on stage. There was an excitement in the air as women began to edge their way, not always with maidenly decorum, towards overtly equal participation in all that life had to offer – a move, more than a century later, not yet completed. One indicator then was the casting off of physical encumbrances. Twenty years earlier they had rid themselves of part of their iron cage, the crinoline. There was at first still some gross distortion of the figure with the bustle, worn even while playing tennis. There remained also the steel and whalebone wasp-waisting which was remarkably persistent. But freedom was growing. The skirt trailing behind a yard or so, which had to be held up with one hand when out of doors, was out. Skirts were shortened just to clear the ground, and the bustle slowly diminished to allow the rear to show its natural curve. The artificial exoskeleton, at least for those whose hard youth had not softened to flow point, was gradually expanding to a 'natural' girdle. This emancipation was recognised and welcomed by both César and Auguste. They were to make it their central marketing theme and in this they would be working, so to speak, with the grain.

The grain was against them, however, in a more general sense. Urbanisation in England had set in, and domesticity was the feature of the day. For the bulk of the population, the least endowed with wealth, it was the era of 'Home Sweet Home'; home building was the fashion. That wasn't a bother to César and Auguste: they had their sights set at levels above such people. More troublesome was that it was still a time of big families in the upper and middle classes, and social contact beyond the wide range of family friends was little sought. Domestic servants were plentiful and cheap – there were more than two million of them – and social entertaining was mostly confined to the home. A way had to be found to change this habit and to entice them into dining out.

When César and Auguste arrived with their teams on 6 April 1890 to start work at the Savoy, they found that the dismissed staff had not departed in good spirit. Much later, Auguste wrote that he never forgot the shock he suffered when he went into the Savoy kitchens on that first day: 'those who had lost their jobs and had left the previous evening had created havoc in the place and destroyed everything that would have been of use to us ... there was not even a grain of salt left'.[7]

They were in a difficult spot: there were tables booked, but no food; and, being Sunday, the shops were closed. Fortunately, there were many well-disposed Frenchmen around in the kitchens of London hotels. One, a good friend, Louis Peyre, who managed the kitchens of the Charing Cross Hotel close by in the Strand, was able to provide all they needed, and Auguste says they got through the day with little difficulty. There were probably many more snags than he chose to recall in getting the kitchens up and running. Economically, he related only this one, showing, on the one hand, a certain pride in his ability to cope with an emergency and, on the other, his relaxed attitude. He was determined to be the reverse of the usual harried and temperamental chef.

It was a formidable task that faced Auguste in those first days at the Savoy. To raise the cuisine from mediocrity needed much more than a rewrite of the recipes. The degree of success could only mirror the extent to which customers were impressed. There had to be a choice wide enough to satisfy their fondest desires, impeccable presentation and timely, efficient service. The changes he had to make included the training of a kitchen staff of some eighty members with no break in the ongoing service. The organisation of a large kitchen to prepare meals à la carte was no mean task, but Auguste knew this did not go far enough. To impress the worldly-wise it was necessary to give something of a personal service, to know their tastes as individuals and to pander to them.

For many years he had kept records of the preferences of prominent customers, many of them international personalities likely to become part of the Savoy's clientele. He intended to continue this practice, enabling him to design special menus for such people from his records.[8] He would need a finely-tuned kitchen organisation to handle at sufficient speed the wide variety of meals that would then have to be served.

In the last quarter of the nineteenth century, rationalisation of working procedures was already fashionable in industry. Frederick W. Taylor, the American promoter of scientific management, was a leader in this movement towards mass-production. Taylorisation, as it was then called, was making industrialists rich and the unions angry long before Henry Ford painted the world black with his automobiles.

The process was finding its way into the professional kitchen and there was often a division of the staff into specialist groups. Auguste's first change was to adopt this *partie* system for his *brigade de cuisine*. The *maître de cuisine* (known as *gros bonnet* since he usually wore the tallest white hat) controlled a number of teams or *parties* each headed by a *chef*.[9] A large kitchen might have a

> Chef *pâtissier*
> Chef *rôtisseur*
> Chef *saucier*
> Chef *entremetier*
> Chef *garde-manger*
> Chef *poissonnier*
> Chef *de nuit*

The responsibilities of each chef would vary to some extent according to his own aptitudes and the staff available. For example, the *chef entremetier*, concerned with second courses, would often have to cope with sweet courses as well as with soups and vegetables.

Auguste took specialisation further. Each man working under a *chef de partie* kept a specialised job for a time, and knew precisely the limits of his activity. Eugéne Herbodeau, who later worked with Auguste, gives the simple example of the preparation of *Deux oeufs sur le plat Meyerbeer*.[10] The *annonceur* – Auguste's quietened *aboyeur* – read out the waiter's order and the *gros bonnet* or his deputy saw that work was properly allocated to *parties*. *Chefs de partie* then assigned the appropriate assistant, *commis*, to his part of the job. In Herbodeau's simple example, the eggs supplied from store by the *garde-manger* were cooked in butter on their dish by a *commis entremettier*. The *chef rôtisseur* would see that a lamb's kidney was opened and grilled, put between the cooked eggs on the dish, and passed to the *commis saucier* who had prepared the truffle sauce (*sauce Périgueux*). Garnished with its sauce, the dish was quickly inspected by the *gros bonnet*, who perhaps took a spoon to the sauce – although Auguste always relied on his keen sense of smell. Checked, the dish was soon on its way to the customer. Five minutes from order to delivery, instead of fifteen by the older process.

Auguste's aim was for speed with quality. He achieved this by a production line technique where processes were carried out in parallel instead of sequentially, and each by a cook well-practised in his allocated procedure. Auguste was able then to reduce the customers' waiting time to a minimum and to serve a quality dish at the right temperature.

Auguste foresaw another difficulty. He didn't think much of an Englishman's finesse in choosing a balanced meal *à la carte* – most couldn't even read the menu.[11] They would defer to the choice proposed by the *maître d'hôtel*, who, Auguste felt, could scarcely be expected to have the necessary skill to make a proper choice. He didn't think providing menus in English would help – it was the basic food sense they lacked with no idea how to blend dishes for a meal. In any case, translation was not really possible: the English language reflected the coarseness of English cooking – cooking for men. It was for that reason Auguste never attempted to learn English. He feared, he said later, that in speaking the language he would come to cook like it.[12] His immediate solution involved one of his great skills, the creation of the balanced menu. He adopted a version of the *prix fixe* meal. For this he took it upon himself to design a menu for each customer with a party of at least four.

When a table was booked, the *maître d'hotel* wrote a chit showing the name of the client, the time he wanted the meal, the composition of the party and any special requests. The chit was sent to Auguste, who composed the menu. The system was immediately popular, and increasingly so as Auguste learned more of his customers' tastes and opinions. For his records, he filed against the name of the client the original chit from the *maître d'hotel* and a copy of the resulting menu.

As to his English, Auguste was not alone among foreign *cuisiniers* in England in his lack of the language. French so dominated the kitchen there was neither the need for English nor the opportunity to practise it. There's a story about Joseph Thouraud who eventually took over from Auguste at the Savoy.[13] Thouraud was borrowed on one occasion to mastermind a dinner given by a duke entertaining Lord Kitchener. Dinner over, the duke called for three cheers for Kitchener. The cheers died away and Thouraud stepped forward into the silence and thanked the company in French. Well, '*cuisinier*' wasn't a bad translation of 'kitchener'.

Auguste did not allow himself to be discouraged by his gloomy view of the English. He knew from his experience of them abroad that they were not savages at heart, only victims of an environment starved of French refinement. He set out with César to change all that. As in Monte Carlo, he and César concentrated on bringing in the ladies with, he felt, their more refined palates – the task was more difficult in England where ladies did not dine in public. That is, not the right sort of ladies. The wrong sort had to go. César 'chased the *cocottes* from the Savoy' – or at least the obvious ones – 'and so helped to bring to an end the reign of the *grande cocotte*, the *demi-mondaine de luxe*, in London, and to make it respectable for a lady to be seen dining in public'.[14] He achieved this mostly by insisting on evening dress in the dining room and by refusing entry to any woman unaccompanied by a man. One lady who doubtless had no difficulty with either the evening dress constraint or in being suitably partnered was Liane de Pougy, who said to César: 'You can lay down the law now, for you have reached the height of your career in your profession – as I have in mine.' 'Alas,' said César, 'I'm afraid with much less pleasure and far more trouble, mademoiselle.'15

César agreed with Auguste that the dining room, despite its ornate wall panels by Whistler, was stark. Direct electric lighting from its magnificent chandeliers was particularly unflattering to feminine diners. César experimented and, eventually, transformed the room by simply using table lamps with rosy silk shades. Auguste noted that, 'the entire décor finally created a ravishing effect for the ladies'. They both paid a great deal of attention to such details, concentrating on producing an environment that women would want to be in.

The clincher came from Lady de Grey – Earl de Grey was on D'Oyly Carte's restaurant committee. On César's suggestion, the earl had little difficulty in persuading his wife to invite some of her friends, all shining lights in Society of the day, to dine with her at the Savoy. A ladies' banquet – for such it turned out to be – in a public restaurant was itself novel. César added another original touch: a string ensemble.16 He made sure the ladies felt discreetly screened but did nothing to prevent the sounds of the music and their animated conversation being overheard. It was, and soon the word was whispered around. The scene was set. It was suddenly highly fashionable and respectable for ladies to dine out at the Savoy.

A new era had started. It has been said that French *grande cuisine* existed only because there were courtesans to be entertained and that civilisation would move backwards with their disappearance.17 This might well have come about but for Auguste and César. They made it respectable for men to dine in feminine company. It was not that adventure was removed: the new practice, as it spread, was in addition to, not instead of, sliding in at a side door to the private room upstairs.

There were still problems to solve. For example, many who might have used the restaurant were theatre-goers, particularly on a Saturday evening. There was little time before the show for a meal, and indeed little after it, since the law said the restaurant must close by 11.30 p. m. César was incensed also with what he regarded as the ridiculous laws on drinking hours and he was determined in the longer term to badger his high-placed friends until they got something done about them.

The Savoy, as Auguste found it, already had the makings of an interim solution to the theatre problem. It had a grillroom, among the first in the country. Its décor was in good taste, if plain, and its furnishings were of mahogany, leather and brocade. As cuisine, it featured chops and steaks and a few made-up dishes that could be served quickly. All very functional but, in Auguste's view, it had little or nothing of an atmosphere a lady would find irresistible. César saw to a softening of the interior, while Auguste changed the cuisine more to the standards of the main restaurant and staffed for rapid service. César renamed the Grill Room the Café Parisien (later the Savoy Grill) and made it a pleasant place for an informal leisurely meal. For those with less time, a four-course meal could be served in as little as half an hour. It was immediately popular, and still is today.

Auguste also continued with his mission to improve working conditions for cooks. He extended his attentions beyond the kitchen and, with César's collaboration, made considerable improvements to the living quarters of both senior and junior staff. One young man, Pierre Bourillon, who joined the team as a junior, wrote later that he was astounded on arrival to be shown to a comfortable bedroom, so different from the verminous attics he had endured in Paris – with a bathroom to use, too.[18]

In a few weeks, César and his team had transformed the Savoy. Auguste's kitchen had been refitted to his exacting requirements, the system of working reorganised, and the staff comfortably housed; the dining room, supper room and grill room had been dressed and lighted anew; there was splendid new tableware, *prix fixe* meals and of course *service à la Russe*. The hotel décor had been lightened and cleared of useless ornamentation and dust-collecting fabrics; it had day-and-night service on all floors and valet service for all. And in all aspects of the service, in the hotel and the restaurant, the Ritz credo was applied: 'The customer is always right.'

Within a few months, the Savoy was an immense success. Having raised its standards to his own, César left nothing to chance. He visited or wrote to the influential clients he had gathered at previous establishments to tell them about the new Savoy. They came – the elite of society, the stars of theatre and opera, millionaires from the Americas and Africa, and 'exiled princes wistful for lost splendours', as Marie Ritz put it. Even die-hard Englishmen were lured from their clubs and brought their ladies.

Interlude 10

The Princely Frog

'The discovery of a new dish does more for the happiness
of the human race than the discovery of a new star.'

Brillat-Savarin's ninth aphorism [1]

An aphorism doesn't have to be a great truth as long as it strikes a chord.
Brillat-Savarin's surely does, but perhaps not one to ring down through the
ages to come: who knows what happiness our growing knowledge of the
Universe may eventually bring. Nevertheless, his claim is probably safe from
disproof for a while yet. Are there, in fact, any new dishes to be found? It
has been said:

> The art of cooking is still centred on the same dozen or so pitifully overworked
> recipes. The same dishes continue to make the rounds of our tables and are merely
> christened and rechristened time and time again with high-sounding names we
> hope will disguise their mediocre uniformity. For three centuries now, no truly
> new dish has been presented to the world.

That pronouncement was made before the First World War by a young
chef named Jules Maincave.[2] He had little chance to alter things for us –
he was killed in the war.

We do have, of course, a built-in conservatism, a sort of 'never had it,
don't like it' tendency – doubtless otherwise, if we had been too adventurous,
we would have poisoned ourselves off at the hunter-gatherer phase of
our evolution. And chefs, too, are similarly human. But, as a scientist, or
rather a statistician, will tell you, there is plenty of variety still awaiting our
discovery. Count the number of basic meats – from duck breasts and chicken
liver to the various parts of the bull, the pig, rattlesnake or frog. List the

fishy things from haddock to John Dory, winkles to lobster, vegetables from aubergine to pine kernels, the sauces, the spices, the modes of cooking (or not), and the methods of display and serving. Of course, not everything goes with everything else, but start counting the sensible combinations and you are soon into the millions.

Auguste Escoffier detailed five thousand or so in his *Le Guide Culinaire*, contemporary with M. Maincave, and a couple of thousand more elsewhere. It would seem that M. Maincave didn't get around very much.

In any case, the argument is academic. A new dish is one you haven't had before, and who cares if it is just a rehash of something someone claimed to have created in the sixteenth century. And there is surely enough to choose from to outlast a lifetime of anyone's desire for novelty. We must be reasonably satisfied with the variety we get since we know of many dishes that millions abroad rave about, which most of us don't bother with. In fact, most of us tend to stick to a round of more or less humdrum dishes with the occasional splash out into the exotic. But not everybody.

Auguste, talking to Emile Zola when he visited the Savoy in the 1890s, found nothing routine about his eating habits. Zola was always searching. He had favourites, but they were widely cast. They talked of them, his *faiblesses de gourmandise*.³ They spoke of a tasty *Pot-au-feu de mouton* with a *Chou farci à la mode de Grasse*. Then there were fresh caught sardines, salted and peppered and sprinkled with olive oil. These would be grilled over vine-shoot embers, served, garnished with chopped parsley in *l'huile d'Aix*, on an earthenware plate lightly rubbed with garlic. An 'unforgettable flavour' according to Auguste.

Zola liked *Blanquette d'agneau de lait à la Provençale* with *Nouilles au safran*; *Les oeufs brouillés au fromage et truffes blanches* in a *Croûte de vol-au-vent*; *Le risotto aux petits oiseaux et truffes noires* and the famous *Plat de polenta aux truffes blanches* so much favoured by the Emperor Napoleon I. Zola liked, too, a *cassoulet* with tomatoes, aubergines, courgettes and sweet peppers cooked *à la mode provençale*.

Simple dishes, but with attention to flavour. Auguste did a great deal to introduce flavour into British lives with his many new dishes. He had a few failures, one of which became for him a minor obsession. It was with *les grenouilles*. He was particularly upset that the English were not only horrified that anyone should eat frogs but were derisive of the French who did, calling them 'frog eaters' or just 'Froggies'. He was determined that he would at least get *Messieurs les Anglais* at the Savoy to try them. He did.

No doubt the frog, not too difficult to catch, fell victim to the early gatherers in Europe, but we get little information about it as a foodstuff until much more recent times. There are records that the frog was a favoured food in the south of China around the first century AD, and in this they were following the habits of South-East Asia – they were also fond of spit-roast elephant trunk and pickled python.

The Romans, not without a spirit of adventure in their feeding, make no mention of the frog in their detailed descriptions of their culinary antics. The frog therefore enters European annals in the twelfth century, when it is mentioned in the literature of the church. During one of the cyclical periods when monks were seen to be getting fat, fasting procedures were tightened up and only fish could be eaten on given days – they got up to some two hundred fast days a year until monks started fading away again. Meanwhile, with the low cunning born of hunger, the monks got the frog classified as fish, and it then enhanced their fast day diet.

The Spanish probably met the little animal peering out of a cooking pot in the early sixteenth century when, as Conquistadors, they were revolted to find that the Aztecs ate them – as well as white worms and water flies. The French crept up on the frog a little warily from about the eleventh century, mostly kicking them back into the water but sometimes popping them into the pan. It took an entrepreneur of the sixteenth century to settle French intentions and to turn them into the world's most celebrated frog eaters. Auguste names the man as Simon from the Auvergne. He saw an opportunity to exploit the frogs that were plentiful in his part of the country and made good eating. He fattened them for sale in Paris and made a fortune. Ease of supply and good quality were the spurs to their popularity and the frog became a national dish. Good for M. Simon's pocket was the fact that only the legs were eaten and that a lot of frogs were needed for a meal.

The French soon spread the idea around their colonies and frog eating is practised, following their influence, in isolated places even in North America. It also found other uses there. A slave would sometimes keep a frog in an ants' nest until the flesh had all been eaten. Then, selecting the heart-shaped bone for himself, he would hang the hook-shaped bone on the clothing of the woman he desired. Magic would then get to work, and her lust for him would be quickly aroused.

In England? Well, most of us are still holding out. Funny about food: many will gorge on rubbery whelks and slimy winkles but blanch at the sight of snails – which are in a category along with frogs and puppy-dog's tails.

Auguste tells of his attempted introduction of the frog to British tables. He confesses in the draft of the memoirs he intended to publish, written towards the end of his life, that he played a trick on the English, serving high society with frogs' legs in disguise.⁴ Having once tasted them, he thought, they would be converted, and the rest would follow. He was encouraged in this idea on learning that in Martinique the English as well as the French preferred the local frogs to chicken. There was also the precedent of the English Prince of Wales being fond of '*le petit batracien*'.

So, at a *grande soirée* at the Savoy, Auguste included a frogs' legs creation in the buffet among a large number of other cold dishes. He named the dish *Cuisses de Nymphes à l'Aurore*. The 'charming and brilliant society', unsuspecting, tucked into the frog dish with some relish. The Prince of Wales, according to Auguste, was amused at the little deception and some days later ordered some *nymphes* for himself. Auguste crowed afterwards that the English could no longer reserve the label 'frog-eaters' for the French alone.

On another occasion, he was stung into print by an accusation that he had made a practice of changing of the names of well-known dishes. In particular he was chided for using the word *nymphes* in the name of the dish of frogs' legs he had served at the Savoy. They were clearly concerned that, thinking of nymphs, a pair of naked frogs' legs arranged in the dish was highly suggestive. This was not mentioned; they merely attacked Auguste's knowledge of mythology.

His rejoinder under the serial heading 'Friendly Chat' was anything but friendly and he managed to expose several chips weighing down his shoulders.⁵ 'Certainly,' he wrote,

> I do not claim to be a scholar, not having remained, as have some people, at school until I was twenty. But I can truthfully say that I know my business thoroughly down to its least details, having climbed up step by step ... The rare intervals of leisure I have had in a life crowded with work have perhaps allowed me to gain some knowledge of history and even of mythology. Since today my famous *nymphes* are brought against me as a reproach, I think it will be useful to give a little lesson to those who, never having made an innovation, yet take it upon themselves to pronounce judgement on their more practical predecessors.

He then gives another version of the story, side-stepping the responsibility for the deception. The lesson intended is not abundantly clear. In this tale it was a 'pretty client' who had ordered the frogs' legs for the dinner she was giving for the Prince of Wales and 600 others. Frogs had never figured on an English menu and she was a little fearful about their reception. The English called the French 'frog-eaters', but, she thought, only in jest. It just seemed to them impossible that civilised people really could eat frogs' legs. 'Christen your frogs as you like,' she had said to Auguste, 'and all will be well.' Auguste went on to say that a French cook is never at a loss, especially when it is a question of being agreeable to a pretty woman.

As for changing names in general, he argued that it was sometimes necessary to do so; many earlier ones did not fit modern circumstances. 'That is why,' he said, 'we may rightly modify some terms such as that of a savoury soufflé fritter, which really cannot be presented everywhere under its other title, which is too vulgar and too ethereal.' These days, doubtless, few would be offended if the term *pet de nonne* appeared in a menu – even in frank translation into English, although 'nun's fart' hasn't quite the same ring to it.

The original *Cuisses de Nymphes à l'Aurore* was prepared with the frogs' legs cooked in a court-bouillon with aromatic herbs, cooled and covered with a *sauce chaud-froid* coloured a golden pink with paprika. He served it decorated with tarragon leaves and covered with a chicken jelly on a square plate. A version of this survives almost a century later in the latest issue of *le Guide*. Now the frogs' legs are poached in white wine and the jelly is champagne-flavoured fish aspic. *Cuisses* has been dropped from the name to avoid any misunderstanding.

11

High Society

'He who ascends to mountain-tops shall find
The loftiest peaks most wrapt in clouds and snow;
He who surpasses or subdues mankind
Must look down on the hate of those below.'

Lord Byron

Sometime in 1890, Delphine came to join Auguste in London, but there is no record of the date. She brought the children, ten-year-old Paul and Daniel, aged five. Marie Ritz, who had stayed behind in Cannes keeping a proprietorial eye on the Hôtel de Provence, made her first visit to London early in the year, during the 'Season'. She and Delphine may well have travelled together.

The reactions of the two wives to London were entirely different. Delphine didn't like it and was unhappy from the start. Auguste was little help. He was totally immersed in his work for most of his waking hours. Delphine, lacking anything of the language, found Londoners cold and unfriendly, and London a lonely place; dismal too – unlike Paris, it still had old-fashioned gas lighting, even in the main streets.

For her part, Marie was only staying a short while, but she was immediately drawn into her usual partnership with César, taking an active interest in the running of the hotel. She was impressed with the Savoy and with London. Mostly it was the people – the handsome, arrogant Englishmen; and the stately beauty of the women with their blonde hair, and slim waists and jewels, and their talk of the new plastic surgery. London was also so foreign – Rotten Row in the Park on Sunday mornings; the costermongers with their hand-barrows shouting or singing their wares in unintelligible argot; the huge electric trams clanging their way past shying horses along the Embankment.

She was impressed again with the association of Auguste and César, 'which,' she said, 'was one of the most fortunate things that ever happened in either of the men's lives'.[1] During the first years he had spent at the Grand Hôtel National in Lucerne, Ritz had evolved almost completely his ideas of what a de luxe hotel could and should be, and had been convinced of the importance in such a hotel organisation of superb cuisine. Until he met Escoffier he had not been able perfectly to apply his ideas in that realm. As to Escoffier, before Ritz no one had fully appreciated his talents nor given him full scope to exercise them. Marie, and perhaps most people at the time, considered the two colleagues entirely responsible for the success of the Savoy. There is, however, another perspective.

Auguste's grandson, Pierre, has said, 'One should not discount D'Oyly Carte: he got the timing right in building the Savoy to catch rich Americans travelling on the new great liners across the Atlantic.'[2] In 1989, Sir Hugh Wontner, then Chairman of the Savoy, looking forward to the hundredth anniversary of the hotel, wrote:

> It was the inspiration of the theatrical impresario, Richard D'Oyly Carte, which provided London with a standard of luxury and good taste it had never seen before, and was not to be found anywhere else in Europe. His inexhaustible energy, drive and business acumen made sure that the Savoy would succeed, as it did beyond all expectations.[3]

He did, however, add:

> While D'Oyly Carte instinctively knew what was needed and had the enterprise and courage to provide it, he still, like in the Gilbert and Sullivan operas he was presenting, needed the artists to play the principal parts. In this, in the early years, he was well served by César Ritz and Escoffier, whose achievements at the Savoy, and later elsewhere, became a legend in the annals of the late Victorian era.

Marie went back to Cannes with César to open the Provençal for the winter. She writes of that time: 'Life was far more marvellous than I had ever supposed. That year which had begun so auspiciously for us drew to and end with a great crowning joy – the knowledge that I was going to be a mother.'[4] There was a problem. A homing instinct usually asserts itself on such occasions and it did for Marie. Home was not in a hotel suite in Cannes, alone, nor in the flat in Baden-Baden awaiting César's next fleeting visit. The solution was provided by her aunt, Alexandrine Jungbluth, who invited her to stay for the critical period. The Jungbluths' château was near Strasbourg in Alsace, under German rule since 1871, but home territory to Marie. Charles was born on 1 August 1891. César was unable to leave London at the time but made the christening a fortnight later.

Perhaps even more pressing was Delphine Escoffier's need to return to her roots. She too was pregnant and anxious to leave London; she certainly would not have considered it a suitable place for the birth of the child, her third. Auguste took her and the two boys back to their new house, Villa Fernand in Monte Carlo. He expected to join them there when he had the kitchens at the Savoy running smoothly and he could return to the Grand for the winter season. As it turned out, since he had not found the English so tedious as he had expected, and had grown to like London, he offered little resistance to the generous offer he was made to stay at the Savoy as *chef de cuisine*. But his daughter Germaine was born French, and Delphine never returned to England.

It was possibly on his way back from his journey home with Delphine that Auguste went to the old university town of Rennes.[5] He was fond of travelling to new places, sampling regional dishes; he was not always flattering in reporting his finds. Rennes seemed to him to be 'asleep in its glorious past'. He went to dine at the Restaurant Gaze and found himself at a dinner attended by Breton poets, which he gatecrashed. He declined an invitation during the meal to recite a poem to the assembly. Finally, he gave in, tired of his neighbour's punning repartee, particularly when he said, 'one often gets *vers* dining at the Gaze' – Auguste had nothing to say on worms so he made do with the other meaning, verse. He quoted one about Pegasus, which Victor Hugo had sent to a famous actress during the siege of Paris when she had declared she was unable to dine with him:

> Si vous étiez venue, belle que j'admire,
> Je vous aurais offert un dîner sans rival.
> J'aurais tu Pégase et j'aurais fais cuire,
> Afin de vous offrir une aile de cheval.

Just plain horse had become a rare luxury in Paris at the time, so a cooked wing of Pegasus would indeed have made an unsurpassable meal for Victor Hugo to have tempted the beautiful actress he admired.

The menu for the poets' dinner was:

> *Consommé à la bisque et aux quenelles*
> *Bar sauce vénitienne*
> *Filet de chevreuil flamande*
> *Dindonneaux à la Montmorency*
> *Perdreaux Bardés au cresson*
> *Salade Moscovite*
> *Terrine de Ruffec*
> *Fond d'artichaut à la Barigoule*
> *Bombe Bibesco*
> *Desserts, Fruits*
> *Café et Liqueurs*

Auguste, so concerned with making his own menus fit an occasion, thought this a strange one, evocative neither of poetry nor Brittany. There were no worms, but he thought the menu 'more suited to a gathering of international firemen than of poets'.

Famous now, and a star attraction at the Savoy, Auguste must nevertheless have been a lonely man – but a private one. He tells something of his professional life in his books, articles and letters, but signs of his inner emotions appear only about his work, France, and the troubles of other people. There's no record for example of his reaction to living away from his family, and nothing about Delphine until much later in life when she became one of the people with troubles. Until then, Delphine was only someone who 'also sends her kind regards' at the end of his letters to intimates.

There was one chink in his shield. It is the one through which his obvious admiration for Sarah Bernhardt appears to be for more than for her genius on stage. They had been friends since his time at the Le Petit Moulin in Paris when she was an *ingénue* at the *Comédie Française*. Since then he had been an *habitué* at her performances and he knew most of her roles by heart. She had never failed to stay where he worked when she was engaged in the area. He always hurried back after shows to prepare one of her favourite dishes, perhaps *Zéphyr de poularde Belle Hélène*, 'dainty slices of chicken's breasts on *pâté de foie gras* ... served with asparagus salad.'[6]

And so she came to the Savoy, and indeed lived there during her periods in London from 1892. They had known each other then for over twenty years and both were well into middle age, although Sarah seemed blessed with eternal youth. Pierre Louÿse, the French poet and novelist, having just seen her Tosca, 'one of Sardou's made-to-measure creations', wrote of her:

> Sarah! Sarah! My God, Sarah! you are as beautiful and graceful as a seventeen year old ... I can understand how one would do anything, leave everything, ruin oneself, kill oneself for a woman like that. But how can one compare Sarah with any other woman? And this woman, this miracle of grace and suppleness, is an old woman of forty-four.[7]

He was only eighteen. Marie Ritz once said she was amazed at the charm the 'Divine Sarah' exerted over everyone. 'But over men,' she wrote, 'no matter what their age – from five to ninety-five – her power was magical.'[8]

Stories of Auguste's relationship with her have circulated around the Savoy staff and its clients for a century, yet none points a finger at more than innocent adoration on Auguste's part. It was said that he 'was Bernhardt's willing slave'. They also spoke of him weeping outside her door 'on the night she came back exhausted to the Savoy and took an overdose of chloral'.[9]

Most suggestive was perhaps that Auguste gave loving care to Sarah's birthday dinners. She took these in her private suite with Auguste as her only guest. Were they in fact lovers? At the time they first met in the Petit Moulin days they were in their late twenties and unmarried – Sarah was two years older than Auguste. Sarah's biographer says 'for Sarah to admire a man was, as often as not, to sleep with him'. The gossip was that 'Sarah slept with all her leading men, her playwrights and her critics, not to speak of a great many artists, politicians and other interesting men of her day'.[10] She was the daughter of a courtesan with aunts of a similar calling and her upbringing was such that casual intimacy with a man would not seem a matter of any great consequence. She was the entirely convincing *cocotte* from *La Dame aux Camélias* continuing her act to consummation.

Little more needs to be said. Sarah and Auguste became lifelong friends. If this arose from a much closer relationship in their younger days there is no direct evidence. But if so, there was a great deal more discretion shown than was usual for Sarah; this was in character for Auguste, but not for Sarah. She spoke airily of her lovers and why would Auguste have rated differently? Later it would scarcely have been a friendly act to expose any intimacy with Auguste, a respected married man with a family. She merely revealed that he made the best scrambled eggs in the world.

Separated from his family, Auguste found time, beyond his long working hours, to involve himself again with his little culinary reference book, on which he had amassed so much material during his time at the Grand in Monte Carlo. He got far enough to seek publication. He was at the time writing a regular article in the periodical *L'Art Culinaire*, under the title *L'Ecole des Menus: Etude et Composition des Menus Modernes à la Maison, à l'Hotel et au Restaurant* and he sent his proposal to the editor, Philéas Gilbert.

He wrote later to his friend Paul Thalamas:

> I acquainted Gilbert ... of my project. I gave him at the same time some recipes and formulas, samples worded as briefly as possible but written clearly to be easily understood. These recipes appeared in the April 1894 issue of *L'Art Culinaire* – at the same time as somebody's study of the banana.[11]

You can hear him grinding his teeth. He went on:

> Monsieur Gilbert did not understand the importance of a pocket dictionary and recognised too late the value, after Dagouret had taken my idea and published his little book.

'Pierre Dagouret was a respected headwaiter in a London hotel. His book, *Le Petit Dagueret*, was very successful – it is still used today, almost a century after first publication.[12] At the time of writing to Thalamas, more than thirty

years after his intended great work was overshadowed by a banana, Auguste
had reason to be upset with Gilbert, but in the long interim they had been
colleagues, successful partners in publication.

Auguste had always been fond of tools and machinery and his kitchens
were amply supplied with up-to-date devices. His upbringing in a family of
ironworkers may have had something to do with this. Perhaps his early
environment also influenced his strong preference for cooking with the coal
or charcoal fire rather than gas or electricity. The only gas ring in the Savoy
kitchen was the *feu éternel* under a great *marmite* constantly replenished to
keep the kitchen supplied with meat stock.

He was apt also to be inventive, often with commercial intent. In the late
1880s he entered into some sort of arrangement with a Monsieur Badin in
Paris 'for the construction, patenting and marketing of their inventions'.
They brought in a third member of the group they refer to as 'old Lumière':
he seems to have been the business brain behind the venture.[13] One of their
devices was an apparatus for treating wine that was too acid, and to fortify
that which was too dilute – it didn't sell. Another device was for a stopper
to recork a wine bottle and another a machine to draw off (rack) wine from
its dregs (lees) by suction, to replace free-air racking which disturbed the
sediment. There is very little information on all this, but such money as is
mentioned changed hands in a direction from Auguste to the others and
by early 1892 his enthusiasm for the arrangement had faded.[14]

Where preserved foodstuffs were concerned he was more persistent. When
he was *chef de cuisine* at the Petit Moulin Rouge in the mid seventies he had
been unable to persuade companies in the south of France to undertake the
canning of tomatoes. He tried again from the Savoy. He 'had an interest',
as he puts it, in a fruit-preserving factory in Saxon-les-Bains in the Swiss
Rhône Valley – it had been a casino which became available when gambling
was banned in Switzerland.[15] One fine summer, when the tomato crop was
much bigger than usual, they were pleased to be able to can the surplus for
sale to the Savoy. Bad weather destroyed the crop the following year and the
business failed. Auguste didn't give up. He went back to the companies who
had previously turned him down. One of them, Maison Caressa in Nice,
agreed to produce some two kilogram tins of tomatoes for him. He points
out that he was one of their best customers for other products. The fame of
the product soon spread and the company sold 60,000 kilograms. the
following year. He says: 'and they thanked me, as a friend, for my advice'.
Those teeth are grinding again. The other company, Maison Fontaine in Paris,
also took his advice and went into production. Soon, Italy and the USA were
in on the act and it was big business. Auguste says: 'my only interest in the
matter was the satisfaction of having perhaps been of some use ...'

Maison Fontaine was also involved in another of his projects. At the Grand in Monte Carlo, Baron Rothschild had always insisted on having green asparagus rather than the anaemic white shoots. Auguste had been able to get Fontaine to separate out the larger green shoots into separate bundles. They charged twice as much for them. He later introduced the green asparagus at the Savoy and it was immediately popular. Fontaine were unable to keep up with the demand and charged heavily for what they did supply. Auguste went to Lauris in the Vaucluse on the banks of the Durance, noted for its fine white asparagus with a faint tinge of violet, and persuaded them to grow larger shoots without blanching. With some reluctance, they complied. Again a new industry grew up. Auguste wrote (in the 1920s) 'Today *l'asperge verte de Lauris* is the only variety known in London and, I must add, but without resentment, that I have never been made a present of even one bunch of asparagus ...'

It was Benoît Constant Coquelin, a French baker's son turned famous actor and gourmet, who spurred César into getting English law changed. Coquelin always stayed at the Savoy when in London. César had first met him in his early days at Voisin's in Paris. At the Savoy he once complimented César saying, 'England will soon be fit to live in. You have revolutionised the habits of society.' Then with a backhand stroke, 'But, alas, you can't change England. You will never, for instance, change the law that prevents us from supping, as we should like to, after eleven. And nothing on earth would convince the English that it is not wicked to dine in public on Sundays – they make a virtue of it.'

According to Marie, César didn't believe he couldn't change England.[16] Had he not converted their Prince of Wales to frogs' legs, by feeding them to him in the guise of Auguste's *Nymphes à l'Aurore*? (In fact he hadn't. The Prince had been eating frogs' legs for years at that time.) But Coquelin had issued a challenge César could not resist, especially as he saw the commercial advantage of such a change. Marie says, 'Ritz moved heaven and earth'. He talked to all the Savoy's clients with any influence, including many members of the Houses of Lords and Commons, and important journalists. They all said, in despair, that he couldn't change England. They were with him, however, and it was probably due to the efforts of Gordon Bennett of the *Daily Telegraph* and of Henry Labouchère who owned and edited *Truth* that they all made moves in the right direction so that Parliament took the subject seriously and hotel law was changed. Thereafter the Savoy could keep its restaurant open until half an hour after midnight, and Sunday dinners could be served. In fact Sunday dinner at the Savoy became an institution which spread subsequently to all Ritz hotels. As Auguste put it, 'the well-to-do began to flock to them on Sundays to give their servants the required weekly rest'.[17] Which is an inverted way of saying they were glad to be able to get a decent meal without having to cook it themselves.

By the middle of the Gay Nineties the Savoy was attracting everybody who mattered, or aimed to matter. The Prince of Wales had followed his favourite hotelier and master chef, and the others followed him. He indulged there his affair with Lillie Langtry more or less discreetly and she complimented César on his discretion. Cesar, knowing the affair to be an open secret already, and as good an advertisement as any, replied: 'The hotelier who cannot learn to keep his own counsel had better choose another *métier.*'

Dining at the Savoy became a Society cult and there was rivalry to produce the most original party. Often, the entire arrangement for such affairs was turned over to César and Auguste with little concern for the expense incurred. Alfred Beit was one who indulged himself in this way. He had been associated with Cecil Rhodes in South Africa and was early in the diamond industry. For one of his parties the Savoy court, which was later to become the lower dining room, was flooded and set as a Venetian scene. The guests were served in gondolas while gondoliers brought from Venice sang to them. Auguste of course suited his menu to the Italian theme. Beit was reputed to be the richest man in the world and, having spent until middle age amassing his great fortune, probably felt he had to splash out to get the fun out of it in the time left to him. The gondola party became so celebrated that it is hard now to distinguish fact from fiction.

A lavish party that particularly appealed to Auguste was given by a group of young Englishmen who had won a tidy fortune on the red in the Casino at Monte Carlo – 350,000 francs. They had decided the theme of the party should be in their favourite colour, red. César offset the red with gold, representing the winnings, and a little black for the inevitable but small losses that colour must have brought them. He reserved a corner of the dining room for the group and their guests and, to represent the south of France, furnished it with floodlit palm trees in red pots. The chairs were red and labelled with a number 9, their final winning number. The tables were sprinkled with red rose petals and the menu cards were red.

First on Auguste's menu was caviar sandwiched between two discs, about two inches diameter, cleanly cut from thin slices of smoked salmon. These *frivolités*, as he called them, were served each on a plaque of thin flaky pastry on a small red serviette, and accompanied by champagne, Clicquot rosé.

Then followed:

Consommé au fumet de perdrix rouges
Suprême de rouget au Chambertin

Laitance de carpes aux écrevisses à la Bordelaise
Cailles Mascotte
Riz pilaw
Vin: Château Lafite – étampé 1870
Selle d'agneau de Galles aux tomates à la Provençale
Purée de haricots rouges
Sauce souveraine au suc de pommes d'amour
Vin: Chateau Lafite – étampé 1870
Poularde truffée aux perles noires du Périgord
Salade de coeurs de laitue rouge des Alpes
Asperges nouvelles sauce 'Coucher de soleil par un beau soir d'été'
Parfait de foie gras en gelée au paprika doux à la Hongroise

The showpiece, the *poularde truffée*, was presented at table with an arrangement called 'Golden Rain'. It comprised of a dwarf Mandarin orange tree with chocolate 100 franc pieces covered with spangles of gold leaf arranged around its base. Segments of glacée mandarins were arranged between each coin. The whole was covered with 'rain' of golden-coloured spun sugar. Auguste said that at the end of their unique meal the diners' faces were also red – due, he thought, to the fine French red wines. They enjoyed their meal so much they said they would try the tables at Monte Carlo again. They didn't return to the Savoy, so Auguste assumed the goddess Fortune had deserted them.

Another celebrated occasion was in June 1895 when the Duke of Orléans gave a dinner and reception for the marriage of his sister, Princesse Hélène, to the Duke of Aosta.[18] Court mourning for Tsar Alexander III and for the assassinated President Carnot of France had just been lifted; Society was ready to blossom again. More than thirty princes and princesses (including Princess Alexandra of Wales), dukes and duchesses were to attend with their retinues and other guests, sixty-four in all.

The Duke gave little notice and, it so happened, the best reception rooms were already booked by the Cornish Club for a regimental dinner over which the Prince of Wales was to preside. There was little love lost between the prince and the Duke and offence was easily taken. Piqued, the Duke said he would go to the Hotel Bristol. He was a highly valued client, with his own private apartment at the Savoy, and César and Auguste had even collaborated in having a special porcelain service designed for him, patterned in gold and bearing his fleur de lys crest. César now had a problem. Undaunted, as usual, he adapted basement rooms for the Duke's party and fashioned them as a fairy palace. This meant removing partition walls, widening windows and doors and redecorating. Masons, carpenters and painters went to work, florists brought in palms and ferns to disguise what could not be changed and to conceal huge blocks of ice used to keep the place cool in the hot summer – ice was even sculptured in the form of vases to display flowers.

César had explained to the Duke what he intended to do and perhaps the fact that the Duke had fractured a knee made it easier for him to yield on his decision to go elsewhere. The banquet got off to a good start with Princess Alexandra insisting on wheeling in the Duke in his wheel chair. Both the basement affair and that upstairs went well.

Auguste's menu for the wedding reception, written on special Bristol paper, was:

Menu for the Duc d'Orléans' Main Table

Cantaloup
Consommé à la Française
Velouté à l'Italien
Truite saumonet Royale
Paupiettes de sole aux fines herbes
Selle de Pré-Salé aux Laitues
Petits pois Bonne Femme
Suprêmes de volailles Montpensier
Mousseline à l'Anglaise
Sorbet au Clicquot Rosé
Cailles aux feuilles de vigne
Brochettes d'ortolans
Salade Alexandra
Soufflé d'écrevisses à la Florentine
Coeurs d'artichauts à la moelle
Pêches Princesse
Biscuit glacé Savoy
Mignardises
Raisins nectarines

The menu is from one kept by César Ritz, which was signed by all at the main table. It differs slightly from that shown in Escoffier's notes – doubtless changes were made on the night. Different again was the menu served in an adjoining room to retinues and other guests. They had fillet of beef instead of mutton *aux laitues*, lobster in aspic instead of the sorbet. Nor were they offered the little buntings.

As for the table upstairs, the menu shows some signs of kitchen economy – the same main ingredients as for downstairs, but somewhat different preparation. Auguste had however popped in three of the Prince of Wales' favourite dishes: *Selle d'agneau à la broche* – it might have been the downstairs mutton dressed up, of course – whitebait *à la diable* and, as a savoury, soft roes on toast.

In 1896 Marie and César lived in a house together for the first time, Westover in Hampstead, furnished, Marie wrote, 'in the stuffiest kind if English taste'.[19] They had been married eight years, their son Charles was five and Marie was pregnant again. Young Charles was the one to object to their moving from the Savoy, since it would take him away from Madame Bernhardt and her grandchild Simone. He loved them both. Sarah Bernhardt of course charmed everybody but a major attraction for Charles was that she usually wore a live green lizard on a chain at her bosom: Simone, although two years Charles's junior, was his playmate. He was distracted for a while when a new brother, René, was born on 14 August.

Marie noted that César was occasionally depressed at this time.[20] She thought this was due to difficulties experienced at the hotel with 'some manoeuvre of Mrs W., the Savoy's annoying housekeeper, whose difficult attitude was troubling César a great deal'. But for the most part he had little time to brood on such problems. Apart from his commitment to the Savoy, his own business was occupying every moment he could find. He was besieged with requests from all over Europe to start new hotels and to run them; the Savoy Company now had the new Grand National Hotel in Rome of which César was managing director; and he was involved in plans with his own financial backers to form a new company, the Ritz Hotel Development Company, to encircle the globe with grand hotels. He was busy.

The following year, César and Marie moved to 'the real country' – Golders Green, then north of London but now well within it. It was the year of the celebrations for Queen Victoria's Diamond Jubilee and London was unusually crowded with visitors from home and abroad. César was involved with the preparation of a succession of Jubilee Dinners and Balls. The Savoy Company had bought Claridges Hotel and he was organising the new staff – the hotel was to be the last word in exclusive luxury – newspaper reports of its opening referred to César as 'the Napoleon of hotel-keepers'.

On his own account César also had a growing number of hotels to look after. He was having some difficulty with one he had leased in the mountains overlooking Aix-les-Bains, and he was reorganising the Frankfurter Hof that he had also leased in Frankfurt-am-Main. The Ritz Hotel Development Company was now a going concern, with César as managing director, and they were at full stretch with projects for new hotels in Cairo, Madrid and Johannesburg. He was also involved in plans for a new hotel in the Place Vendôme, Paris. He was still busy.

There is little doubt that Auguste was content in his job at the Savoy. There were culinary heights still to scale and vast scope for his talents; he was essentially his own master; he was very well paid; and he was much esteemed by the great and the good. While he gave then no indication that he was in any way anxious to move on, he still made various sallies into commercial activity. Perhaps there was something in him that remained unsatisfied. One probe in this direction aimed at setting up a company with a factory to produce bottled sauces. He succeeded in getting financial backing for this and started the process of registering a company to be called Escoffier's Food Preparations.[21]

He was also active in some of Ritz's adventures abroad. For example, he planned, staffed and organised the kitchens of the Savoy Company's Grand National Hotel in Rome which César had brought to a high standard – it was the first hotel in the world to have a bathroom for every bedroom, all two hundred of them. The new hotel changed Rome. The city's brief social season in the spring was extended back three months into winter. It suffered the tyranny of fashion imposed by visiting nomadic socialite tribes that came *en masse* to camp at the Grand. They found the Escoffier-Ritz formula irresistible. Rome gained the patronage of the cosmopolitan idle rich that it has never since lost. Both Auguste and César were entranced by Rome, and both found time to explore its ancient beauty. César said, on first entering St Peter's, 'What a magnificent banqueting hall this would make'. Auguste's activities also took him with César beyond the Savoy Company's boundaries. He was involved along with Louis Echenard, the manager of the Savoy under César, with the Ritz Company's mountain establishment, the Chalet du Mont Revard at Aix-les-Bains. So, like César, Auguste was busy – and both were probably rather pleased with their considerable achievements together. There was a summit still to be reached but they were high, head in the clouds. If there were hazards ahead, they were not obvious.

Despite all this activity they managed a little relaxation. Whenever possible, César spent his Sundays at the new country home and it became a routine for Auguste, Louis Echenard and others to drop in for tea on the lawn. It was on one such occasion, Marie recalled that she complained about the toast, saying that it was never thin enough for her.[22] César said 'Why not toast thin slices of bread once, then slice it through and toast it again?' He and Auguste then went off to the kitchen to see if it could be done. They brought out on the lawn a plate full of thin, crisp, curled wafers and Auguste said, 'Behold! A new dish: it is called toast Marie'. Marie said it was a name 'too anonymous to suit me'. She knew, however, that Nellie

Melba had just returned from America very ill and she had heard Auguste discussing the diet the famous singer was constrained to. It included dry toast. 'Call it *Toast Melba*', she said. They did, and Marie sampled it a day before Nellie herself.

According to Marie, Melba Toast was invented by her husband and named by her. But it has come down to us as an Escoffier first. It's too simple a fabrication to squabble over, but it was unlikely to have been a new concept anyway. Many a housewife must have made thin curly toast that way before. In any case, the formula was given more than four hundred years earlier by Platina.[23]

Interlude 11

The Frying Pan

'La bonne cuisine est la base du véritable bonheur.'

Auguste Escoffier

Like most aphorisms this one of Escoffier's, with which he signed many of his presentation photographs, will not stand close analysis as a universal truth. Perhaps good cooking can lift a lever on the lock of happiness – leaving aside unfortunate dyspeptics and weight-watchers – but it is a complex key that opens the door.

In Auguste's opinion, good cooking was not possible without the *poêle*. That eliminated Britain in the happiness stakes. He had been astounded to find that the French *poêle* was scarcely known to the English. How could they expect to cook properly without such a fundamental utensil? They didn't seem to realise that a whole meal from soup to pudding could be cooked in the *poêle*. All the English knew was the 'fraying-pan', which 'looked a little like a *poêle* but was of very limited use'.

He often recalled in later years the occasion when he was visited at the Savoy by *une dame du meilleur monde*, who asked him if he would kindly show her cook how she should make an omelette. She was very fond of omelettes and had found those at the hotel exquisite, while those made for her at home were uneatable. When he visited the lady's house he found that her kitchen was very well appointed and lacked nothing – nothing, that is, except the indispensable, the *poêle*. The cook had never heard of such a utensil. The happy ending to Auguste's little story was of course that the cook was amazed by the French *poêle* he brought her, and her omelettes thereafter, to the delight of her mistress, were always succulent.

Why so much fuss? Superficially there's little difference between a *poêle* and a frying pan: each is a shallow pan with sloping sides and a long handle. At the time, Auguste would mostly have seen the heavy iron pan devised for use with the bar-grate coal fire. This was similar to the pan used in the seventeenth century for 'downhearth' cooking in a wood-burning fireplace, except for a much shorter handle. There were also identically shaped pans in tin-lined copper. Some thick-bottomed frying pans of today are still similarly shaped. He would also have seen the beginning of the era of the cheap, thin, tin-plate pans, an abomination in French or English.

The main difference between a French and the traditional English pan, each of high quality, is that in the latter the sloping straight sides meet the flat bottom at an angle, while in the *poêle* the sides curve down to merge into the base. It is, of course, not impossible to cook well in an English pan, unless, like Auguste you have been brought up on a *poêle*. The good English cook was even managing to produce a good omelette long before Auguste came on the scene. Nevertheless, it doesn't take long to acquire the taste for the *poêle*. It is certainly easier to mix and stir in one when there is no sharp angle the spoon won't go in. And it is so much easier to slide an omelette out over the curved sides. Anyhow, we have the rounded ones now – although we still call them frying pans whatever the advertising blurb says.

Tools are like that: apparently trivial differences are often significant to the expert user. A carpenter will prefer one chisel to another seemingly similar, a violinist will pay a fortune for a Stradivarius. And the differences as affecting performance in the experts' hands are real. But there are some strong preferences with no real basis, as much in the cooking world as anywhere. Some of these are simply due to long experience in one mode or another. How many food processors fret under their covers while their owners beat away as they always have done with the old fork that was their mother's. But there are traditions too, which assume the stature of firm rules.

Take, for example, the frying of a steak: quickly brown the meat to seal in the juices. Do that, but don't expect to seal in the juices. The searing, in fact, shrinks the protein of the cross-cut muscle-fibre ends, effectively leaving larger pores for the escape of juices – the sizzling during cooking is due to the juices boiling off. The usual process is to brown one side, turn the steak over in the pan and cook until the red juices begin to show. The steak is then done to 'rare'. Turn it over and cook for a minute or two more and it will be 'medium rare' And so, while pre-browning doesn't save juices, it does provide a built-in timing mechanism. We are also told that a thicker cut will give us a juicier finished product. It will if you cook it for the same time as the thinner piece, but not if you cook the thicker piece longer until its centre is as well done (or as rare) as the thinner.[1]

Stop! Leave us our illusions. How can we cook at all if our myths are denied us? We'd then only have the cookery books to go on. And each tells a different story – often a myth.

12

Fall and Rise

'Never dreamed, though right were worsted, wrong would triumph,
Held we fall to rise, are baffled to fight better.'

Robert Browning

César Ritz's departure from the Savoy was precipitate. He told his colleagues he had been unable to agree policy with the board and had resigned. He stressed, however, that there was no difficulty for them. They should stay with the company.[1] It was advice none of them took. Apart from their loyalty to César, who had moulded successful careers for them all, they feared the Savoy would soon get back into its original difficulties without his leadership. They resigned as a body, as they had arrived: Agostini, Autour, Echenard, Henry Elles, Rainjoux and Auguste Escoffier. With over seven years experience at the now famous Savoy, none of them expected difficulty in getting other employment, but they were prepared to leave secure and lucrative positions to take their chances on the job market.

César had other ideas. He offered his fellow directors of the Ritz Hotel Development Company his resignation, which they refused. He then had no difficulty persuading them that his powerful Savoy team should not be dispersed. The board agreed to take them over from the Savoy Hotel Company at full salary pending the opening of their own new hotels. There was no fuss outside the immediate circle of those involved. A well-known hotelier was changing his job along with his team. Men of achievement tended to move on to achieve even more. Prosper Montagné, himself a great chef, wrote forty years later that Auguste 'for personal reasons gave up the direction of the Savoy kitchens to take charge of those at the Carlton Hotel'.[2] Eugéne Herbodeau also knew Auguste well and in his posthumous biography of him says only: 'Suddenly difficulties arose between Ritz and the directors of the Savoy Company ...'[3]

In 1938 César's wife, Marie, gave some further explanation for the abrupt departure. She wrote that, from his earliest days at the Savoy, César had been in conflict with the housekeeper she names only as Mrs W., in fact, probably Helen, D'Oyly Carte's second wife.[4] She had considerably influenced the original concept of the Savoy and its furniture and fittings, and had been the main adviser to the board on housekeeping matters – until the arrival of Marie and César Ritz. César had not favoured the housekeeper's methods and had restricted her dominion. As D'Oyly Carte's wife, Helen doubtless had strong influence with the board, and César had been unable to remove her from the staff. She continued to criticise and make trouble for César with the board. As time went on and César's influence increased, her 'hatred of him was fanned to white heat'. He was very busy with his many commitments – showing every sign of overwork in Marie's opinion – and inclined perhaps to intolerance and apt to intensify conflict, making it the more obvious. It was thus easier for the housekeeper to sway the board into presenting César with an ultimatum to restore her lost rights. He preferred to cut himself adrift from the Savoy Hotel Company. All concerned in César's resignation seem to have played their cards close to the chest – unless of course there was nothing to hide. Marie's quaint explanation has the ring of a story told by a prevaricating husband, but we shall see later why it was not an unreasonable one – although by no means the whole story.

César seems to have left immediately for Paris where his new hotel was taking shape in the Place Vendôme. Marie, who stayed to tidy up and arrange the move, found things irksome. She wrote that the housekeeper at the Savoy 'was a bad winner'. She continued her campaign of recriminations and accusations against César and also hustled Marie in her arrangements:

> She was in a great hurry to rid our apartment at the Savoy of all our personal belongings. Indeed, she practically threw them out into the street, sending pieces of Saxe and Sèvres, fragile Venetian glass and Roman pottery, precious to us, packed anyhow, helter-skelter, in cardboard boxes. The whole thing was incredible.

Marie went on to say that she received many declarations of goodwill from important customers of the Savoy.[5] There were many bouquets of roses, and Lady de Grey called specially to tell her the Prince of Wales had cancelled a party he had arranged at the Savoy and had said, 'Where Ritz goes I go'. Friends too rallied round. Mr Neuschwander of the Charing Cross Hotel, a few minutes walk along the Strand from the Savoy, reserved a pleasant apartment for her use. She was then able to close down the Golders Green house.

The arrangements for the continued employment of Auguste and the rest of César Ritz's team soon became complicated. César was keen on the promotion of hotels around the world, the declared objective of the Ritz Hotel Development Company, but his great dream centred on building his ideal hotel at No. 15 Place Vendôme in Paris. The existing building had been a bank, Crédit-Mobilier. He had taken the proposal to the Ritz Hotel Company, his own board. They had considered the site too small for a first-class hotel, and certainly too expensive to enable a profit to be made from a hotel built on it. Even the cost of an eight-day option on purchase had been daunting and he had been outvoted. Undismayed, César trawled his many patrons for financial backing, right back to those gained in his days at the Grand in Monte Carlo, including the Rothschilds. None was ready to support his dream. Then he had remembered Monsieur Marnier Lapostolle.[6] M. Lapostolle had been a client at the Savoy. He had invented a liqueur that he had brought to César for an opinion. César had liked it and had said so. 'Then you shall name it', the inventor had said. César, well aware of Marnier Lapostolle's well-developed sense of his own dignity, had said, 'Let's call it Grand Marnier'. The liqueur had been a huge success and M. Lapostolle now felt he owed César something: he financed the eight-day option. Thus armed, César found little difficulty in attracting further support.

One of his backers, Henry Higgins, the fashionable English lawyer, said: 'Kings and princes will be jealous of you, Ritz. You are going to teach the world how to live.'[7] Others came in, including the Armenian oil magnate Calouste Gulbenkian and the South African Alfred Beit, enabling César to form a new company in May 1896 with a capital of six million francs to buy and develop the site. The company, Ritz Hotel Syndicate Ltd, was registered in the names of César Ritz, Henry Higgins and members of César's team: Auguste Escoffier, Louis Echenard the *maître d'hotel*, the cashier Agostini, the staff manager Baumgarten, and Collins, César's private secretary. César was the major shareholder with 37 per cent. Higgins, Arthur Brand, a banker, and Lord de Grey, a friend of the Prince of Wales, also held deferred shares. Auguste was credited with 2½ per cent of the ordinary shares.

Work on the building had started in the same year, 1896, the year before the débâcle at the Savoy. César, of course, now wanted Auguste for his new hotel. Auguste was also wanted by the original Ritz Hotel Development Company, which was paying him a retainer: he was expected eventually to plan, staff and oversee the kitchens of their many proposed hotels. The matter was soon settled. A large and prestigious hotel was being built on a corner of the Haymarket in London by another firm, the Carlton Hotel Company. There was a strong link between this company and César's new syndicate: Henry Higgins was on both boards. The Carlton board of directors, hearing that Ritz and his team had left the Savoy, put in a bid for the services of Ritz, Escoffier and Echenard to run their new hotel when it was finished. The directors were scarcely able to believe their luck when their offer was accepted. As Auguste wrote: 'They profited from the error of the Savoy Hotel Company.'[8]

Their terms were generous: they agreed to the three staying in Paris to launch the Place Vendôme establishment – to be called Hôtel Ritz – paying them handsome retainers during that period. They would then move to the Carlton. The board agreed too that when the Carlton was up and running the team would turn its expert attention to the Ritz Hotel Development Company's new hotels as they were completed. The business network, with César and his team as the common denominator, was growing fast.

Auguste was pleased with the new arrangement and in particular that his absence from England would be temporary. 'It was a matter of my self-respect. I didn't want to leave England without finishing the task I'd started at the Savoy: the development of French cuisine not only in England but also across the world.' This was a pretty staggering ambition. There was, too, the small matter of the Escoffier's Food Preparations Syndicate Ltd, the sauce company due for its commercial launch he had left stranded in London without a sauce expert.

In Paris, Auguste set about planning the kitchens of the Ritz and seeking out suitable staff. He and César made no bones about attracting the better staff from the Savoy Hotel Company's establishments, a veritable host of smart young waiters, many of them drawn from the Savoy or the Grand Hôtel in Rome.[9] Since César was being quite obsessionally exacting in everything to do with the setting up of his new hotel, both Auguste and Marie spent a lot of time selecting the furnishings and fittings. Marie combed not only Paris but across Europe and beyond to get just the right rugs and tapestries, brocades and silks, and the linens. She toured museums and galleries for inspiration, and even studied the colour balances of the old masters in the Louvre to get room decoration just right.

The two of them were the chief advisers to César in all his dealings with the architect, Charles Mewès, who was concerned in every aspect of the design from cellar to roof and all that went between as furniture or decoration. Marie once had him change the design of the cupboards in the bedrooms because no deep drawer had been provided to hold all the false curls, buns, rolls and 'rats' that were then being worn.

César involved Auguste in the development of the restaurant, its decoration and the table equipment – much of the glass, silver and china was made to order from the selections they made from Mewès's designs. It was at the Paris Ritz that Auguste first introduced silver-plated dinner plates to the restaurant. The plates were square. This was no flash of inspiration: it was the realisation of the youthful dream he had had as an apprentice at the Restaurant Français in Nice, when his uncle had bought at auction some square plates in pewter with covers. Auguste modified the original pewter design. He replaced the handles on top of the covers by *deux petites oreilles placées aux extrémités du couvercle*, and had plates and covers made in three sizes. Ears instead of top handles made stacking possible, and the covers could be used as plates for cold entrées. The silver service for the Ritz was made by Christofle of Paris, who named the square plate '*plat Escoffier*'.

César was particularly concerned with the lighting and spent many weeks, with Marie as the model, experimenting with indirect lighting to suit the ladies. His solutions eventually became commonplace, but they were revolutionary at the time. He had large alabaster urns throwing light upwards to reflect from tinted ceilings – 'a delicate apricot pink' was found the most flattering – and centre lights behind translucent bowls hung from silken cords. And all this at a time, says Marie, 'when the last word in artistic lighting was considered to be a bronze nymph holding up a cluster of naked electric-light bulbs in lieu of flowers'.[10]

Auguste had little difficulty finding the more senior staff for his kitchen. Like César, he simply poached them from the Savoy, including Joseph Vigeard who had been his assistant chef. They were French and delighted to be well paid to work in Paris with *le maître*. This action did not endear him to the directors of the Savoy, and probably didn't help his case in the later negotiations he was to have with them. He also took on M. Gimon, a fine and well-travelled chef, who had worked in many famous restaurants and as *chef de cuisine* at the Russian Embassy in Madrid. It was Gimon who had said that even English dishes were quite good if cooked by a French chef.[11] He was Auguste's understudy.

Auguste and César made a superb partnership in hotel and restaurant development, yet they were very different in temperament and attitude to the work. César was mercurial, quick to act on ideas of which he had a constant stream, while Auguste worked long and hard on ideas developed over years. César suffered an internal tension striving to reconcile two sides of his nature. He said, for example, to the architect Charles Mewès, 'My hotel must be the last word in modernity. Mine will be the first modern hotel in Paris; and it must be hygienic, efficient and beautiful.'[12] There was the dilemma: his idea of beauty was along classical lines and difficult to reconcile with the modernity he sought.

Mewès was of course appalled at the thought of developing in modern style a building designed by the great Jules Mansart, the seventeenth-century architect who had put the gloss on Versailles. But a good architect understands people, especially paying clients, and Mewès soon recognised César's quandary and tactfully blended the best of the hotelier's ideas with his own to produce a masterpiece.

Auguste, his concepts solidly based on his own experience, knew what he wanted. His kitchens displayed only heavy iron or shining rows of copper pots and pans. No enamel or the new-fangled aluminium.[13] They had their uses, he said, in kitchens where labour was a problem. 'Here we are not concerned with that. We are concerned only with means to produce perfect cooking.'[14] This attitude was expressed everywhere in his kitchens at the Ritz. He surprised the Press by not using electricity or gas for cooking. 'Gas and electricity do have certain uses in the kitchen,' he said to an interviewing journalist, 'but they are, as you see, quite limited.' He indicated his usual gas ring, '*le feu éternel*', under the huge copper *marmite* constantly simmering to produce his meat stock, and the electric lights over stoves and preparation tables precisely hung for best effect. He explained that 'no steak could be properly grilled, no chicken properly broiled, no joint roasted just to the proper degree except with the natural heat and flames of wood and coke'. Auguste in the kitchen or restaurant knew no standard less than the best, and this was the one attitude he had in common with César. Their bond was their meticulous search together for perfection, the basis of their friendship and the secret of their success.

By the end of the year, Auguste felt he had his task at the Ritz well in hand. He was kept busy planning and conferring, but still, with no kitchens to run or menus to concoct, clients to talk to, or consultancy trips abroad, he was relatively free. And so, early in 1898, twenty years after his discussions with Urban Dubois in Monte Carlo about writing a book, he consulted his friend Philéas Gilbert, editor-in-chief of *L'Art Culinaire*, and they started to plan the book together. This time his sights were set higher. The book was to be a comprehensive cookery book for the professional.[15]

The Hôtel Ritz in Paris was to open 1 June 1898. The English version of the brochure produced to celebrate the opening announced:

> The Hôtel Ritz in La Place Vendôme, was erected on the site of the Palace of the Seigneurs de Vieuville.[16] It is unique. Each apartment has its own bathroom and is decorated in the style of Louis XIV, Louis XV, Empire, or English (Sheraton, Adams).[17] It is the very best hotel where English comfort is to be found combined with French tastes and excellence. The cuisine under Mr Escoffier the well known chef is without doubt the best in Paris.[18]

There was a series of last-minute crises precipitated by César's insistent search for perfection. The chairs for the Regency dining room arrived a week before opening day; César sent several dozen back to have arms fitted. They were back in time, but there were still no tables. The tables arrived early on the opening morning; César decided they were two centimetres too high and sent them all back to be cut down. They were 'returned just in time for the waiters, working at high speed, to get them arranged with the satiny new damask, the bright silver, the finely traced glassware, before the first guest's carriage rolled under the arcade'.[19]

The opening of the Ritz was to be signalled with a sumptuous gala to which Parisian society and international celebrities had been invited.[20] César was fearful right up to the moment the doors were opened to the first guests. Would they come? Marie thought César was remembering his departure from the Savoy and wondering how Society of the day had viewed the 'miserable scandal the Savoy housekeeper had made'.[21] It is doubtful whether Society had in fact detected any sort of a scandal. They came all right – the princes and princesses, the dukes and duchesses, counts and countesses, financiers, hostesses, beauties, sportsmen, writers, artists, gourmands, kings and queens of fashion – all that governed the world's tastes and destinies. The opening was a triumph. Then came the lull. After the opening, Parisian Society went back to whatever it was doing before. The ladies of Paris had not taken to the idea of dining in public. They saw no reason to change from what they were good at, entertaining at home. César was despondent. He had changed the traditions of life in the provinces, in London and in Rome. Why was Paris resistant?

Then Izzet Bey arrived, a francophile Egyptian Pasha. He booked at the Ritz for a dinner party with some of his friends. With one glance at the guest list – there was the best of Paris, as well as several famous hostesses who would be dining in a hotel restaurant for the first time – César and Auguste knew what they had to do. They spared no effort or expense to impress. The décor, reception arrangements, the menu and service were all discussed for days and fine-tuned for the occasion. *Le Tout Paris* was at the party and was impressed. Thereafter the Ritz overflowed with the elite of Paris. It became the meeting-place *à la mode*, a place of beauty, the place to be at extravagant ease – and to be seen.

César added another opportunity to be seen. He introduced Parisians to the English habit of afternoon tea, despite Auguste's objections. 'It breaks my heart', Auguste said. 'The bread and butter, the jam, the cake and pastries – oh, how can one eat and enjoy a dinner, the king of meals, an hour or so later? How can one appreciate the cooking, the food or the wines?' But the Paris Ritz saw the genesis of *le five-o'clock* taken at four in the afternoon.

Did the Ritz represent the last elegance of a century of elegance? Was it the last bastion soon to fall before the encroaching tide of technology? Already, even at tea, talk was of the new technical advances. There was the latest daredevil aeronautical exploit, the Curies' discovery of radium or 'Have you seen Dubois's new Daimler-Benz? Such an expensive way to frighten the horse from under you.' If it was the beginning of an end, those of the age cannot have realised it, but they nevertheless crowded into Hôtel Ritz and its restaurant as though they had.

Interlude 12

Little Devils

Auguste was instrumental in the launching of several periodicals on the culinary theme. The first of these was in 1883, *L'Art Culinaire*, then ten years later *Le Pot au Feu*, both in Paris. In London, he saw the need for a magazine in French for the ever-growing population of French cooks and kitchen staff and *Le Carnet d'Epicure* saw publication in 1911 which ceased with the Great War in 1914. *La Revue Culinaire* took its place in 1920.

For all these publications Auguste kept up a steady stream of articles. He drew mostly on personal experiences, both in his own kitchens and on his travels, but he would often spring into print with a piece of information that had intrigued him during his wide reading and researches. Typical is the following little contribution to the *Carnet d'Epicure*.[1]

Diablotin

What are they exactly, these 'Diablotins'?

The dictionary will tell you they are, quite simply, little devils, and you would be kind enough to assume that culinary diablotins must be benign little devils.[2]

The name is not new: Diablotins were invented by Duc de Richelieu towards the end of the rein of Louis XV – the one who during the siege of Port Mahon ordered a menu composed entirely of beef.

But the Diablotins of the Duc de Richelieu, or rather the *Diablotins Louis XV*,

which were very much in fashion up to the Revolution, were made as an aphrodisiac and were intended to give… certain ideas to the sovereign who, like some of
Courteline's heroes, had a devastating youth.[3]

The formula was more medical than culinary and it is still used sometimes
today, but for more than a hundred years we have left it entirely to the disciples
of Hippocrates. They only prescribe *Diablotins Louis XV* for their jaded patients
with wise circumspection.

The peculiar stimulants that Brillat-Savarin doesn't hesitate to recommend in
his *Physiologie du Gout* are not dissimilar to *Diablotins Louis XV*, although they
are more nearly actual cuisine. But I think of our objective as entirely one of
satisfying the taste and the stomach of our clients and to prepare for them agreeable
and healthy food. We know in any case how to make little intimate suppers to
inspire all the … virtue required – and I use the word 'virtue' in its original sense.

The French *vertu* comes from the Latin *virtus*, manliness. Auguste goes
on to give a recipe, but only for the culinary version:

Diablotins d'Epicure

The recipe is very simple. Little slices of bread, cut very thin, are grilled and
covered with a mixture comprising one half mashed Roquefort cheese, a quarter
fresh butter, and a quarter very finely chopped walnuts. Sprinkle with a pinch of
red pepper and serve hot. Note: the bread must be crusty.

13

The Carlton

'To know how to eat is to know how to live.'

Auguste Escoffier

By the end of the nineteenth century the railways had made the journey between London and Paris quick and comfortable. Even so, César and Marie Ritz were able to refine the journey, to ease as much as possible their frequent trips between Paris and London while the Ritz and the Carlton were both under development.[1] They would catch the 3.45 p. m. train from Paris-Nord, change at Amiens to the express from Basle, dine in the restaurant car on the way to Calais, take the steamer to Dover and the boat-train of the South Eastern and Chatham Railway to London, all in less than eight hours.[2] A century later, before the Channel Tunnel, Paris to London still took over six hours by the surface route and not, in practice, much less by air. Auguste doubtless took this route when he returned to London in March 1899[3] He was then a man in his early fifties, usually austerely dressed in a double-breasted, black, three-quarter coat, wearing built-up shoes, a bowler hat and carrying a silver-headed cane. He was clean shaven except for a rather bushy 'Prussian' (he would have preferred 'French') moustache, carefully combed but unwaxed, and his receding dark hair was beginning to grey. He undoubtedly had a lot to ponder on his journey. He was going to oversee the fitting up and organisation of the kitchen complex of what was to be the most up-to-date and luxurious hotel in the world, the London Carlton. It all had to be completed by the end of June. The hotel must open before rival constructions by the Savoy Company, the large annexe to the Savoy itself and Claridges.[4] Doubtless excited at the prospect of this new job, it would not have been a worry to him; he was now used to starting up new kitchens, each one grander than the one before. He was confident about his side of the business. He knew what had to be done and that it could be done in time. His real worries were less tangible. They centred on César Ritz. It was clear that César had taken on too much, so that, with his dogged pursuit of perfection and his insistence on being closely involved with every aspect of his projects, he was overworked. Marie was very concerned about him and spoke of his bouts of black despair which only another burst of intense activity would dispel. Auguste was sure his indispensable colleague and friend was heading for a serious illness.

Then there was the matter of leaving the Savoy, the hotel they had saved from liquidation and built up to international prominence. It was generally understood that César had resigned over policy differences with the board and, Auguste felt, had not been sorry to be able to break his contract and give himself more much needed time on his many hotel projects. But apparently for some reason the affair still rankled. Now, however, the secret was out. César had often ranted on, swearing dire revenge, but recently he had declared his intention to sue the Savoy Hotel Company for wrongful dismissal. He was, of course, taking his cue from the first general manager of the Savoy, Hardwicke, whom he had displaced at the Savoy and who had similarly sued the company – and had won. César was admitting he had not resigned but had been dismissed.

César's attitude gave Auguste a feeling of insecurity. They were firm friends and they had need of each other in continuing business success. Nothing surely could break this relationship. Yet César, without concern for Auguste's views, now seemed set on a course of action which could bring them both down. Auguste knew that in the end he would go along with Ritz in suing the Savoy, although he would much rather not have raised the issue again. While he thought they could win the case, there was no telling what mud might be slung in the public court. He felt however that, provided they stayed together, they would survive.

Such worries aside, Auguste had pleasanter thoughts to dwell on. He had enjoyed his time in Paris. Chaotic Paris, where the traffic was now so congested that talk was of greater use of the motor car to relieve the blockages and reduce the danger from runaway horses and overturning horse-drawn omnibuses. Paris that was divided two ways on every conceivable issue by the Dreyfus affair. If you were for or against this army officer's conviction for selling military secrets to the Germans, you were for or against the Jews, the Roman Catholics, the church, France, social order – or even croissants for breakfast. Auguste was French: he was comfortable in this atmosphere. To him it had a logical form and he understood it.

His task during the setting up of the Paris Ritz had been a demanding one at first, but once the hotel had opened he had more time at his disposal. He was able to indulge his favourite pastime – going to the theatre. The last show he had been to before leaving was in Sarah Bernhardt's new theatre that she had leased and rechristened with her own name: she had opened there successfully with a revival of Sardou's *La Tosca*. [5]

Had he rushed back from the theatre to cook Sarah's supper as usual, or had he left it to Gimon, the new *chef de cuisine*? He would not have doubted Gimon's ability – he had turned out to be a splendid chef. But he worked very differently from Auguste. For example, he used his very powerful voice to act as his own *aboyeur*, and Auguste expected the kitchen would be a much noisier place now he had left.

Clients for Gimon were just numbers on the chits that came to the kitchen. He made no attempt at the personal touch. He was happy to leave all that to Henry Elles, who had stayed as manager, and to Olivier Dabescat, the *maître d'hotel* César had taken over from the Restaurant Paillard in Paris. Dabescat, a Basque, started hotel work in London at the age of twelve. He stayed almost sixty years at the Paris hotel, and as Olivier of the Ritz became a celebrity to the celebrities of the world.

Auguste had regretted having to abandon his book again for a while. He wrote later, 'I was recalled to London for the opening of the Carlton Hotel, and kept extremely busy by the organising of the kitchens of this great hotel. I was forced to put off my writing to a less busy time.'⁶ He had, however, been glad to go back to the London he had grown fond of. And, for him, London started at Charing Cross. From there it was a few minutes walk eastwards up the Strand to the Savoy Hotel, and a similar distance down the Strand and across Trafalgar Square to the Carlton.

Charing (originally Cheeringe – from *chère reine*, Queen Eleanor) was once a small village between Westminster and the City of London. In 1291 the funeral procession of Queen Eleanor made its last stop there on its journey from Lincolnshire to Westminster Abbey. The grieving King Edward I had ordered a memorial cross erected at each of the thirteen stops made on the way. They were constructed in stone and elaborately carved. The cross at Charing was torn down by enthusiastic Puritans in 1647 and the stones used to pave the roadway in front of the Palace of Whitehall. A replacement cross, seventy feet high, was built in 1865 in accordance with surviving records of the original. It has since been moved closer to the station to permit widening of the Strand.

London's welcome to Auguste would have been the view of Queen Eleanor's cross in the station forecourt, and the acrid-sweet smell of horse dung from the day's accumulation on the cab rank. Like the Ritzes, he would have been welcomed in the Charing Cross Hotel by Mr Neuschwander. They knew each other well, and had spent many a Sunday afternoon together with the Ritzes and their children in their house in Golders Green.

When the Carlton Hotel Company acquired the building on the corner of Pall Mall and the Haymarket, it had already imposed itself on the landscape as a shell structure, rising on the site of the old Carlton House, the Prince Regent's London house. Auguste had last seen the building disguised in an insubstantial mantle, a scaffolding of thin, rope-tied pine trunks. He had not expected its undressed appearance, foursquare and solid, its complex of windows and pillars sharp and clean, its classical lines disguising a steel-framed structure, a method of construction new to hotel building.[7]

On César's insistence, the original front steps to the Haymarket entrance had been removed, and the entrance reconstructed to the edge of pavement, leaving room within the building for a large Palm Court, almost at pavement level. At the far end of the court, a wide stairway was to descend from the great dining room. César said it was to show off the ladies to best advantage. Waring, the board member watching costs, said, 'What, thousands of pounds just for that?'[8]

A gallery was also to be raised each side of the steps down into the Palm Court – these features had also been questioned by the board. César had said: 'The Prince of Wales will appreciate having a corner of the Palm Room to himself, and a little removed, where he and his friends can have their coffee and listen to the orchestra undisturbed.' To the next obvious question he had replied confidently that the prince would dine at the Carlton frequently. César got his galleries – a design adopted in 1908 by the Waldorf Hotel of London for its Palm Court.

It is possible to imagine the scene that confronted Auguste as he walked into what was to be the grand entrance hall: a chaos of pipes, baths and lavatory basins for installation in the hotel's three hundred bathrooms – the Carlton was to be the first hotel in London to have a bathroom for every bedroom – step-ladders and boards, paint tins and trestles, noise and bustle. And, doubtless Mewès, the architect, was waiting there to get down to kitchen planning with him.

From that moment on, Auguste was immersed in a tide of work: arguing amendments to plans, inspecting and approving, visiting suppliers of equipment, testing installations, looking after the paper work, meeting with contractors and attending design conferences. Then there were the hectic periods when César came over from Paris. Auguste was called into board meetings for discussions, particularly with Lord de Grey, J. H. Stephens, the Marquis d'Hautpoul and Harry Higgins, all of whom were closely interested in the success of the Carlton. And then came the long process of seeking and interviewing prospective kitchen staff, to form a *brigade de cuisine* with its hierarchy of a dozen *chefs* and four dozen *sous-chefs* and their assistants – sufficient, under Escoffier's direction, to serve 500 clients at each meal, *à la carte*, with no fuss and without delays.[9]

He emerged at the end of June to find that suddenly it had all been done.

He had moved some weeks previously into his fifth floor apartment, and his office on the first floor was in working order. The kitchens were fitted and tested out and the staff was trained to his ways. Mewès was making the rounds with Warings, on a final inspection of the furniture they had installed throughout the hotel, so carefully matched to the décor. An army of cleaners had arrived and was in full occupation.

César and Marie Ritz arrived from Paris on 2 July with Charles and René, their two boys now aged eight and three years respectively. The Channel boat that brought them into Southampton gave them a view of a new yacht, the *Shamrock*, at anchor at Hythe. It belonged to the newly knighted Sir Thomas Lipton. Superstitious César said, 'Foolish to paint a yacht green that you want to be a winner.' [10]

Marie's mother had come over with the household staff some time before to open up their house in Golders Green. César and Marie were in the hotel the next day where they had reserved an apartment – they were not to see much of their house for some weeks to come. César called a management meeting to include Louis Echenard, William Autour, Jacques Kramer and, of course, Auguste – all veteran members of the Ritz team – and the fine-tuning started for the grand opening on the 15 July 1899. The date usually quoted is 1 July 1899, but that was the originally planned date. Escoffier said the opening coincided with the declaration of war on South Africa, the Boer War, which was, in fact, three months later still.

Auguste was aware that, even during the last-minute checks to discover anything that might go wrong on the day, there was little tension among staff or management. Everyone seemed quietly confident in a job well done. He felt their faith was probably not misplaced, so many of them were experienced hotel openers. If more evidence of relaxation were needed it emerged the night before the opening: the staff set up an impromptu party.[11] The men came in dressed as Romans with bath-towel togas. They chanted 'Hail, César' with uplifted arms, until Ritz responded with a speech in the manner a Roman Caesar might have adopted in the Forum. Auguste was there dressed impeccably as usual in cravat and Louis-Philippe dress-coat, but nobody laughed with more abandon.

The opening was a success. There were many notables, and the whole affair was a high-society fashion parade, but the day was made for Auguste by the presence of Nellie Melba. And, in a sense, the day made him. He had last seen Nellie, his *gracieuse diva*, at the Ritz in Paris in January. She had recalled then with obvious pleasure the dessert, his *Pêches au cygne*, he had produced for her at the Savoy six years earlier, after seeing her in *Lohengrin* at Covent Garden. His own pleasure at the time had been at least threefold: the sensuous satisfaction in sculpting an elegant swan from a large block of ice; the triumph of discovery of the subtle blend of flavours of cold peach and vanilla; and the gratification in Nellie's delight. He had known for some time that she had booked in for the Carlton's opening day and he was determined to mark the occasion with a dish in some way special to her. He produced in fact a dish – which it is difficult to regard as a work of genius unless genius is the art of simplification – but undoubtedly it was the one he was to be best known for across the world. It was its première, its first public appearance. After days of worrying about the problem, the solution was in the end a simple adaptation of an existing peach dish. It was *Pêche Melba* and it was a success.

The first weeks in the new hotel were intensely busy for Auguste. The rapid growth of business was very stressful in its effect on a staff not yet fully welded into a team. Nevertheless, it was a source of great satisfaction to him that the Prince of Wales, true to his word, had followed Ritz and was frequently to be seen after dinner on his balcony in the Palm Room. The Prince's custom ensured that his friends, the so-called Marlborough House set, could be counted on, as well as the rest of the clientele of the Savoy, including theatre and opera stars who were a draw to others.

As at the Savoy, Auguste had introduced *prix-fixe* menus. This would wholly have eased the burden of a straight *à la carte* service, except that his system of designing menus individually to suit his known customers had so much increased the number of dishes to be served. Unflurried, he dealt with problems as they arose in his usual systematic way. One of his *prix-fixe* menus was priced at twelve shillings and sixpence per head for four people:

Melon Cocktail
Velouté Saint-Germain
Truite de rivière Meunière
Blanc de poulet Toulousain
Riz pilaw
Noisette d'agneau à la moelle
Haricots verts à l'Anglaise
Pommes Byron
Caille en gelée à la Richelieu
Salade romaine
Asperges d'Argenteuil au beurre fondu
Mousse glacé aux fraises
Friandises

At the other extreme was a menu for twenty people at one guinea each:

Caviar frais
Crêpes au blé noir

Huitres natives
Tortue claire au Frontignan
Velouté Princess Mary
Paillettes dorées
Homard Carmélita
Riz Creole
Eperlans à l'Anglaise
Selle de chevreuil Grand Veneur
Crème de marrons
Sauce aigre-douce au raifort
Parfait de foie gras en gelée au Champagne
Punch à la Romaine
Poularde Périgourdine
Salade de laitues aux oeufs
Coeurs d'artichauts à la moelle et
pointes d'asperges au beurre
Ananas glacé à l'Orientale
Mignardises gourmandes

As the London season drew to a close, rapid growth settled to a steady increase and Auguste fell into a routine, which suited him well. True, his working day still extended often to eighteen hours or so, but he was soon achieving three hours free in the afternoon most days, when he would often take a walk in St James's Park, play billiards or read.

The policemen on the route of his afternoon walk knew him well and the constable on duty would stop the traffic in Pall Mall for him to cross to the park. Auguste would bow his thanks and give the officer a sixpenny piece. On Sundays, the routine changed. As a practising Catholic, he went to a mid-morning church service, having seen breakfast through and before preparations for luncheon. In the afternoon his favourite pastime was to visit César and Marie at Golders Green, where they would have tea on the lawn and play with the children.

With a more settled life he thought again about the book which first Urbain Dubois then Philéas Gilbert had encouraged him to write. It would be a great book. It would encompass all his experience and detail all his innovations. It would give the world an insight into all that was good in French cooking. Then doubt assailed him. He was not so much worried about his ability to write to the necessary standard. He had had a great deal of practice over the years, with his many articles, and his friend Gringoire, editor of *L'Art Culinaire*, had always accepted his work. He admired Gringoire's own polished prose, as well as his poetry, both of which he seemed to achieve so effortlessly, but Auguste did not aspire to such standards. He still felt sure that with editorial help he would be able to produce the quality of writing the book demanded. That then was not the worry. It was the sheer size of the task he found daunting. He would need help. He talked again to Philéas Gilbert, a great chef who wrote well, but there was to be further delay.

Several of Auguste's colleagues have recalled his almost invariable morning routine after his habitual short period in bed. Invariably he would have slept well. His long working hours may have had something to do with that, but he put it down to his bedtime drink.[12] It was one he had invented and regarded not just as a nightcap but also as a great aid to longevity. It comprised the yolk of one fresh egg beaten in several spoonfuls of sugar, mixed with a pony of champagne and a glass of hot milk. He got up at 6.30 a. m., bathed and dressed carefully and brushed his black Louis-Philippe dress coat before putting it on to leave his apartment. He took the lift from the fifth to the first floor to go to his office, perhaps to leave the draft of an article for *L'Art Culinaire* he had worked on before bed the night before. He exchanged compliments with Frank, the night porter who presided over the lifts, although conversation was restricted by the language difficulty mostly to mutually friendly and respectful smiles. Leaving his office, he walked with extra heavy tread on the stairs to the kitchens and smiled as the noise of chat and banging pans died down. The difficulty for the kitchen workers was that there were two staircases to the kitchen and they never knew which one he would come down.[13] It was now about seven o'clock and preparations for breakfast were well in hand. He walked round the kitchen not missing any detail of what was going on. He stopped to have a word with a *chef de partie*, then again to give a word of advice to a young *commis*. The language was French and he was comfortable. He stayed to see the early breakfasts ready for room delivery.

Before leaving, he checked over the early morning market deliveries – what was not available in London would come from Les Halles in Paris in hampers and baskets labelled 'Reserved for the Carlton Hotel, London'. He had appointed all the suppliers himself but he kept a constant check on quality. Early vegetables, foie gras, lamb, fowls and fruit came from France, while soles, small turbot, salmon trout and Scotch salmon came from the local market. He was no believer in food from cold storage and, apart from his own crushed tomatoes, he rarely used tinned food.

On the way out from the kitchen he had a word with the *chef de nuit* who was just going off duty, and heard his report of the night shift.[14] Auguste said,

'Ah, *Monsieur*, someone had been smoking when I came down last night, I didn't see who it was. Please be strict about it, *Monsieur*. It is of course important for discipline and for hygiene, but also what do you think would become of our good name if an English Lord found a French cigarette-end in his *sauce Anglaise*, huh?'

'Sorry, *maître*, I'll see to it.'

Upstairs again, Auguste took his usual route, out under the balcony where the Prince of Wales liked to sit after dinner, through the red-carpeted entrance hall with its green-painted walls and tall palms, to the front doors. There he exchanged greetings with Kresig, the Swiss hall porter, who swung open a door for him to go out into the Haymarket. He consulted his pocket-watch as little groups of women with print-cloth turbans giggled their way past on their way home from cleaning government offices. Big Ben started its chime and on the first stroke of eight he nodded at his watch, clicked it shut and returned it to his waistcoat pocket.

Back inside, he collected his French newspaper at the gentlemen's cloak-room from Harris – who eventually knew every hat from that of the Maharajah of Bikaner to that of the King of Spain – and then went up the stairs to his office on the first floor where his own breakfast was brought in. Having seen the market deliveries, he got down to finalising the menus for the day. In the kitchen, the day staff were starting preparations for luncheon, and Auguste spent some time walking around watching techniques and occasionally tasting dishes in preparation. The calm that reigned while he was in the kitchen had become habitual, and the noise level was little raised when he left around eleven o'clock.

He next visited the restaurant to talk to the manager and the headwaiters. He was mostly concerned to discuss the clients booked in for the meals. He wanted to know the size of each party and the ratio of men to women, their nationality and anything that was known about their likes and dislikes, and what they would normally spend.

When César was in, he and Auguste ate luncheon together, unless one or other of them had been invited to the table of a client. Many of these customers were indeed friends. Auguste, for example, would invariably lunch with Alfred Harmsworth when he was in. Harmsworth was already a great newspaper magnate. He had acquired the *Evening News* in 1894, founded (with his brother Harold) the *Daily Mail* as a halfpenny morning paper in 1896, founded the *Daily Mirror* in 1893 and was to be chief proprietor of *The Times* in 1908. Later, as Viscount Northcliffe, he said of Auguste, 'I love Escoffier, a fine chap and such a restful man'.

In those early days at the Carlton, César was away a lot and Auguste did not see a great deal of him. César was now supervising the management not only of the Carlton but also of the Hôtel Ritz in Paris and the Frankfurter Hof in Frankfurt-am-Main. He was also still involved with the Grand Hôtel

National in Lucerne, and he had leased a restaurant in Biarritz – renamed Restaurant Ritz, of course – and was advising on the remodelling of the Hyde Park Hotel. He was negotiating the purchase of the Grand Hôtel des Thermes in Salsomaggiore and was in discussions with his board on opening Ritz hotels in New York, Madrid and Cairo.[15]

At one lunchtime meeting César had announced: 'One piece of interesting news, Auguste. The Walsingham and Bath Hotels are for sale.' 'They are terrible places, César, you wouldn't want those, would you?' 'Not the hotels, they are only fit to be torn down. It's their Piccadilly site overlooking Green Park that's important, the best hotel site in London and the board has agreed we should bid for it.'[16]

At such a luncheon César dropped a bombshell. Just at a time when Auguste was beginning to hope he had given up the idea, César said he had started things going on suing the Savoy Hotel Company. He hoped he could count on Auguste's backing.[17] That was in October 1899. If the Press had wind of any such activity it was probably swamped out by the news from South Africa, culminating on 11 October with the British declaration of war on the Boers – essentially for control of the gold and diamonds in the Transvaal. The Boer War had started.

Interlude 13

Out of the Jungle

'It seems a pity that more people who enjoy their food do
not enjoy the primary pleasure of preparation – as in most
cases they employ chefs, such as myself.'

Auguste Escoffier

Modern chickens have an ancestry in common with the sacred wild jungle
fowl of ancient India. So revered were the Indian fowl that on their death
their entrails were searched for clues on the ultimate meaning of life.
Domestication of those distinguished birds probably started earlier than
their sanctification. Certainly the Indian jungle fowl was used as food in
the valley of the Indus as early as 2300 BC and probably more than a
thousand years earlier. The best guess is that domestication started about
then around the fully evolved town of Rehman Dehri, where field peas,
wheat and barley had by then been cultivated for centuries.[1] Chicken breeds
then found their way to Siam, China, South-East Asia and Indonesia. They
also made their way to the Mediterranean and the chicken is recorded in
the paintings dated as 1350 BC in the tomb of Tutankhamun. The Israelites
seem not to have got around to chicken in biblical times, since it is not
included in prescribed diets in the Bible – perhaps they just didn't go for
Egyptian specialities. The Greeks around 700 BC didn't think much of the
chicken, but they liked the eggs. They were also way ahead of their time

in banning crowing cocks from the cities. The Romans, a couple of centuries later, thought the chicken too scrawny to eat, until they discovered that by feeding them instead of letting them scratch around for themselves they became plump, tender and succulent.

By the first century AD they had many chicken recipes in their portfolio.[2] These they rendered anonymous with their usual battery of condiments and sauces, mixing in, for example, dill, mint, dates, asafoetida, a reduction of grape juice, olive oil, mustard and the ubiquitous fishy liquamen. No quantities are recorded and so, to be generous, one might suppose that, carefully balanced, such concoctions were ambrosial. One snag was that the grape juice was probably boiled down in lead-lined vessels and took a horrendous quantity of the brain-rotting metal into solution, contributing, perhaps, to the dose the Romans acquired from their water transported in lead ducts, and leading supposedly to the downfall of the Roman Empire. Meanwhile, the Romans spread the chicken around their empire, and left it part of the staple diet of the whole of Europe. Chicken is now one of the world's most popular meats – and is becoming more so as people eat less red meat, apparently for health reasons.

Chicken featured well to the fore in Auguste's best-known dishes. A recipe for one of these, which has stood the test of a long time, he acquired intact on a visit in 1885 to Châtillon, near Bresse, in the area of France famed for the chickens it rears:

Volaille aux Ecrevisses

Choose a fine bird and divide it into five parts: the two wings, the breast and the two legs (separate thighs from drumsticks at the joint), divide the carcass into two, remove the pinions from the wings.

Put all the parts into a casserole with four or five spoonfuls of melted butter; season lightly with pepper and salt; cook slowly so as not to darken the butter.

After 20 to 25 minutes (depending on the size of the bird), add a soupspoonful of finely chopped onions and two dozen very fresh chicken kidneys.

As soon as the onions have acquired a light golden colour, add a glass of dry white wine. When the wine is reduced add two large glasses of fresh cream; simmer for 10 to 12 minutes.

While the chicken is cooking, cook three dozen prawns in *court bouillon*, peel them and add the tail meat to the casserole; season as required and serve hot.

Auguste notes: 'This is an excellent dish worthy of the most sumptuous table and to be classed with the marvels of great cooking. But it was in a little county town of the Bresse district that this recipe was given to me by Mme Edouard, the charming wife of a farmer.'

In writing about the occasion a quarter of a century later, he says the memory of the meal he enjoyed on the farm 'still haunted him'. He still served the *volaille aux écrevisses* made to the recipe just as it was given to him. He sometimes added thickly-sliced truffles or morilles. And occasionally he would add to the sauce a spoonful of good curry or of fine paprika. At the time of his visit to Bresse he was directing the kitchens of the Grand Hotel in Monte Carlo and he first prepared Mme Edouard's chicken dish for a small lunch party given by someone of importance in the principality. On this occasion he added the truffles and took the opportunity to name the dish after M. Blanc, the founder of the Grand.

M. Blanc's name however, was destined for posterity for other reasons. The recipe comes to us in *Le Guide* as *Poulet Sauté à la Bressane*,[3] where crayfish replace the prawns, and then with the same name in *Ma Cuisine* where mushrooms replace the crustaceans – supermarkets now package something like that, too.[4] It was at the Grand Hôtel in 1881 that Auguste devised his famous *Poularde Derby*, at a time when, with the Grand's growing popularity, Auguste's cuisine was edging towards international renown – it was then that D'Oyly Carte, who was to be such an influence on Auguste's career, fell under the spell of his menus. Auguste served the *Poularde Derby* for the first time when Albert Edward, Prince of Wales, stayed at the hotel. The prince pronounced it 'a truly royal dish'

Poularde Derby

Stuff a *poulet* with 7oz. Riz Pilaw mixed with 3½ oz. *foie gras* and 3½ oz. truffle cut into large dice.

Poêle the bird, then place it on a dish and surround with alternate large truffles cooked in Champagne and slices of sautéed *foie gras* each placed on a small croûton of bread fried in butter.

Serve separately the cooking liquid from the pan to which 3½ fl. oz. veal gravy and the cooking liquid of the truffles has been added; reduce to 7 fl. oz. and lightly thicken with arrowroot.[5]

Auguste presumably recognised the extravagance of the recipe since in presenting it to the housewife in his *Ma Cuisine* he invited her to cook the truffles in Madeira rather than champagne. He couldn't have known of course the truffles alone would cost more than the champagne at today's prices in Britain. And then there's the *foie gras*.

His first published recipe for chicken (1883) is one less greedy for truffles:

Poulets à la Broche à la Russe

Take two corn-fed chickens [why two?]: after larding (with pork fat and anchovy) and, seasoning well, you stuff them with fine forcemeat with chopped truffles added; cook them on a spit. When they are nearly cooked you keep them basted

with hot fat to keep them from blackening.
  Serve with:

Sauce Rémoulade

½ pt. mayonnaise	pinch of chopped parsley
2 tbsp. Dijon mustard	pinch of chopped chervil
1 tbsp. chopped gherkins	pinch of chopped tarragon
½ tbsp. chopped capers	½ tbsp. anchovy essence

Mix all the ingredients together.[6]

Auguste needed little encouragement to include truffles in his chicken recipes and what a medium they are for the black beauties. Roll on the day when we have learned to cultivate them.

If the bird is to be served jointed, he still preferred where possible to cook the whole bird first. Elizabeth David is firm about this, too, indicating that, if the French cook is in a hurry, he or she will cut a roasting chicken into joints, fry it gently in butter or oil, add wine or stock, and perhaps vegetables and little cubes of salt pork.[7] The result will be the *poulet sauté*. Such a dish in a restaurant would be uplifted with a regional label, or named after a dignitary. 'I must confess,' she says, 'these cut-up chickens seldom appeal to me. However good and carefully cooked the dish, one nearly always finds the chicken is a trifle dry …' These days the market does not encourage us to take this line. Rows of plastic covered thighs, drumsticks and breasts, in cold display cabinets, pale flaccid flesh lit in pink disguise, tempt us to take the sinful line of least resistance, away from the path of whole-bird righteousness. Despite his view on cooking chicken joints, Auguste declared himself 'ecstatic' over *Chicken à la Maryland* he had at Martin's in New York in 1908. Strangely, he already had the recipe in *Le Guide* as *Poulet sauté Maryland*. He also included over sixty other recipes for *poulet sauté* among the 350 or so chicken recipes he gives in *Le Guide*. An admission perhaps that even seasoned professionals are sometimes in a hurry.

Auguste was a great marketeer when it came to popularising his cuisine, ever seeking the famous or the topical to embellish his wares. In 1879 an American explorer, Commander G. W. De Long, set out in the ship *Jeannette* in search of new lands north of Siberia. His ship was trapped in the ice and drifted eastwards for two years before she was finally crushed and sank. Two of the crew survived. Auguste came across this romantic story many years after the event and found its appeal irresistible. A chicken dish, aptly designed and named, soon headlined a menu for three hundred people gathered in the Savoy dining room one Sunday evening in June 1896. The dish remained one of his specialities:

Les Suprèmes de Volailles Jeannette

Poached chicken breasts, skinned and cold, each cut in four slices, are trimmed to a neat oval and coated with white sauce *chaud-froid*. Each slice is placed on a slice of parfait of foie gras shaped to match. These are laid in a timbale on a bed of chicken aspic jelly, on which are arranged thin slices of truffle. Decorate with blanched tarragon leaves and cover the whole with more jelly and allow to set. To serve, the timbale representing the ship is inset into ice by sculpting a hole the right size. Otherwise it can be pressed into crushed ice. The *chaud-froid* sauce is a reduction to one third of equal quantities of chicken aspic jelly and ordinary velouté and a little cream. Season and finish with cream equal in volume to the reduction

14

The Summit

'The pleasures of the table belong to all times and all ages,
to every country and every day; they go hand in hand with
all our other pleasures, outlast them, and remain to console
us for their loss.'

Brillat-Savarin's Seventh Aphorism

On 22 January 1901, Queen Victoria's death drew a line under an era. Her
implacable respectability had changed the character of the monarchy and
ensured its survival, but among those less concerned with such respectability
was her eldest son Albert Edward, Prince of Wales. During the decades she
had kept him from the throne, he had preferred travel around Europe to
staying at home under her austere gaze, but while his diplomatic antics
excused the use of his small allowance from public funds, his taste for life,
especially its food and its women, ran through it rapidly. He was, however,
a popular figure with many rich and influential friends, so shortage of funds
was never more than a temporary embarrassment. He, with his large social
following, was also a boon to hoteliers across Europe. He was particularly
attracted to hotels and restaurants associated with the Ritz-Escoffier team.

Suddenly, he was King Edward VII of Great Britain and Ireland, of British
Dominions beyond the Seas, and Emperor of India; many purveyors of the
good life had lost a client. The Ritzes were in Paris when the news broke.
César was sombre at first but soon brightened: King Edward's reign would
be a merry one. César hastened to London to prepare first for the onslaught
of royalty and people from the provinces visiting for the funeral, and then
to plan for the Coronation. He was overoptimistic. The South African war
dragged on and news was not good. It was no time for festivities, and the
date for the Coronation was not set. Kitchener called for more young men
to face the deadly accurate rifle fire of the Boer guerrillas.[1] A commentary
on the nutrition of the time was that forty per cent were rejected on medical
grounds – mostly for bad teeth.

There seems to be nothing recorded on whether César had done anything
about his threatened suit against the Savoy Company. He was working away

almost in a frenzy between his many projects, travelling from one to the other ceaselessly. Auguste settled into his job at the Carlton, content to run an efficient kitchen and always devising new menus and developing new dishes. Soon, as he settled to his routine, he found time to look again to his writing. Still he was sure he would need help to produce the comprehensive book he had in mind. His main hope originally had been Philéas Gilbert, but as Gilbert was in Paris close collaboration would not be possible. Nevertheless Auguste approached him, and Gilbert said he would help all he could, but went on 'I have a friend in Anvers, Emile Fétu, an intelligent fellow, who should be better known. He is not going to find a way to make himself known in Belgium. Could you not interest yourself in him?' [2]

Auguste followed up Gilbert's suggestion and, with the collaboration of both Gilbert and Fétu, the book was restarted in earnest. They published the book themselves. Auguste describes the process:

> Fétu spent nine to eleven hours each day editing the formulas and recipes for the future book. I'd had some little scales sent from Paris with which he could weigh exactly each ingredient before it was incorporated into the composition of a dish. He made fair copies of the recipes and despatched them to Gilbert (in Paris), who took them himself to the printers in Lagny (E. Colin) and kept an eye on the composition. He then sent us the proofs and after verifying them we sent them back to him with authority to print ... [3]

Eugéne Herbodeau said later that most people Auguste consulted were of the opinion that it was a book of recipes that should be compiled for the use specifically of professional chefs. Auguste thought differently. His aims for the book have been variously reported, for example that it was as much for the housewife as the professional. He says himself that he wanted the book to be more 'a useful tool rather than just a recipe book', an instrument to be kept close at hand by every cook who wished to learn, but, in particular, 'those who, starting work today, will in twenty years' time be at the top of their profession in charge of a large organisation'.[4]

It was not until May 1902 that the Peace of Vereeniging was at last signed to end the Boer War, and the date for the Coronation set as 26 June 1902. The Carlton in Pall Mall was on the route the Coronation procession would take from Buckingham Palace, and César planned a gala dinner for the night. He was 'determined preparations for it be brought to their ultimate perfection. The hotel which the King as Prince had so often honoured should now spare no plans or expense in honouring the King'.[5]

It soon looked as though the expense was not going to be a worry. Every room and every table for the gala dinner was booked weeks in advance. As for viewing the procession, César used all his guile and persuasive powers to get those lucky enough to be booked into rooms overlooking the route, to take in others less fortunately placed in the hotel.

At this very busy time at the Carlton, and in addition to his overseas commitments, César was in the last stages of negotiation for the purchase of the site in Piccadilly for the new Ritz Hotel. Marie was sometimes quite frightened by his exhausted condition.[6] 'Don't worry, Mimi,' he would say, 'I'm not ill; only tired ... I'm an old man now.' He was nearly fifty-two.

On 24 July 1902, with the Coronation two days away, the King was taken ill with appendicitis – this at a time when removal of the offending organ was scarcely a practised procedure, and anaesthesia was often provided by a porter with a rag and a chloroform bottle. Risk of death was far from negligible. The King was operated on successfully. In fact he kept his appendix – the surgeon drained the abscess. Nevertheless, from then on appendectomy was fashionable and soon became routine. The Coronation was of course postponed. Cancellations of hotel and restaurant bookings flooded in.

Auguste heard the news from César at noon while supervising the preparation of Sunday luncheon, a popular meal at the Carlton at which he would often serve as many as five hundred clients. Many of the provisions for the great gala dinner the following Tuesday had been bought and delivered, and some dishes had even been prepared, but he had to set about cancelling what he could of remaining arrangements. This was not simple since most suppliers would not have been available on a Sunday and many despatches to the hotel would already have been arranged for early Monday morning. César announced the news in the luncheon room, which was quite full. A Press report said:

> All at once there was an instantaneous and striking silence. We looked with surprise, and as the silence continued we rose from our seats. Everybody was standing motionless and as if petrified. In the middle of the room M. Ritz, the managing director of the hotel, pale and dejected, was speaking with a voice muffled but clearly audible to the taciturn gathering. He said, 'The Coronation will not take place. The King, after consultation of the leading physicians, is now undergoing an operation, dangerous, perhaps mortal, which has been declared absolutely and immediately necessary ...'[7]

César, too, had many cancellations to make at this late hour and he calmly set about doing so. Then suddenly, in mid-afternoon, talking to one of the staff, he collapsed.

When he came to he was delirious. His carriage was called and he was taken home to Golders Green. In two weeks the King was out of danger but César was not. The date of the Coronation was set for 9 August; the Ritzes went off to stay with the Pfyffers in Lucerne to get 'complete rest, no work' as prescribed for him. The change in César may be judged from his response to Mewès, now directing his architectural skills on to the new Ritz in London, who consulted him on important design aspects of the hotel. 'Do what you like', César said.

Marie felt that news of how ill César really was would do nobody any good. She decided that with the help of Defente, César's secretary, she could cover for him and carry on his business affairs. She did this successfully and the outside world was not aware that the inimitable César Ritz was not still at the helm. A newspaper report, said:

> Various rumours have been in circulation for some weeks past as to the health of M. César Ritz of the Carlton Hotel, London, England. We are pleased to be able to state on the most reliable authority that M. Ritz is now in good health, and is at present busily occupied with his plans for the transformation of the Walsingham into a *hôtel de luxe*, which is to bear his name.[8]

Transformation indeed; the old Walsingham and its neighbour, the Bath, were being completely torn down to make room for the new Ritz Hotel.

In the pleasant surroundings of Lucerne and with the kindly care and attention lavished by the Pfyffers, César's rest cure was beneficial. He was able to take a holiday with Marie in Egypt, and to lay the foundation stone of a Ritz hotel that was to be erected in Cairo. After a short stay at the Grand Hôtel des Thermes, Salsomaggiore, at the beginning of its spring season, they then returned to London and, against the doctor's advice, César got back to work with some semblance of his old enthusiasm. Marie was greatly cheered too when he again entered into family life and paid a lot of attention to the children. She realised, however, that he was still ill and took on a great deal of the work herself. But at home he was happy again. Auguste would come to tea on Sundays and it sometimes seemed like old times. In play, César would plot with the children to play tricks on Marie. She wrote of one occasion:

> I was always scolding them for leaving money around carelessly. 'You never catch me doing such things', I said. Then one day we were going out for a drive. It was raining. As I opened my umbrella to cross the courtyard, out fell a five hundred franc note. All the family stood in a circle and nearly suffocated with laughter at my discomfiture.

'You do things on a large scale, Mimi', César said, and they all laughed again. Marie says, 'That is the last happy memory I have of my husband.'[9]

The Gala Dinner was again planned for 9 August 1902, the day of the Coronation, and it was again fully booked. Auguste's menu was:

Caviar frais
Melon Cantaloup
Consommé aux nids d'hirondelles
Velouté Royal aux champignons blancs
Paillettes au parmesan
Mousseline de sole Victoria
Poularde Edouard VII
Concombres au curry
Noisettes d'agneau de Galles souveraine
Petits pois à l'Anglaise
Suprèmes de caneton de Rouen en gelée
Neige au Clicquot
Ortolans au suc d'Ananas
Blanc de romaine aux oeufs
Coeurs d'artichauts Favourite
Pêches Alexandra
Biscuit Mon Désir
Mignardises
Café Mode Orientale
Les vins et liqueurs au choix des dîneurs

César was not there.

Auguste first met Rosa Lewis soon after he was installed at the Carlton. They had a great deal in common. Rosa was born on 27 September 1867 in the village of Leyton before it became part of London. Her father, originally a watchmaker, became an undertaker. She battled her way from kitchen maid to fame as a cook. Like Auguste, she went to cook in great houses and spent her life among the upper crust of society of her day. Working for Lady Randolph Churchill, she had chased the red-headed Winston Churchill out of her kitchen wielding a soup ladle and shouting, 'Hop it, copper knob'.[10] He was ten at the time.

She was a favourite of the Prince of Wales, later Edward VII – as a cook, that is. They first met – says one of the several stories – at a shooting party at Chieveley Park where Rosa was doing the cooking.[11] Rosa, never one for looking like one of the servants, was elegantly dressed as usual that evening. She was sipping champagne in the dining room having supervised the layout of the cold collation. The Prince, came in, kissed her and went back to the drawing room. He asked the hostess later what had happened to the beautiful guest in white, and learned that it was probably Mrs Lewis, the cook. 'But, I kissed her.' 'Then we shall certainly have a very excellent dinner.' There were rumours of course that their relationship was an intimate one, but her biographer, who was a close friend of Rosa's, said there was no evidence of this.[12] She does say though that Rosa kept some corsets which many notables had signed, including King Edward.

In 1892 she bought the Cavendish Hotel in Jermyn Street, London, a pleasant walk from the Carlton, through St James's Park, where Auguste took his walk most afternoons. She was determined that her hotel should not be available to just anyone and, at first, it had no public restaurant. Every apartment had its own private dining room. King Edward had a suite permanently reserved and would dine there incognito. The dining arrangements remained exclusive for some sixteen years but, responding to public pressure, she then extended the hotel to accommodate a public dining room.

Rosa was beautiful, gregarious and friendly, but sparing with her more intimate favours. As for Rosa's relationship with Auguste, the two cooks certainly saw a lot of each other. The great chef called her 'Queen of Cooks' and, Rosa claimed, taught her more about cooking than anyone else. Rosa was well known for reliable discretion about the affairs of others, and this was no bad thing for her business. No one had any doubts that she had a lot to keep quiet about. It was said of her, 'she knew who really were the fathers of one's friends'. She was equally reserved when others had their affairs with her – she said nothing, wrote no letters and kept none. With a Londoner's turn of phrase, softened perhaps in the telling, she was supposed to have said, 'No letters, no lawyers, and kiss my baby's bottom'.[13] She kept some things, however. One of three photographs that survived the bombing of her hotel in the Second World War was of Auguste. She kept it in a silver frame in her parlour where it had been for forty years. Maurice Ithurbure who worked with Auguste at the Carlton knew of his great friendship with Rosa. Asked about it, he tapped the side of his nose, an involuntary gesture he made when he was about to release no information. He said only, 'He was very fond of the ladies, you know'.[14]

During the first year or so of the new century, with increasing work at the Carlton, and the effort on his book, Auguste could not have had much time for Rosa. He finished the book in November 1902 and it was published in Paris in 1903 as *Le Guide Culinaire*. Some of the recipes were certainly culled from the great chefs of the past, particularly Carême, Dubois and Bernard, but they were mostly those he had updated for his own use.

Eugéne Herbodeau wrote:

The great masters of French cuisine were invaluable to Escoffier, and their recipes served him as the foundations of countless of his own. But he knew how to adapt his works to the customs and tastes of the times and his book bears the marks of his genius. An enormous number of cookery books are now published, many written without discrimination. The recipes they contain have rarely been sub-jected to experiment, and for the most part they are copied from other sources and grossly deformed in order to give them some semblance of originality.[15]

He says elsewhere that every single recipe in Auguste's book 'was not only composed with care and intelligence but was considered and pondered ... The *Guide Culinaire* attempted to end the age of empiricism in the kitchen. Everything was now weighed and calculated and recipes classified.'[16]

To end empiricism? Auguste was nothing if not an experimentalist. Was it more to end sloppiness – often applied with a flourish – and to add precision so that a dish once designed could be reproduced time and time again? He was not actually the first to attempt precision. Jules Gouffé, the chef of the Jockey Club in Paris, was finely detailed in his *Royal Cookery Book* of 1869. His motive, however, for meticulous timing and weighing was a somewhat futile attempt to frustrate plagiarism.[17]

Auguste's book sold in French wherever French cooks were to be found – which was across the world. The first edition in German was in 1904 to be followed by versions in Italian and Swedish and, in 1909, in Danish. Translated into English, both in USA and England, the book was called *A Guide to Modern Cookery*. First publication in each country was in 1907 with the number of recipes reduced to a little under three thousand. In England there were fifteen impressions from 1907 to 1952. There was a second edition in 1957 reprinted regularly until 1979, when a new translation was undertaken of the whole French edition of 1921. The new title was *The Complete Guide to the Art of Modern Cookery* and it gives over five thousand recipes again. There were ten reprints up to 1995 and a softback edition. It has been a long-lasting success.

If anything were needed to consolidate Auguste's renown at the time, *Le Guide Culinaire* was it. He was now widely known and his patronage was sought – as it was when Emile Fétu and Pierre Traisneau founded the Union des Cuisiniers, Patissiers et Glaciers de Londres in 1903, with 'the cordial goodwill of Auguste Escoffier'.[18] The Union, a Friendly Society for French cooks working in England, was later named L'Association Culinaire Fran-çaise de Secours Mutuels and still exists today.

With *Le Guide* successfully launched, Auguste missed the insistent press-ure of writing it. His was a life of goals to be achieved, and his main one of reaching the top of his profession was now on a maintenance basis. His position at the summit also facilitated his realisation of another aim: the spread internationally of French cuisine. That was, however, mostly a matter of grasping the best of the many opportunities that now arose. Writing articles provided a medium for conveying messages he thought the world should have. He had mostly written about cooking but he had also long wanted to spread himself on the subject of government contracts for army rations and the urge to write a book persisted. He started work on *Mémoires d'un Cuisinier de l'Armée du Rhin* to express his recommendations.

The book was to tell the story of his involvement as an army cook in the Franco-Prussian war and so present his credentials for criticising the method used for selecting suppliers of food for the army. His theme was that to select contractors submitting the lowest tender asked for trouble. Obviously, suppliers would cut to the bone and beyond to get the contract. Selected, they would then have to cheat to stay in profit, 'cheat the patriot fighting for his country'. Auguste's friend and confident, the poet Gringoire, liked the idea of a book and suggested that the story of cooking during the war would also make excellent copy for the publication to which they both regularly contributed, *L'Art Culinaire*. Auguste then wrote the story as a serial for the magazine over a period of two years.

Auguste's time was again fully taken up, but there were breaks in the routine, a series of highlights for many years to come. The first highlight after the publication of *Le Guide* was his meeting with the President of the French Republic, Emile-François Loubet. Auguste's menu for dinner on the first evening of the President's stay at the Carlton was:

Visit of the President of the French Republic
to the Carlton Hotel Restaurant, London

6 July 1903

Caviar frais – Melon Cantaloup
Potage béarnais
Consommé aux nids d'hirondelle
Filet de truite au chambertin
Poularde aux perles du Périgord
Nouilles au beurre noisette
Mignonette d'agneau Clarence
Petits pois à la française
Suprême d'écrevisse
Neige au champagne
Caille escortée d'ortolans
Coeur de laitue
Asperge crème d'Isigny
Pêches Alexandra
Parfait aux trois couleurs
Mignardises

The peach dish dedicated to the new Queen had doubtless been a success at the Coronation Dinner since Auguste reproduced it for this important occasion. He favoured, too, the birds' nest soup – which he persisted in ascribing to swallows.

The next evening the President went to the opera, and then back to supper at the Carlton. He was served lamb again, *Côtelette d'agneau au beurre noisette*. Recognising Auguste's precision in menu design, it can only be assumed that he knew Monsieur Loubet was fond of lamb. Perhaps they spoke of the two dishes after supper when Auguste was presented to him. Auguste would have been keen to learn more of his likes and dislikes.

It is clear from various letters that Auguste managed to visit his family occasionally, but nothing has survived that he might have written referring directly to such trips during this period. He seems to have taken advantage of visits on behalf of the Carlton to suppliers in France to spend a few days in Monte Carlo. One such excursion was over Christmas 1903. His daughter Germaine, still at school, was living at home with Delphine. Daniel at eighteen and Paul, twenty-three, might well have left home by this time. Paul was courting Jeanne Dupré, the girl he was to marry. But Auguste has left us nothing about his developing family. Only a letter to him at the Carlton several years later from a Monsieur Monteille, a wholesaler in butter, poultry and game, refers to the visit.[19]

Auguste also extended his duty trips to visit the regions of France for research purposes. He tells of an adventure in Lyon. He was invited to dinner with some friends who were above all else preoccupied with politics. As this was the time when the separation of state and church in France was still unsettled, he expected dinner to be contentious. He had very much in mind a recent strip cartoon by Caran d'Ache – the pseudonym for Emmanuel Poiré – *karandash* being Russian for pencil – where, in one frame, the hostess had forbidden talk at dinner on *l'Affaire Dreyfus*. All at the table was serene. In the second frame there had been no constraint on the subject of conversation: 'the soup bowl, the plates, the bottles were dancing a furious tango; guests had each other by the throat, menacing with their knives or forks; it was a desperate battle, a war to the death without mercy. The caption read simply, 'They spoke of it!' Auguste wrote, 'I feared something like that at the dinner. I had never had the time to busy myself with politics and I wondered what I could possibly do at such a *mêlée*.'

In the event, talk was at first quite noisily political. Auguste was amused to notice that the maid was unaffected by the exuberant discourse – she turned out to be deaf. But talk soon became essentially epicurean and Auguste was able to take part. He had no doubt that it was the excellence of the meal that had kept the peace, and who could doubt it? First, *oysters au piment*, helped down with an excellent Chablis – politics going well, but muted. Trout in a *beaujolais court-bouillon*; a Mercurey to drink – politics faint. *Poulardes de Bresse en gelée*, accompanied by a Chambertin – no politics. Some little thrushes – *Terrine de grives à la Bourgeoise* – the burgundy was still helping things along – happy talk. *Pâté de foie gras Sainte-Alliance* – burgundy. It was as well, Auguste thought at this stage of the male conversation, that providence had had the wisdom to plug up the ears of the chaste maidservant. *Jambon glacé a l'Epicurienne* – burgundy. *Salade des Fines Gueules*, 'a marvellous surprise' said Auguste, served, of course, with a fine champagne.

On that same trip, Auguste went to spend a few days with his old friend Lecoq in Auch, Gascony. The two had met in 1870 as prisoners of war in Mayence when Lecoq, a captured sniper, had been reprieved at the very last minute from death by firing squad. They had not seen each other since those days but, clearly, Auguste was known by repute to the rest of the family, presumably from Lecoq's war stories. Auguste was treated by Madame Lecoq, the children and the grandchildren almost as a member of the family.

The first evening's dinner in the Lecoq's smart dining room was:

Pot-au-feu familial
Perdreaux à la Bonne-Maman
Galettes de mas [20]
Salade de beteraves
Flan de cèpes
Poires Mariette
Crème Chantilly
Café
Vieil Armagnac

Auguste described the menu as a simple one, but dainty. It was the partridge casserole that interested him most. Mme Lecoq, naturally enough, had been apprehensive in producing a meal for so famous a master chef but she was soon at her ease talking to Auguste about it. She said the casserole recipe was one of her grandmother's. Auguste said he thought many of the best dishes would not be known if our grandmothers had not carefully preserved and passed on their secrets. He congratulated her on her menu and its preparation. Auguste passed on the recipe to us as *Les perdreaux de grand'mère*.[21]

In July 1903 César had become very ill again. He had taken to his bed with an attack of influenza. Recovered from that, he had remained in a depressed state and again he collapsed. The crisis had passed but, Marie remarked, 'it left him a broken man. A dark cloud seemed to envelop his mind'. She went on to say that it lifted only for very brief intervals thereafter. His memory was failing and at times he blanked out almost completely. For fear of these lapses he avoided meeting people. He said to Marie, 'I am worse than a dead man, my working life is ended'.[22]

It was during one of his more lucid periods in 1905 that the Ritz Hotel in Piccadilly opened its doors and he was able to be there for the ceremony. During the same period he sold his interests in the Frankfurter Hof and the Grand Hôtel des Thermes in Salsomaggiore, among the many luxurious palaces he had laboured to perfect, probably at the expense of his health. They went out of his life, no longer meaning anything to him. He also retired then from the board of directors of the Ritz Hotel Development Company, but Marie kept his name on the board of the Hôtel Ritz in Paris.

Auguste's next highlight resulted from his being commissioned by a German shipping company, the Hamburg-Amerika Line, to plan, staff and organise the kitchen and restaurant on their new de luxe liner, *Amerika*, which was to ply the Atlantic between Hamburg and New York. They approached the Carlton Hotel Company Board, which accepted the commission and agreed to the use of the name 'Ritz-Carlton Restaurant'. The liner was finished on time, and was to leave Cuxhaven on her inaugural voyage on 19 June 1906. The evening before sailing, the German Kaiser, Wilhelm II, was to dine on board. Auguste was asked to compose a suitable menu.

His previous work with Germans had been for César and his companies. This time a German company was the direct beneficiary. To Auguste, the French patriot, Germans were the enemy. At the same time, he was a firm believer in the power of discussion, and even compromise was acceptable if it made for progress in the desired direction. He tells a story about the *mousse d'écrevisse* which was to be part of the Kaiser's meal. The translator rewriting the menu in German did not understand *mousse*. His dictionary gave the meaning 'cabin boy'. He said to Auguste 'What do you think, we Germans are, cannibals?' Auguste was not happy to have his menu expressed in coarse German, but he explained that it was the masculine form of the word he had found. He added: 'A nice tender cabin boy might make a more appetising dish than the old *bavarois* we've had on our menus for the last couple of centuries.'[23] A compromise emerged. The German laughed at the joke and left the menu in French: Auguste changed the name of the dish to *Ecrevisses à la Moscovite*.

There are many stories told of the various meetings of Auguste with the Kaiser and it is difficult to separate fact from fancy. Several of these emerged after their meeting at the Adlon in Berlin, one of the new hotels to which he and Ritz had applied their particular brand of magic while at the Savoy. After the inaugural dinner, the Kaiser, the guest of honour, asked Auguste how he could thank him for all his trouble.[24] 'Your Majesty,' said Auguste, 'give us back Alsace-Lorraine.' It was probably also at the Adlon the Kaiser drew Auguste aside to ask him to draw up a menu for a late dinner with a noted French actress, 'knowing his ability to suit such an occasion'. This was reported as an example of the sort of insight Auguste gained into the private lives of the great ones.[25]

Fortunately Auguste tells his own tale of what happened on the *Amerika*:

> The Kaiser came aboard at seven o'clock in the evening with his suite having just returned from Kiel where he had been watching a regatta. He had scarcely sat at the table when one of his aides said to him, 'Your Majesty sent for Escoffier from London. Is Your Majesty aware that he was a prisoner of war in 1870 and he could be planning to poison us?' [26]
>
> I was immediately warned of this observation which could have had quite unpleasant consequences for me. A few minutes later an enormous fellow came to the kitchen 'to cast an eye over the place', he said. It certainly was not the object of his visit as he immediately asked me whether it was true I'd been a prisoner of war in 1870. I told him that I had been a prisoner in the camp at Mayence but that I wasn't on board to poison them. I went on to say that if one day there was trouble again between his country and France, if I was still able, I would do my duty. Meanwhile they shouldn't worry, as that would upset their digestion.

A newspaper obituary reported Escoffier as saying that he regretted missing the opportunity to poison the Kaiser.[27] Auguste always vigorously denied the story.

After dinner, the Kaiser went to the kitchen and Auguste received him 'with all the honours due to his rank'. The Kaiser was very friendly and put Auguste at his ease so that he was able to reply to questions without embarrassment. The Kaiser said, 'I understand you were a captive of my grandfather', then asked Auguste where he had been taken prisoner, where he had been kept, and whether he had been well treated. Auguste said he had nothing personally to complain about, but he had seen on all sides, German, French, English, and Italian, the inhumanity of war. 'Why do we have wars?' he said. 'When one thinks of the crimes committed, the widows, the orphans, the maimed of war, and the unfortunate women victims of the brutality of the invader, one cannot help being angry.' The Kaiser smiled. 'I'm sorry not to have been there,' he said, 'I would have released you.' Auguste said, 'I appreciate very much Your Majesty's sentiments, but it would have been most unlikely Your Majesty would have met me.'

They then went on to talk about cooking. Auguste learned that the Kaiser favoured an English-style breakfast: coffee, tea, cream; eggs and bacon, kidneys, chops, various steaks, grilled fish, fruit. Luncheon was a heavier meal. At dinner, light dishes were preferred so that a full stomach did not discourage spirited conversation. The Kaiser left for bed at about ten o'clock. The next morning after breakfast he went ashore to go back to Berlin. Auguste wished him *bon voyage* and the Kaiser shook hands with him saying, 'Au revoir et à bientôt.' And indeed they did meet again.

The light dinner menu for the Kaiser was:

Hors-d'oeuvres Suédois
Potages
Consommé en gelée
Tortue claire
Suprèmes de sole au vin du Rhin
Selle de mouton de pré-salé aux laitues
à la grecque
Petits pois à la Bourgeoise
Poularde au paprika rose gelée au Champagne
Cailles aux raisins
Coeurs de romaine aux oeufs
Asperges sauce Mousseline
Ecrevisses à la Moscovite
Soufflé surprise
Friandises
Fruits
Pêches, fraises, nectarines
Raisins Muscats
Café à la mode orientale
Vins: Eitchbacher 1897
Château Fourteau 1888
Liedricher Berg Auslese 1893
Château Rausan Séglar 1878
Veuve Clicquot
Ponsardin Rosé, Heidseick & Co., 1900
Fine Champagne
La Grande Marque de l'Empereur

The *Amerika* left on her maiden voyage to New York while Auguste returned to London with mixed feelings. He was sad that César had not been involved with him on this new adventure, designing a kitchen and luxury restaurant to send to sea. But he also had a sense of excitement that it had been his own show, and that the German company had asked for him. He was emerging from the shadow of César Ritz. Auguste Escoffier was now a celebrity in his own right.

Interlude 14

Peaches

'What woman wills, God wills. There, in five
words, you have the whole of Parisian law.' [1]

Anthelme Brillat-Savarin

In 1907 Auguste published a simple recipe for a simple dish: 'Poach the
peaches in vanilla-flavoured syrup. Dish them in a timbale upon a bed of
vanilla ice cream, and coat them with a raspberry purée.' Not imposing; in
fact, the recipe is something of an understatement, as we shall see. And it
has a name – the name of a woman. She didn't 'will' it directly in the
Brillat-Savarin sense; she just willed service in general.

A dish of this name, variously constructed, appears on menus across the
world every day and has done so for almost a century. Only a small
proportion of the millions preparing it or eating it know the original was
created by Auguste Escoffier, or know whether it is as it should be. It has
outgrown the image of its maker, gone far beyond those who would know
the name of any great chef. But it has taken with it the name of a silver-voiced
singer from Australia – Melba, later Dame Nellie Melba. There must be few
who have gained such vast publicity for so long at such little cost.

Pêche Melba to Auguste was just another carefully considered dessert. As
a Frenchman, the English idea of a pudding was anathema to him. A meal
should tail off to cheese after the entrée with nothing sweet between to
spoil the palate for the wine. Then the table is cleared, *la table est dessert.*
After that something light and sweet can be allowed to invade the taste
buds – the dessert.

Peach Melba we have all known since childhood, when (if you are old enough) it was a treat, a relief perhaps from something heavily roly-poly. It is indeed a simple dish and is, when it conforms to the original, incomparably the best way to eat a peach. Auguste makes no bones about it: '*Pêche Melba* in effect reigns supreme in the most sumptuous feasts, and its renown crosses the seas.'[2] Not everyone is as enthusiastic. 'The *Pêche Melba* is typical of much of Escoffier's cuisine – garish, colourful, vulgar: easily mass-produced yet giving the illusion of a rare delicacy and then dedicated to a world figure to ensure its publicity', wrote a Dr Plumb.

The peach, with its overtones of brazen, sensuous luxury, would seem to fit well the image of some Caligulan orgy. Indeed the ancient Romans, not perhaps given to subtlety in their feasting, were strong on the unusual and the exotic, and the peach, *persicum malum* to them, was both novel and foreign to Italy. It soon found its way onto patrician shopping lists. They had the peach with them in Gaul, and they brought it to Britain. Their Persian Apple became the medieval *persica*, then the Italian *pesca*, which devolved to the *pesche* of old French, now *pêche* and our peach. With its origins in Persia, it might be easier to believe that Eve was tempted from a Mesopotamian Eden by such a delicacy rather than by a rough old wild apple, except that the luscious peach, fruit of the *prunus persica*, a cousin of the rose, probably came from China.

The peach features in Chinese legend much as the apple does in ours. But, more than just saving doctors' bills, they have it that 'a peach eaten at the right moment will preserve the body from dissolution until the end of the world'. Not just any old peach, however – a special one for the gods, from a secret tree that fruits every six thousand years. The gods have to eat them to keep on living forever.

It was the Romans, who brought us the peach. But the picture of a Roman ruler lying back, fat on his couch, sinking his teeth into a ripe peach, may not be a true one. They made funny things with their fruits, *patinae* for example. These were fruits pounded up with wine in a mortar together with such unlikely partners as brains and eggs.

There is not much evidence of the peach in England for a long time after the Romans went back to the sunshine, although they left us peach trees. Cultivation of these continued in a few sheltered places, so the Roman skills of grafting and layering were not lost. In the thirteenth century new planting in sheltered gardens in the south of the country became more widespread.

The peach was first mentioned in print in England in a book on diet from Caxton's press around 1490 – predating the first English printed cookery book by about a decade.[3] It passes on the advice of Galen, the distinguished Greek physician of the second century AD, that for a long life we should abstain from eating any sort of fruit. But, if we must, it had better be peaches, which do the least harm. The father of the book's unknown author had taken Galen's advice. He lived a hundred years.

By the Elizabethan era an open tart filled with a peach purée was a favourite pudding:

> You must boil your fruit … and when they be boiled enough, put them into a bowl, and bruise them with a ladle, and when they be cold, strain them; and put in red wine or claret wine, and so season it with sugar, cinnamon and ginger.[4]

In the time of Charles I there were no less than twenty varieties of peach commercially available to growers. Certainly one of these would have been the nectarine, *prunus persica nectarina*. This is a smooth-skinned, genetic variety of the fuzzy-skinned peach and has been known as long in the West. The variety can occur spontaneously as a 'bud sport' on a fuzzy-peach tree. Under the skin it is indistinguishable from the basic stock and the two fruits are interchangeable in recipes.

Preserving of the peach had changed since Roman times and was mostly by candying or as a marmalade, but they were also kept in covered stoneware jars with sugar syrup and brandy. Just jamming down the peaches and boiling the mass quickly in sugar syrup produced what was called by the housewife her 'jam', a noun that later followed the verb into the language. The peach was also pickled towards the end of the seventeenth century in imitation of pickled mango arriving from the East. In the eighteenth century, peach flummery was invented, a snack eaten before the meat. In this, peaches were incorporated into an oatmeal paste, dyed red with cochineal and set in moulds.

Long ubiquitous, the peach has been viewed variously across the world. Texans made a tea from the leaves to treat diarrhoea, while the Navaho Indians used the dried fruit as a purgative. The Italians, unlike the English, buried peach leaves instead of beans to cure warts. In many places peach blossom is a bridal emblem, and to the Japanese it is a fertility symbol. The Arabs thought of the deep downy cleft of the peach as a female symbol, an attitude reflected in England where a 'peach' is a pretty girl particularly appealing to basic male instincts, and at one time a Peach House was a brothel.

Victor Hugo was not beyond an erotic allusion:

> The fruit seduces all men's eyes
> And all their senses gratifies;
> Its velvet cool our touch can teach
> How roses may be blent with lilies;
> This golden form could well be Phyllis –
> Were it not a tender peach.

Auguste is said to have served his *pêche Melba* to the famous singer for the first time at the Savoy hotel at a dinner celebrating her appearance as Elsa in *Lohengrin* at Covent Garden. This may not be the true story. Auguste first met the *gracieuse diva*, as he calls her, in 1893 at the Savoy where she stayed while performing at Covent Garden. She continued to use the Savoy as her base during London engagements. Auguste went often to her performances but was once particularly impressed with her rendering of Elsa and wanted afterwards to show his appreciation. Nellie was just back from an American tour and she was to give a small dinner the next day, to be attended by some of her co-stars from Covent Garden. The Duke of Orléans was to be there too.[5] Auguste seized the opportunity to produce a special dish for her. It is often said that he then produced the first *pêche Melba*, but perhaps it wasn't so.

Remembering the majestic swan that appeared in the first act of *Lohengrin*, he carved a representation of it from a block of ice – it was an impressive piece of sculpture. Between its wings he put a silver terrine, in which there were peaches on a bed of vanilla ice cream. The whole swan and its burden he then dusted with icing sugar and overlaid with a veil of spun sugar. It was this *pêches au cygne* he presented to Nellie at the table, delighting her and also the rest of the distinguished party. Auguste said later that he was amazed that she should have been so impressed with just peaches on ice cream.[6] It would be difficult not to agree with him, but it was probably the swan that did it, its aptness and its rendering.

Pêche Melba didn't evolve directly from *Pêches au cygne*, or so Auguste tells us.[7] The story begins after he left the Savoy:

> It was at the opening of the Hôtel Ritz in Paris that Mme Melba told me how she adored *Pêche Cardinal au coulis de framboise*, and asked me for the recipe, which I was pleased to give her.
>
> It was in writing out the recipe that I conceived the idea of creating the *Pêche Melba*; but it was important to keep the character of the *Pêche Cardinal* while finding something new which, rather than changing the flavour of raspberry and peach, augmented it.
>
> I found that nothing was more perfect than to lay the delicate *pêche* on a bed of vanilla ice cream and to cover it with its cardinal robe (*le coulis de framboise*).
>
> It was at that moment that *Pêche Melba* was created, and it was at the opening of the Carlton Hotel in London that for the first time it took the stage.

This story of the origin of the dessert, largely from its creator, fits all the pieces of evidence available – except one. Nellie Melba's version is different. She says:

> I was lunching alone in a little room upstairs at the Savoy Hotel on one of those glorious mornings in early spring when London is the nearest approach to

paradise that most of us ever attain. I was particularly hungry, and I was given a most excellent luncheon. Towards the end of it there arrived a little silver dish, which was uncovered before me with a message that Mr Escoffier had prepared it specially for me.

'It's delicious', I said. 'Ask Mr Escoffier what it is called.'

Word came back that it had no name, but that Mr Escoffier would be honoured if he might call it *Pêche Melba*. I said that he might with the greatest of pleasure, and thought no more about it. But, very soon afterwards, *Pêche Melba* was the rage of London.[8]

Opposing stories. History was ever thus. Perhaps the greater detail from Auguste's memory adds verisimilitude.

He published an expanded version of his recipe he claimed to be the original:

Original Recipe for Pêche Melba

Choose six perfectly ripe peaches. Montreuil peaches are best for this dessert. Immerse the peaches in boiling water for a few seconds and then transfer them quickly to ice water using a skimmer ladle. Peel them, put them on a plate, cover lightly with sugar and keep them cold.

Make some very creamy vanilla ice cream. Press 250g. of fresh raspberries through a fine sieve and add to the purée 150g. caster sugar. Keep cold.

Make a bed of the ice cream in a silver serving dish. Arrange the peaches carefully on the ice cream and cover with the raspberry purée. Optionally, chopped fresh almonds may be scattered over, but only when they are in season. Never use dried almonds.

When ready to serve, embed the dish in a block of ice and cover the peaches with a light veil of spun sugar.

The recipe was written after he had retired, probably in the late twenties.[9] Montreuil, where the peaches were grown in small gardens as espaliers, is east of Paris, a couple of kilometres from the *Périphérique*, the ring road, a Saturnine annulus of trucks spinning fast around the city. Montreuil is now all concrete and high-rise, and if you ask for peaches, they fetch a tin. A famous tale of Montreuil peaches is about Edward VII who was overcharged for them when dining incognito in Paris with a young lady. 'They must be very rare this year', he commented. 'Not as rare as kings', answered the waiter.

Prior to his 'original recipe' above, Auguste had published a somewhat similar one back in 1911 in which he makes no mention of the hot-water dunking of the peaches.[10] He merely calls for them to be covered with vanilla syrup and kept on ice until ready to serve. He says 'This is the original recipe', which it isn't: the original was years earlier in *Le Guide* 'and should not', he goes on, 'be departed from' – except of course by him.

He was quite troubled at the time by the lack of protection for recipes. Invent a new cooking pot and it could be protected by patent, but anybody could profit from the new dish he had created, or just make it badly and spoil its market. It sickened him to see his new peach dessert ravaged; all subtlety removed for example by using strawberry or gooseberry jam and kirsch, and smarming it over with *crème Chantilly*. As Auguste says, apart from presentation, the sole difference between Nellie's new dish and the ancestral *Pêche Cardinal* is the bed of vanilla ice cream for the Melba version. These days even that distinction has gone, and usually the Cardinal also has cold feet. The peach from a tin gets used for *Pêche Melba* of course, and did in Auguste's time. He bowed to the inevitable and claimed virtue. Commenting in 1928 he said:

> The world success of *Pêche Melba* is beyond all doubt. Its creation was not only a success for *la cuisine* but at the same time has done even more for the food canning industry. Half a million more peaches are now tinned every year to meet the demands, still increasing, of the lovers of this delicious dessert.[11]

Auguste honoured many ladies with dishes, who were thus sometimes immortalised. One story is that Auguste was dining with the Duchênes at Frascati's – Monsieur Duchêne was a manager at the Carlton and later at the London Ritz – when Madame Duchêne asked: 'What do you yourself consider to be the secret of your art, Monsieur Escoffier? I have heard other people say, but I would like to hear your opinion.' 'Madame,' Auguste replied, 'the secret is that most of my best dishes were created for the ladies.'[12] He honoured with the peach many ladies whose names still appear on menus, some having done so for over a century. Of the many, an early tipping of the cap was to Blanche d'Antigny, the bright young actress, when she was dined by Prince Galitzin at the Petit Moulin Rouge about 1874:

Coupe d'Antigny

Half-peach poached in vanilla flavoured syrup set on Alpine strawberry ice cream combined with 'very light and strongly flavoured raw cream'.

He cites *Crème niçoise* from Alpine pastures as a strong-flavoured cream.[13]

For the celebration at the Carlton of King Edward VII's coronation, Queen Alexandra got a mention with:

Pêches Alexandra

Peeled peaches with Kirsch and maraschino liqueur, covered with boiling syrup and allowed to cool.[14]

Auguste named a peach dessert for Sarah Bernhardt. He first served it at a dinner in 1901 given in her honour at the Carlton by the actor Benoît-Constant Coquelin. The dinner was to celebrate her triumph in Rostand's *L'Aiglon*, and the dish was named accordingly. (*Filet de Sole Coquelin* made its debut at the same table.) The dish did not cause much of a stir. For one thing, the idea was a noticeably second-hand:

Pêches Aiglon

Peaches poached in vanilla-flavoured syrup are laid on a bed of vanilla ice cream in a silver timbale and set in an ice sculpture of an eagle. The peaches are sprinkled with crystallised violets and veiled with spun sugar.

The published version does not demand ice sculpture.[15]

Napoléon III's Empress had:

Pêches Eugénie

Peaches garnished with wild strawberries sprinkled with Kirsch and maraschino liqueur and dressed with champagne *sabayon*.[16]

For the Duchesse de Guise, Princesse Isabelle of France he created:

Pêche Isabelle

Choose a dozen or so nicely ripe peaches and remove the skin. Halve each of them and remove the stone. Cover the bottom of a silver timbale with caster sugar and sprinkle it with a few spoonfuls of old red wine of the Clos du Papes – the sugar should be scarcely moistened. Arrange the peach halves side by side, cut side down, in the timbale. Powder the peaches with castor sugar and sprinkle with the wine. Repeat with further layers of peaches as necessary.

Make several hours in advance and keep cold. Serve with *crème Chantilly* (whipped cream with caster sugar) flavoured with vanilla.[17]

Auguste's puckish humour comes out in:

Coupe Vénus

Two peach halves poached in vanilla flavoured syrup side by side in a bed of vanilla ice cream. Each half is decorated with a red cherry.[18]

He changed from the cherry later to use, more suggestively, 'a small, red strawberry'.

15

Celebrity

'Let fame, that all hunt after in their lives,
Live register'd upon our brazen tombs,
And then grace us in the disgrace of death.'

Shakespeare, *Love's Labour Lost*

Auguste's conversations with the Kaiser on board the *Amerika* in June 1906 attracted the attention of the Press, and soon after his return to the Carlton, one newspaper, the *Tribune*, invited him to give a lecture in London on the art of cooking.[1] It seemed not to worry them or, on the day, his audience of *jolies Anglaises*, that he would have to make his presentation in French. His talk involved little preparation: he had written so often about the effect of cooking on happiness in the family, and on the indispensable nature of the *poêle*. His surprise was that his audience seemed to understand what he was saying.

At about this time he received a letter from a friend in Paris, Comte Becheval, which gave an indication of the circles in which he was by then moving, and perhaps of what was seen to be his financial standing. Becheval wrote of his wife having had an accident – she had broken her leg rather badly.[2] He went on to ask whether Auguste knew anyone who would like to open a hotel on the Champs Elysées on a site he had to sell – a quarter of a million pounds would buy a half share. The offer was obviously directed at Auguste himself. The letter finished, 'The Comtesse asked to be remembered to you'. A few years earlier, with César active, a deal might well have been struck and the money raised, but Auguste had learned his lesson on his adventure in Cannes with his Faisan d'Or. He knew about running kitchens but managing establishments that contained them was a different matter.

César had now moved with Marie into a villa, 'Eich Matt', on Lake Küssnacht, near Lucerne. By then the outside world had ceased to exist for César. Reports in newspapers of people he had known well had no meaning for him. Out there, says Marie, was 'a world grown unreal, peopled with harmless phantoms'.[3]

Early in 1907 the Ritz-Carlton Company wanted to consult Auguste about the kitchens of the hotel they had under development in New York. Also, following the success of the Ritz-Carlton Restaurant on the German liner *Amerika*, the company had been approached by the Hambourg-Amerika Company for advice on the installation of a grillroom, to be positioned forward on their smaller liner, the *Deutschland*. Auguste crossed to New York on the German ship so as to comment on the grillroom proposition. This was Auguste's first experience of the open ocean and he remarked that he didn't miss a single meal in the main dining room amidships, where the ship seemed remarkably stable.[4] He felt, however, that taking a meal forward of the dining room would have been impossible because of the marked pitching. He advised against the construction of a grillroom there, much to the captain's relief.

He stayed a week in New York and spent some time with Robert Goelet, the owner of the estate on which the new Ritz-Carlton was being built, and his architect, Wetmore. Auguste was now so experienced in setting up high-class kitchens that, with his business soon complete, he had time to visit friends, mostly *cuisiniers* whom he had recommended from time to time from his own staff for jobs in America. He mentions in particular the kitchen staff at the Knickerbocker Hotel.[5] The proprietors, Mr and Mrs Regan, had been to London to recruit high quality staff and had visited him at the Carlton, wondering whether he could recommend a good *chef de cuisine*. Auguste had done them proud. He had recommended his own *sous-chef*, M. Gastaud, and several good *chefs de parties* from his own *brigade*. He stayed with them in New York at their newly opened hotel, and it was clear they were delighted with the staff he had provided.

It was surely unusual to give away expensively trained staff in their productive years. Auguste was indeed liberal in staff matters. He saw himself at the top of the hill others must want to climb, emulating his standards to gain such eminence. But it was a hard steep track which the best people would avoid while he blocked the summit – he remembered his own dilemma when his advance was barred by Rahaut at the Petit Moulin Rouge. If, however, it was clear that working with him provided a safe stepping-stone to more senior positions elsewhere that was different. There were many chefs already, across Europe and beyond, claiming their tuition was by Escoffier – often where this comprised nothing more than a nod and a smile from him in their younger days while they washed pots and pans. Eugéne Herbodeau, eventually a successor to Escoffier at the Carlton, started there as a young *commis*. He says *le maître* usually gave no tuition, He thought he was probably Auguste's only pupil – perhaps they all thought they were.

Was Auguste in fact just commercially motivated? There is no evidence of this and it would have been out of character. From his early days he had declared his objective to promote French cuisine and to encourage its use across the world. What better way than to train cooks and dispatch them to spread not just the word but also the practice? And, although it was probably not part of his motivation, what better way to spread his own fame?

On the way back from America, Auguste sailed to Hamburg on the *Deutschland* and then by train to Monte Carlo to visit Delphine, stopping overnight in Paris where he still maintained a little flat. From Monte Carlo he would usually visit his son Paul and old friends in Villeneuve-Loubet. This time he found Paul less than happy with the family business. It was not a job he liked, and with increasing industrialisation in the south it was more difficult to compete with factory-made agricultural implements. He felt, too, that the automobile would soon oust the horse and the farrier. Auguste had for some time fretted about the company he had set up in England to market sauces and pickles, which he had never found the time to get properly off the ground. When he suggested that Paul could run it for him, Paul jumped at the idea.

Auguste was on very good terms with the Marquis de Panisse-Passis and often went to see him at the château above Villeneuve-Loubet. On one occasion he was invited to luncheon.[6] After the meal the Marquis said to him, 'What did you think of the cooking, Auguste?' Auguste had noticed a change of style and had been impressed. 'Excellent', he said. 'We have a new young *chef* in training and I wonder if you would give him a few words of encouragement – it would mean a lot to him, coming from you.' It did indeed mean a great deal to the seventeen-year-old Joseph Donon who had put everything he knew into his cooking that evening, just hoping to be noticed by the Master. 'If you ever want a job, my lad, come and see me in London', Auguste said. Joseph turned up at the Carlton six weeks later and Auguste took him on for the season as an assistant chef.[7]

After a month away, Auguste was back at the Carlton. Easter was over and London's high season was getting into its stride. He settled again to tailoring menus to the tastes of clients and inventing new delights for their palates, still pandering mostly to the women. There was no doubt now that his and César's aims to change the attitude of women in England towards dining in public had worked. Fashionable journals openly fostered the idea. One such magazine, *Gentlewoman*, featured 'the new popularity of dining out' with a picture on its front cover of women with their menfolk so engaged.[8]

Auguste lost no time re-registering his company, with his son, Paul, as a director. Paul came to London to take up his job managing Escoffier Ltd.[9] Auguste published at this time a little fifty-page booklet, *A Few Recipes by A. Escoffier of the Carlton Hotel, London*. It was intended to advertise the company's wares and says lengthily what a modern version would condense into a snappy slogan. We are told that, by following his instructions, the most unpretentious of cooks would be able 'to prepare delicacies calculated pleasurably to excite the most refined and dainty palate ...', and so on in the trade vernacular of the time. The instructions were not taxing. For example:

> *Crème de Tomate au Riz* is a very nourishing soup, rich in cream, and thus most useful to yachting or exploring parties, expeditions, etc ...
>
> To prepare: pour the contents into a saucepan, bring to boiling point and serve immediately. Should the soup be too thick, a few tablespoonfuls of water, milk or stock may be added.

It was also at about this time that Auguste started talks with the Swiss company producing 'Maggi' foodstuffs about marketing his products, although nothing came of the negotiations at the time.

When Auguste had first set up his company there had been little competition for bottled sauces other than from the Victorian attitude: people were suspicious of novelty and most were brought up to an ideal of 'plain, wholesome, food'; a cold, dreary market for his products. True, the enlightened middle class had been served since the late eighteenth century with sauces in the bottle. Harvey's Sauce and Lazenby's were the best known. Then, early in the nineteenth century, came Lea and Perrin's sauce from Worcester, and later the exotic sounding 'Mandarin' and 'Empress of India' sauces. But a sauce for the masses had not emerged, although a Mr Edwin Samson Moore, a vinegar manufacturer in the midlands, had produced pickles that were appearing on the tables of those who dined in the kitchen.

When Paul launched Auguste's sauces and pickles in 1907, Edwin Moore and his son had a sizeable pickles market and, four years earlier, had given the world Garton's HP Sauce.[10] Competition indeed, but the market was no longer cold; pickles were commonplace and the sauce bottle was read at many a table. Such products were on the edge of respectability; 'Escoffier of the Carlton' gave Auguste's wares a superior gloss that nudged them over the line. They sold into a niche market of Edwardian novelty seekers – which either couldn't quite bend to the products of the industrial north or wished to reach above them.

Fifty years later the products, or their derivatives, were still being marketed under Escoffier's name – but by another company, Brown and Polson Ltd. The original nine sauces had grown to fifteen, the soups had disappeared, but there were tubes of tomato paste, jars of pickles, potted patés and a puffer of 'lazy garlic'. A nicely produced pamphlet of 1966 gave sixty recipes incorporating their wares – with the implication that using them would bring your cooking up to Escoffier standards.

In 1908 Marie Ritz bought a villa in Saint-Cloud, not far from the Sèvres porcelain factory, just to the west of Paris. Marie says, 'and there Ritz gradually sank out of life until 1912, when, to all intents and purposes, his life finished'. Marie had taken over all César's responsibilities

Auguste's next departure from routine was in 1908, again with the Hamburg-Amerika Line to organise the kitchen for their second Ritz-Carlton Restaurant, this time on their liner, the *Kaiserin Auguste Victoria*.[11] He travelled on her maiden voyage to New York. A great deal of his time on board was spent overseeing the operation of the kitchen, intent on detailed adjustments for highest quality of service and general efficiency. For relaxation he was not one for deck games or sitting around on deck chairs: he spent his spare time on the voyage reading and writing. The manuscript survives of an article for *L'Art Culinaire*.[12] In it he wrote:

> At the moment, on a short excursion to New York – short in time if not in distance. The Paris papers and *L'Art Culinaire* I brought with me to occupy the leisure time on the journey echo to the recent military scandals.
>
> Fraud in supplying food to the military is not out of date, unfortunately. But, ever since I have been writing in *L'Art Culinaire*, that is since its foundation, I have never given up emphasising the fundamental cause of these troubles.

He went on to reiterate the case against the government's method of contract by tender for army supplies, continuing the campaign started in his *Mémoires d'un Cuisinier de l'Armée du Rhin* fourteen years earlier. Auguste's main memory of his brief stopover in New York was of his first meeting with soft clams – clams caught early in the process of building themselves more spacious accommodation – with which he was 'entranced'. Other firsts were *Chicken à la Maryland* at Martin's Restaurant, canvasback duck and terrapin, all of which impressed him.

In October 1909 Auguste was sixty-three years old and had completed half a century as a *cuisinier*, climbing from the bottom to the top of the profession. L'Association Culinaire de Londres organised a celebration of his Jubilee, his *Noces d'Or Culinaires*, at the Monico Restaurant in London.[13] They also raised a subscription of 6000 francs for a gift to him, but he asked that the money be used to provide a bed at *la Maison Dugny*, a home for retired kitchen workers – it doesn't sound so drab in French: *la maison de retraite des vieux cuisiniers.*[14] He went on to say that to the subscriptions from his colleagues he would like to add his own. It would be a ticket in the Panama lottery, 'in the hope,' he said, 'that the lucky draw of a first prize will ease the lot of our old comrades'.[15]

The banquet was for a hundred and eighty people: master chefs and others from all over the country attended, as well as a delegation from France. In his reply to the presentation – improvised, he claimed – Auguste gave a résumé of his 'fifty years at the stove'. Speaking of leaving the Savoy after seven and a half years managing the kitchens, he said: 'I had to leave following dishonest intrigue, but, for all the unhappiness at the time, it all turned out for the best. The results are evident in my being with you on this celebration today.' This appears to have been the first public acknowledgement that there was anything other than a normal change of job in his leaving the Savoy. He continued, saying, 'If I had looked after my own monetary interests I should have left London at the time, but dignity and conscience insisted that in the face of such monstrous and incredible manoeuvres I had a moral duty to stay'. He said his decision had meant considerable sacrifice. Results, however, had exceeded his expectations due to the support he had received from the board of directors of the Ritz-Carlton Hotel Company over the dozen years he had been in their service. He took the presence at the banquet of the chairman of the board, and the presentation by the company of the silver cup inscribed with the signatures of the directors, as further signs of the trust the company had in him. Auguste's speech was faithfully recorded in *L'Art Culinaire*, which appeared a week later, but nobody had the nose for news or the curiosity to dig out the facts behind his scarcely veiled accusation of the board of directors of the Savoy Hotel Company.

Why had Auguste changed his attitude about leaving the Savoy? He had left quietly enough as though making a career move, as had César Ritz, although talking to Auguste César had referred to being dismissed. It was now ten years since César had declared his intention to sue the company for wrongful dismissal, but nothing had emerged as a result. Surely, had such eminent people as Escoffier and Ritz taken the world-famous Savoy Hotel to court, it would have been extremely newsworthy. We could only conclude that perhaps Ritz had been already too ill to carry out his threat, or that he had followed Auguste's advice and backed down, or, of course, that the matter had been settled quietly out of court. However, since César Ritz's declared intention to sue and Auguste's change of attitude were little publicised, the reason for them leaving the Savoy remained unquestioned. And that was the situation for the next three-quarters of a century. In all those years among the gossip about their popularity, their love affairs and other activities, there was no hint of anything unusual about their departure. Then, in 1984, a book written by a journalist on the *Observer* newspaper stated that Escoffier had been caught out by the directors of the Savoy in the 'chef's oldest trick, arranging with his suppliers to be invoiced for more than was actually received and pocketing a commission'.[16] He expanded on this in a second book, two years later, declaring that he had been sent, anonymously, copies of documents which included a confession signed by Escoffier admitting that he had accepted 'commission' and had creamed off overpayments from the hotel's suppliers amounting to some £16,000. Tradespeople had paid back about half the sum and £500 had been accepted from Auguste to represent his share. César Ritz and and his *maître d'hôtel*, Louis Echenard, had also signed a note admitting the use of the Savoy's wine stock's for themselves, other staff and personal guests. They paid over some £10,000 between them in recompense.[17] The Savoy's chairman, then Sir Hugh Wontner, confirmed that the original documents were in the secret archives of the hotel and that the story was true: he said that the directors at the time had not wanted to disclose the matter, nor to disgrace the three miscreants. Now, so many years had passed there was no longer any reason to keep quiet about the affair. He later wrote in his welcome to the hundredth anniversary of the Savoy that the founder, Richard D'Oyly Carte, had been well served by Escoffier and Ritz. The evidence of the documents shows at least that César Ritz had gone ahead with his intention to sue and that there had been a quiet, if startling, out of court settlement. The question remains, then, why was he dismissed?

To those around at the time of the exodus, Ritz had admitted that he was dismissed, and Escoffier had referred to dishonest intrigue and incredible manoeuvres. Escoffier modified this later in his draft memoirs saying that 'Following a disagreement, or rather a misunderstanding between M. d'Oyly Carte (sic), chairman of the board of directors, and Monsieur C. Ritz, the Savoy manager, we had to leave in 1897 this establishment into which we had put all our heart and soul to save fom disaster, to raise it to the peak of its glory, and to give the shareholders the satisfaction they had the right to expect'.[18] Again in the memoirs: 'one of the causes of the quarrel between the owners of the Savoy and César Ritz was his building of the Ritz in Paris'. Marie Ritz wrote forty years after the event that César had resigned because of the machinations of the housekeeper, Mrs W., who had continually made trouble for him with the directors. Then the documents sent to the newspaper introduced the Savoy's 'committee of investigation' and evidence of roguery, new evidence – and, because of Sir Hugh Wontner's declaration of its validity, we can presumably take it as such. It is relevant, however, to note that the committee of investigation had not been set up until a couple of years after the team had left the hotel, presumably when Ritz filed his suit against the directors. And so, the committee's findings, which led to the confessions, were not necessarily the basis of Ritz's dismissal. That is all the evidence from those that were there, but taken together with what we have learned of those concerned, and the timing of events, it is possible to piece together an hypothesis.

Marie Ritz's explanation for the break with the Savoy might seem a bit naïve, but it would be wrong to dismiss it as such; she was certainly in a position to know directly about the friction with the housekeeper, although it is interesting to know why she referred to her as Mrs W. It would be far-fetched to suppose that Ritz was bothered into resignation by some middle-ranking employee. On the other hand, D'Oyly Carte's second wife, Helen, had been a power in the land of the Savoy before the arrival of the Ritz team. She had inspired her husband in the first place to build the splendid hotel based on her experience of American establishments. She had been at his elbow during the design, building, launching and early development phases. All that stopped when Ritz and his wife Marie arrived. Marie not only usurped Helen's position as adviser on furnishings and design, but also took over her office. Helen, however, as wife of the chairman, remained in a position to ferment trouble for Ritz with the board. She was certainly a prime candidate for Marie's 'housekeeper' Mrs W. She doubtless did not fail to drum home the obvious fact that Ritz entertained his business contacts in the restaurant where plans were made for new ventures in direct competition with the Savoy, and that he was also involving Escoffier in such dealings, as well as taking him abroad on similar affairs. The Savoy was nurturing the competition.

For his part, Ritz was now well backed financially. With his powerful Ritz Hotel Development Company, he was planning Ritz hotels around the world. Even though his contract with the Savoy allowed him six months of the year free time, he still had more to organise than he could handle: he needed more time, despite the fact that he was under contract to the Savoy.

The position was, then, that the Savoy board, with their chairman encouraged by his wife, would not have been sorry to lose Ritz, and could afford to do so now that the hotel was brilliantly well established. Ritz would not be sorry to leave to have more time for his own business. Both were restricted by their mutual contract. Under such pent-up conditions, perhaps at a board meeting to answer an accusation inspired by Helen, Ritz, overworked and fed up with such constant nagging, may well have exploded, a reaction echoed by the board. The accusation – perhaps of using Savoy facilities, meals and expensive wine for his own business meetings – was pressed, and dismissal threatened. But to sack Ritz in fact would have risked him suing for breach of contract, and they knew from their previous experience with Hardwick, Ritz's predecessor, who had sued and won, that win or lose they would risk bad publicity. Moreover, influential followers such as the Marlborough House set would be unlikely to use the Savoy again after the field day Ritz would give the Press. Similarly, Ritz, knew that such a scandal was likely to ruin his reputation, then at a peak. A deal was struck: Ritz would resign and the Savoy would not pursue the question of contract.

A couple of years later, Ritz, with the reluctant backing of Escoffier and Echenard, in fact sued. The directors then had to consolidate a case against them, one that would stand up in court. It would not have been difficult for an investigating committee to find shortages whether or not any of the three was involved – petty larceny is as old as commercial kitchens, as are kickbacks and commissions from suppliers. As for the admissions by suppliers, with the promise of silence by the board, and knowing which side their bread was buttered, they complied. In this way, plausibly indictable offences were easily constructed against the three of them. Win or lose, mud would stick and they would be finished in the hotel business. The Savoy in effect said, 'Drop your case and we'll drop ours. We'll keep the papers, of course, but we'll not reveal them to anyone'. And they didn't for eighty years and even then it took some sort of clandestine leak. The Savoy archives are today professionally run and members of staff are very welcoming to anyone seeking knowledge of the history of the hotel. Anything they have is available, including board minutes, except, even after the leak, for one short period at the turn of the nineteenth century.

This is only a hypothesis of course, but it fits and we shall know no better until someone gets a look at the Savoy's board minutes for that secret period. Meanwhile, the leaked papers can only be regarded as the prosecution's case, so to speak, not proven fact. The confessions are meaningless, merely the price of settlement out of court to save careers sensitive to public opinion, and hostages to future silence. As the jury, we must until then bring in a verdict of not guilty.

One small rider: it is clear now why Marie Ritz invented a housekeeper called Mrs W. rather than naming Helen D'Oyly Carte: Marie, too, had to keep quiet or risk the release of evidence purporting to incriminate her husband.

On 6 May 1910, King Edward VII, who had drawn High Society from dull Victorianism to the frank hedonism of his own reign, died. His second son, George, Duke of York, succeeded him – his first son, Prince Albert Victor, had died in 1892. There was no sudden change under King George V. It was going to take a world war to dull the shine of the Edwardian Era.

Over the next year or so Auguste expanded into the world beyond the kitchen. In his marketing for the Carlton he was looking further afield than Britain and France for supplies, intent on importing quality direct from wherever it could be found. He wanted also to maintain constant supplies of seasonal foodstuffs and dealt, for example, with South Africa for fruit – buying apricots, peaches, pears and exotic naartjes from Natal.[19] Such imports, commonplace now, were unusual then.

His name was growing generally in the food-manufacturing industry and he was often approached with business suggestions. Monsieur Monteille, the proprietor of Maison Lenoble, a wholesale supplier of butter, poultry and game near Paris, wrote that a client of his had a proposition:

> Monsieur Petit ... has been fostering the idea of an arrangement where you, he, a notary from Argenteuil, as well as myself, should form a food company to which you and I could bring our inventions. Petit had me taste one of the products you had made from an extract of yeast from beer, and I can certify that gourmets and connoisseurs were certainly deceived by your extract; they could not differentiate it from an extract of meat. I congratulate you on it. Your discovery is superb.[20]

The letter went on to say that M. Petit was anxious for a reply about forming the new company, but Auguste was unenthusiastic; he had suffered in such partnerships before.

Despite the many distractions, writing was still a major interest. He had had one book planned since Savoy days. Not cooking this time but a subject he felt deeply about. He had not been able to interest a publisher in it. He went into the attack again in a letter to the managing editor of *Figaro*:

> You will remember the project of which I gave you a general outline in one of your visits to London. I have waited for twelve years for a voice ... more authoritative than mine and more eloquent, to be raised in favour of those defeated in life. But three legislatures have come and gone since then and although the question was to some extent the basis of their programmes ...

This in the end led to the publication of his *Projet d'Assistance Mutuelle pour l'Extinction du Paupérisme*. In this he presents *un plan d'aide* for workers and the aged. It was essentially a scheme of social insurance and a universal old-age pension. The idea of a social program on a national scale was not new. Germany had brought in health insurance, workman's compensation, old age and invalidity pensions in stages from 1883 to 1889. Auguste had one proposal, however, which rings familiarly in our ears today. He deplored the fact that people lived in impoverished misery while huge sums were spent maintaining military forces, expenditure only necessary because Europe comprised separate states always on the edge of conflict. He wrote:

> The vital interests of all countries today are the same; they each want more than anything else peace, not armed peace, which is just hypocritical preparation for war, but a sincere and definitive peace. Why should not an attempt now be made to found the European confederation the greatest thinkers of the last half-century considered essential? Why not unite to form one great country? There need be no change in the various constitutions and forms of government each nation has freely chosen. Of necessity, in the not too distant future, this vision will become reality – but not until mankind has undergone the most absurd and most fearful of wars.

We now have our social services, but only after two world wars and a further half century have we started the painful process towards confederation. Even now it could be said that as fast as European nations edge themselves closer together, composite states are being dismantled elsewhere.

In his book Auguste did not leave his social scheme reliant upon the transfer of funds from defence. He calculated the taxation necessary to build up a capital fund 'sufficient to do away with poverty for ever'. Eugéne Herbodeau comments, 'Escoffier, while kindly and sympathetic, was no sentimentalist ... he excluded pampering from his scheme of social justice'.[21] He quotes Auguste: 'Since by this scheme all poor, old people and all invalids would, without exception, are permanently assured of food and lodging, all forms of begging should be forbidden. This plan would also put an end to professional begging and those who tried it would no longer have any excuse and should therefore be punished severely.' To finance rest homes for the aged, Auguste proposed a national lottery, village fêtes and a tax on horse-race betting. The rest homes were to be healthily sited and the buildings simple in design. 'Maintenance of those living in them', he said, 'should not be costly. The basis of the diet should be fresh or dried vegetables, which are more easily digestible for old people and just as nourishing as meat. One or two rations of meat each week would be sufficient.' The cooking, Auguste said, might be entrusted to former cooks among the occupants 'who would prefer to be usefully employed'.

Auguste was not the first Frenchman living in England to see the need for such a work. Napoleon III, who had also lived in England for a time, wrote his *Extinction du Paupérisme* in 1844 while incarcerated in France. Auguste not only wrote of his feelings about provision for the poor but took direct action too where he could. He had a highly developed social conscience and was impelled to do what he could for those less fortunate than himself. Charity was not his answer to the problem. He saw always that there was plenty for everyone if it could be better distributed. His military experience had instilled in him a sense of duty that he applied to his own life and in his regard for others. He saw efficiency as the key.

One of his activities was on behalf of the Little Sisters of the Poor, nuns who did a great deal to feed the poor in London. He found appalling the waste of food regarded as inevitable from grand hotels, while people went hungry – particularly as the food thrown away was of such high quality. It was a matter of efficiency to see such food distributed where it could do some good. At the Savoy, Auguste had suggested that the nuns came each morning to the kitchens with their horse-drawn cart, and he had arranged that any surpluses should be kept for them. He would check frequently on the quality of the food they were given. He set up the routine again at the Carlton. The arrangement went as far as keeping for the nuns the coffee surplus that was still fresh and had not lost its aroma. The tea leaves, too, would make another brew. The toast trimmings from hotels of such a size provided an appreciable quantity of bread, and 'bottom pieces' of carved joints made up to substantial dishes of meat.

The great treats came with the frequent large dinners served at the hotel when, for example, a quail dish was ordered which used only the breasts of the birds. The legs and carcasses surplus to requirements for menus the next day were left for the nuns to distribute. Auguste got a lot of satisfaction from the thought of the needy dining on such luxury food. One day, the Little Sisters arrived without their cart. Their old horse had died and there was no money to buy another. Without hesitation Auguste gave them the necessary sum. His generosity was repaid some years later. The bullying *chef de cuisine* from Auguste's early days at the Petit Moulin Rouge, Ulysse Rahaut, was now destitute, old and friendless. Auguste had no difficulty persuading the mother superior of the Little Sisters to take him into care.

Another of Auguste's activities resulted from an initiative of Isidore Salmon, the chairman of J. Lyons & Co. Auguste told the *Caterer and Hotel-Keepers' Gazette* that 99 per cent of chefs employed in clubs, hotels and restaurants in London were foreigners. His report concluded: 'As things stand at present, an Englishman with a taste for cookery would have no chance in his native land.' He then petitioned London County Council to establish 'a cookery technical school for boys'. The council consulted several people in the profession, including Auguste, and decided to act. So, in 1910, Britain's first catering school was opened at Westminster Technical Institute. A catering advisory committee was set up with Auguste Escoffier a founder member. On his visits to the college he would go around and talk to the students to encourage them. If nothing else, talking to him must have been good practice for their menu French.

The first course at the institute was for a professional chef's diploma and the three years practical training it offered was to fit students for employment as chefs. The course still runs today. A restaurant and a school for waiters were added in 1912. In November 1953 a plaque, a large bronze medallion with Auguste's profile in bas-relief, was unveiled by M. R. Massigli, the French Ambassador. It was set in the wall of a new dining room at the college to be called the Escoffier Room. The inscription includes the citation: 'for many years *chef des cuisines* at the Savoy and Carlton Hotels, London, an acknowledged master and teacher of the art of cookery, the originator of modern restauration'.

At this period, Auguste was seeing a good deal of his friend Gringoire, the poet. Auguste admired him greatly as a writer, and they often met to chat in the afternoons at the Carlton, when Auguste would consult him on his own writing. Gringoire was also writing a book about great chefs (French of course) up to and including Auguste, and they discussed this. One outcome of these meetings arose from Auguste's idea that cooking was an art form and deserved appropriate treatment in writing. Gringoire was very much in agreement and they decided to launch a suitable periodical with Gringoire as editor-in-chief.

Auguste's enthusiasm bubbled over and soon they were planning to add, to the treatment of French cuisine, articles on fine wines and liqueurs, and on other aspects of the table, the silver and glass, fine china, napery and lighting. Why stop there? Auguste was also keen to do something to boost tourism in France, to bring to the attention of readers abroad the beauties of the country, its history, its art and its products. And of course they couldn't neglect a subject important to the ladies. They had to deal with 'les mille petites fantaisies qui complètent la toilette de la femme, dont nos grands couturiers et modistes ont le secret'.[22]

Plans for launching the journal were more or less complete by the end of October, when Auguste left for New York where the new Ritz-Carlton Hotel was to open at the end of November. He had already sent over the more senior staff for the kitchens, who had finished recruiting staff there, set up the kitchens and trained the team along Escoffier lines. Auguste would need to put the final touches to the organisation and oversee the preparation of the inaugural dinner. The opening went well, but the dinner achieved an unexpected notoriety. The next morning, newspapers headlined the 'Scandal at the Ritz-Carlton'. Diners had smoked after dinner in the dining room.

Auguste later remarked that things have changed since then.[23] Not only had people begun to smoke after dinner, which was deplorable, they also did so during the meal. Surely every course must then have the same flavour, a disagreeable one; perhaps there should be one-course menus for such people headed *'dîner à la nicotine'*. He had one other job to do during his six-week stay in America. The Ritz-Carlton Company had taken on the Grand Hotel in Pittsburgh. Auguste spent some time there staffing and reorganising the kitchens. He was so practised he had it all up and running in a fortnight.

Auguste's most pleasant memory of this period in America was the time he spent with Sarah Bernhardt, 'la grande tragédienne adorée du peuple américaine', as he described her. He lunched with her several times – in company with her doctor, he added – at the Hotel Marie-Antoinette where she was staying. At one of these lunches he asked her the secret of her youthful energy that everyone admired. She answered, 'You are so inquisitive, my dear Escoffier. There are secrets a woman is born with which she takes with her to the grave'. When he said it was perhaps sheer egoism to guard so jealously such secrets, she said: 'Maybe. It's just that if you have natural gifts, you have to have the strength to say "I will" and to overcome any obstacles raised. Come to lunch next Sunday and I'll let you know how it's done.'

He wrote:

> The following Sunday while we were savouring an excellent *pâté de foie gras de Strasbourg*, that treasure of French products, the most attractive of women told me the secret of her youthfulness. It was very simple: just willpower, sustained with an excellent champagne. She took with every meal a half-bottle of Moët et Chandon. The bubbles, she said, had a miraculous effect on her.[24]

Auguste spent Christmas in New York and travelled to England on Cunard's *Lusitania*. As usual, he spent some time on board writing. He prepared some recipes for the new journal, which he hoped Gringoire had got well into shape during his absence. These were not on his usual lines. They were not for the professional cook. He was sure the only reason the English housewife couldn't cook was because she hadn't been brought up, as were all French girls, to do so. He would tell them what to do. And, to be sure there was no misunderstanding due to language difficulties, he would have the recipes printed in English as well as French in each issue.

He arrived back at the Carlton on 4 January 1911. The year 1911 saw important legislation in Britain on subjects still front-page news in newspapers today. The Shops Act legalised the principle of a half-day holiday a week for staff; and the Official Secrets Act became necessary because of a fear of increased German espionage. Lloyd George's National Insurance Bill, signalling a great change in the country's social attitudes, was made law, and the vast contributory insurance scheme against sickness and unemployment for some of the working population was instituted – another nine years and a world war had to pass before it was extended to all.

The first issue of Escoffier and Gringoire's magazine appeared in April 1911, entitled *Le Carnet d'Epicure: Revue Mensuelle des Arts de la Table, Littèraire, Philosophique et Gourmande*. The intention was to use as a frontispiece a different portrait each month of a notable chef. Auguste graced the first issue – the second showed Urbain Dubois, but he had signed the portrait adding 'Au vaillant et bienvaillant artiste A. Escoffier, souvenir d'amitié'. Advertisements in the first issue included one for the London, Brighton and South Coast Railway which gave the fare from London to Paris, via Newhaven, Dieppe, Rouen to Paris as £1 13s. 3d. third class return and about double that first class. Gringoire's book, *Anthologie Culinaire et Gourmande de Vatel à Carême, de Carême à Escoffier*, was also publicised, as were some of the products of Escoffier Ltd:

The Escoffier Sauce Robert	*La sauce de table par excellence*
The Escoffier Derby Sauce	*La meilleure Sauce Anglaise*
The Escoffier Abricoma Sauce	*Jus de fruits pour entremets*
The Escoffier Sauce Melba	*Jus de fruits pour entremets*
The Escoffier Pickles	*A base de tomates*

Ces conserves sont fabriquées selon les formules et sous le contrôle de Monsieur A. Escoffier du Carlton Hôtel.

Spécialités Escoffier, dans toutes bonnes épiceries.

The publication was not without critics. One of them wondered: 'Who would read it? The French? Perhaps a few ladies of station?'

In his reply, Gringoire pointed to the success of *L'Art Culinaire* over thirty years, written in French and published in England. It was founded under the auspices of French *maîtres de la cuisine* of the highest rank, including 'our eminent collaborator, A. Escoffier. This name will suffice I think to convince you that *L'Art Culinaire* is, as indicated in its title, a very artistic revue, written by excellent gastrologues and consecrated to the most delicate and the most French of all the arts.' Not the greatest advertisement for *Le Carnet d'Epicure*. The critic probably went out immediately to buy *L'Art Culinaire*.

Interlude 15

Pommes d'Amour

'Fair and goodly apples, chamfered, uneven, and bunched
out in many places; of a bright red colour and the bigness
of a goose egg or a large pippin.'

John Gerard, 1597

The tomato, *Lycopersicon esculentum,* a member of the nightshade family,
was grown in Britain at first just for decorative purposes, as it was thought
to be poisonous. It didn't gain popularity here as a food until well into the
nineteenth century. It is now considered, of course, an indispensable part
of our diet. It is rich in vitamins, A, C and E, which are not influenced by
canning. It is low in carbohydrate, has plenty of dietary fibre, negligible
protein, no fat, and no cholesterol.

Auguste used the tomato a lot in his cooking, as might be expected from
his Provençal origins, and he needed a continuous supply throughout the
year. He was surely not alone in this, and it is surprising that he had difficulty
in France, where tomatoes were popular, persuading companies to can
tomatoes. In the end he did get commercial canning of whole tomatoes
started. This ensured him year-round supplies, but he gained nothing more
from his efforts.

He wrote of the tomato:

Quite recently I had occasion to see how popular it is in the New World;
considerably more so than with us, the industry of preserving tomatoes having
made immense strides in the United States.

The tomato is at once excellent and very economic, and has therefore become the basis of quite a number of culinary preparations, occupying a very important place in the food of the privileged as well as of the workers.

It is used as hors d'oeuvre, in soups, sauces, constituting a delicious adjunct to fish, fowl, butcher's meat, and certain game. It is further used in salads with various dressings and finally it makes excellent sweet jellies and preserves.[1]

He also said that the tomato was introduced into France from South America early in the nineteenth century. That seems a bit late. The yellow tomato was introduced into Italy from Mexico late in the sixteenth century. Known as the golden apple, *pomo d'oro*, it was popular as an aphrodisiac. Perhaps they do have this property, and the famed 'Latin lover' is nothing more than a doped-up automaton. On the other hand, to speak of an effect on sexual attraction or prowess was a common market ploy with a product in those days, and many a market was found through man's excess of desire over ability. Is our own advertising any more subtle, with the 'hunk' in the sleek new car shown turning nubile heads? The mandrake, a relative of the tomato, had been known for its powers in this respect since ancient times. Anyone with a black dog and a long cord who could pull one from the ground without hearing its shrieks could enjoy its effects. Sir Walter Raleigh is supposed to have introduced the Irish to the potato, another of the tomato's cousins, with the idea that it too was an aphrodisiac. They didn't consider it food back in 1584, but you could dine out luxuriously for the equivalent of what the Irish paid then for an ounce of potato bought for a love potion.

It is unlikely that the southern French, immediate neighbours of the Italians, would have missed such a promotional puff for the tomato – they were Latins too. Perhaps Gallic pride forbad the use of such an aid. But, by 1600, the cultivation of the *pomo d'oro* as a foodstuff started just across the border to go with the pasta; the French would surely have found then how well it went with the olive and its oil in an incipient *à la Provençal*. Probably, then, the tomato arrived in Provence long before Auguste thought it did. In an article on the tomato he mentions that the old name for *la tomate* was *pomme d'amour*. He doesn't give the origin of the name, although it fits its history, but he often used it subsequently in his menus, thus carrying on the tradition of sexual allusion as a sales technique. Auguste's recipe in his article is for *Tomates à la génoise*, an hors d'oeuvre:

> Slices of tomatoes, deseeded, are arranged on a dish alternating with thin slices of tunny fish, sprinkled with a vinaigrette sauce flavoured with anchovy essence, and bordered with thick slices of boiled potatoes.

The tomato was in the news a few years ago when the aluminium scare was on, when many over a certain age scrapped their aluminium saucepans and bought stainless steel. Tomatoes apparently took up aluminium from pans they were cooked in and the spectre of Alois Alzheimer hovered over us all. Common sense eventually prevailed. Aluminium is concentrated in the outer ten miles of the crust of the earth and nearly all rocks, soil, vegetation and animals contain it. Pans or no pans, we can't escape aluminium. On average, we take in about ten milligrams of aluminium a day in our normal food, which gets aluminium one way or another from the soil. We can easily double that at a heavy meal, and then ten times that from the subsequent indigestion tablet. As well as from food and the water we drink, we get aluminium from the very dust we inhale.

Tomatoes have their natural aluminium content like all other vegetation, a small amount compared with our daily intake. It might be doubled when the tomatoes are cooked for a few hours in aluminium, but it's still a minuscule amount. So, neither aluminium saucepans nor tomatoes make much of a contribution to our aluminium intake. We also excrete more than 99 per cent of the aluminium we ingest.

It is true that brain cells of an Alzheimer patient contain slightly more aluminium than normal, but the whole brain would contain no more than is found naturally in a single tomato. Whether the aluminium in the brain is a cause of the disease, incidental to it or accumulates as a result of it is not known. But plenty gets into the body to provide the quantity involved without worrying about the small contribution of a few tomatoes, cooked in aluminium or not. The present view of most pundits is that we should not be too fussed about cooking in aluminium, although the last word has not yet been said. But, then, probably the first word has not yet been said about many unsuspected hazards.

Escoffier didn't take to aluminium utensils, but his reasons were different. Like most people who have built up a system to a proven degree of perfection, he would not change a vital element without demonstrable advantage. Such proof would not have been easy with the thin aluminium pans available in his time, as compared with those in heavy iron or copper that he used.

16

Phoenix

'The bird of wonder dies – the maiden phoenix –
Her ashes new create another heir
As great in admiration as herself.'

Shakespeare, *Henry VIII*

On the afternoon of 9 Auguste 1911, Auguste and his friend Gringoire had been going through the proofs of the September issue of the *Le Carnet*. At 7.20 in the evening they came down in the lift together from Auguste's apartment on the fifth floor and took leave of each other in the foyer. Gringoire had just reached the door when the fire alarm sounded. He turned to see the lift doors close on his friend and the lift depart for the upper floors. Smoke was coming from another lift shaft and people running down the stairs into the foyer were shouting that the top floors were ablaze. Then the lift that Auguste had taken crashed down its shaft. It was not possible to tell if anyone was still in it, but Gringoire was sure there had been time enough for Auguste to get to his floor and leave the lift. But the top floors were on fire. Outside, crowds had gathered and were staring up in horror at the now blazing roof and soon word spread of the drama in the hotel; fifteen or more people, including the great Escoffier, were trapped above the fourth floor in the hotel. Fire engines soon arrived from all directions but after half an hour, with the blaze getting fiercer by the minute, there seemed no possibility that anybody in the upper floors could have survived.

Just after 8 o'clock, looking up Charles II Street from Haymarket, figures could be seen descending the iron ladder on the wall of His Majesty's Theatre that adjoined the Carlton Hotel. Leading them was the diminutive figure of Auguste Escoffier. Auguste, who of course knew his way around the hotel very well, had collected the people from the upper floors and led them to safety. Applause started in the crowd nearby and spread all the way to Pall Mall. Gringoire said that there was something so moving, and yet tragic, in this applause in the sinister light of the blaze that no one who was there was ever likely to forget it. There was unfortunately one victim, an American artist, Jameson L. Finney, who had been trapped in his bathroom. The two upper floors of the Carlton were totally destroyed by the fire and all the rest of the hotel was very badly damaged by the water from fifty powerful pumps at work for more than four hours.

At one o'clock in the morning, it was at last possible to get back through the flooded grillroom into the only saloon relatively undamaged. Auguste was there looking as though he had just dressed for dinner, with his principal colleagues in various states of disarray. They had been congratulating him on his escape and for saving the others. Auguste expressed his deep regret for the death of Jameson Finney. It was not just that he always had a way of saying the right thing at the right time, he really felt for people. Perhaps there was, too, something of guilt, though unwarranted, for not having checked the bathroom. As for the immense material damage, he treated it philosophically and with his usual wry humour: 'What do you expect?' he said, 'I have roasted so many millions of chickens in a dozen years in this hotel! Perhaps they wanted to roast me in revenge ... Anyhow, they have only managed to singe my feathers; I shall only have to renew my wardrobe.'

A few days after the fire at the Carlton, despite damage to all the bedrooms and suites, the hotel was able to open its doors again, but only to the restaurant. Auguste kept a copy of the first menu he produced:

Melon fine Champagne
Consommé de volaille froid
Soles Coquelin
Selle d'agneau aux aubergines
Riz à l'orientale
Grouse à l'Ecossaise
Salade verte
Fonds d'artichauts aux fines herbes
Soufflé glacé aux framboises
Friandises

During the winter of 1911, Auguste, always thinking of ways to promote French cuisine, had the idea of starting a society with that as its primary aim. He discussed the thought with his friend Gringoire, who was immediately enthusiastic. They drew in two colleagues, M. Bozeray and M. Görög, and on 25 February 1912 a dining society, the *Ligue des Gourmands*, was launched. They invited others to join them to form the committee. They had their inaugural dinner, *le Dîner de Douze*, in London, on 25 March. The committee set itself the task of spreading word of the *Ligue*, which each member did through his personal contacts. Membership was soon growing rapidly, and local chapters were being started across Europe and beyond.

At about this time, Auguste had been taking renewed interest in Joseph

Donon, the lad he had taken on at the Carlton in 1907 from the château at Villeneuve-Loubet. He had shown immediate promise, but there had been a check in his career when he had had to go back to France for two years for his military service. That done, he had returned to the Carlton. Auguste had promoted him to *garde-manger et poisson*.

In the spring of 1912, Henry Clay Frick, the steel king of America, staying at the Carlton, was particularly impressed with the fish courses and asked after the cook, who was indeed Joseph Donon. Frick persuaded Auguste to release Donon to become his personal chef. Frick and his wife were booked for their return to New York on the maiden voyage of the new Atlantic liner that was astonishing the world – the *Titanic*. He was able to get another ticket for Joseph. Fate then made a two-pronged intercession: Mrs Frick sprained her ankle and Joseph was unable to get his visa in time. They all took the next boat.

On the night of April 14 the boat they had missed, the great White Star liner that 'even God couldn't sink', hit an iceberg. With a 300-foot gash below the water line she went down, and 1500 people died in the freezing sea. All but one of the cooks aboard perished, but only Escoffier sought out the details: he made a point of publishing photographs of each of them with carefully researched obituaries in *Le Carnet d'Epicure*.

That of course was the great event of the year for the press, although other things were of course going on. Some of these were setting the scene for the great events of our own time. Montenegro, Serbia, Bulgaria and Greece went to war with Turkey – and won. They then squabbled among themselves. Lenin coopted Stalin onto the first Central Committee of the Bolshevik Party and Sun Yat-Sen founded the Chinese National Party. In Britain the GPO took over the various telephone systems and Samuel Woodhead's Piltdown man upstaged the Neanderthals, a hoax sustained for forty years.

But newspapers still found room to report the first scheme of the *Ligue des Gourmands*, an ambitious one. Auguste's committee was organising a *dîner d'épicure*, where groups of *Ligue* members would sit down to dinner in their cities in various countries, all at the same time, with the same menu. The scheme caught the imagination of the press, which not only prepared the world for the event but also publicised its outcome immediately. Reporters transmitted copy in great detail by telephone and telegraph '*aux quatre coins du globe*', wrote Auguste.[1] 'The event was, way beyond our expectations, the finest promotion of French cooking that had ever been attempted.'

He was overjoyed with the success of his scheme. They had expected to cater for about a hundred members in London, but nearer three hundred sat down to dinner at the Hotel Cecil, which, Auguste wrote, then became the 'gastronomic centre of the Universe'. He was intrigued to think of some four thousand *gourmands* simultaneously enjoying a French meal from his menu in thirty-seven different towns. The more remarkable in that *la Ligue* had not yet been in existence three months, and the *Carnet d'Epicure* was not yet a year old. If he had had any doubt about the success of the venture, it certainly had not been with any thought of failure of his part of the plan: the menu. 'The menu I had designed was, naturally, warmly welcomed by all.'[2]

The highlight of the event for Auguste was early in the evening at the Cecil. They had scarcely sat at table when the first telegram arrived and was read by a M. Bizeray, standing on a chair:

> I am there with you; I am taking part in your celebration, so French; I extend a hand to our great poet Richepin, to my dear friend Escoffier, to you Gringoire who writes so well of fruits and flowers, and finally to you all, friends of poetry and lovers of good fare ...[3]

Before Bizeray could say whom the telegram was from, Auguste was on his feet calling, 'It's her, it's her'. And it was, indeed, from Sarah Bernhardt. Auguste was so emotional, Gringoire says, that he thought *le Maître* might dissolve in tears.

Auguste wrote to Delphine about the dinner:

> Dear Delphine, enclosed two newspaper cuttings, one from *Le Matin* and the other from an English paper. These are only two among forty or fifty from French and English newspapers. I am sending at the same time my little talk as chairman of the *Ligue des Gourmands*.
>
> Many of our customers wanted to have the same dinner yesterday evening, Sunday, here at the Carlton, and especially the *Fraises Sarah* which all the diners wanted to add. It goes without saying that it was a great success, and I believe all the large restaurants in London served *Fraises Sarah* yesterday evening. Personally I must admit it is dainty and nice.
>
> Much love. I will write in a couple of days.
>
> And sweet kisses – sweeter than *Fraises Sarah*. Georges[4]

The letter may not be typical of his communications with Delphine, but no others seem to have survived for comparison. Even in the original French it has little poetic appeal, but it wastes few words. 'Georges' seems to have been a pet name: it occurs neither on Auguste's birth certificate nor on his grave. He was apparently happy to adopt the name: his by-line in early issues of *L'Art Culinaire* was G. A. Escoffier, and a visiting card with these initials has survived. Herbodeau, one-time *sous-chef* to Auguste, entitled his book about him, 'Georges Auguste Escoffier'. On the other hand, Maurice

Ithurbure, also *sous-chef* to Escoffier, knew him to be Auguste, but had never heard him called anything but *Monsieur*, or *Maître* – except for *Papa*, which the staff called him out of his hearing.

By this time, Auguste, aged sixty-four, was an experienced writer and had developed a distinctive style. His articles, in L*e Carnet d'Epicure* for example, have an engaging lyricism. Clearly he read a lot and researched his articles well. Never one for missing an opportunity to bring in an interesting sideline to a culinary theme, he strays with some skill and to good effect. In reporting a visit to Touraine seeking local dishes, he describes economically its terrain and climate, and outlines its history from the time of the Gauls.[5] He deals with the etymology of *martiner* a word in Old French, 'to drink too much' – which comes from Saint Martin de Tours, who apparently often did. Not content with classing a meal as a *fête pantagruélique* he goes on to quote several stanzas of selectively mild Rabelais. It is all apposite and has form. There can be little doubt, however, of the influence of his friend Gringoire who, as editor of *le Carnet d'Epicure*, was of course concerned with Auguste's input to the journal. Nevertheless, Auguste had his own style, which had grown from early naivety to what might be regarded as Victorian simplicity without its convolutions.

In *Le Carnet d'Epicure* he wrote regular articles and used them to express opinions over a wide range and sometimes with some strength. In one, under the serial heading of *Les Trésors Culinaires*, he fairly jumps up and down on the subject of non-French wines:

> For some years there has been sold in England, under the name of Burgundy or Burgoyne, a wine made in Australia, California, or even in London, which obviously does not possess either the delicate aroma, the rich flavour or the beneficial qualities of our divine Burgundy.
>
> The English of the higher classes are too good connoisseurs not to distinguish these wines from those of France. But in many families they are accepted as true Burgundies. It is indeed annoying ... that such a confusion should be tolerated.[6]

These days, of course, even those of us of lesser blood can appreciate that some of the wines now produced in these un-French countries are splendid.

Auguste makes no bones about class distinction, but that was the norm at the time. Moreover, he was exposed to the widest possible range, from those at the back door of the kitchens begging scraps to royalty picking a way through many courses at dinner.

He had another series going called *Causeries Familières*. The articles were directed to housewives, 'many of whom', he says, 'I have often found on my world travels to be almost ignorant of the most elementary culinary ideas. There should be practical courses for girls at school. Even in France students learn only to use excellent produce to cook deplorably.' There is something of a reversal here of his previously expressed views on the impeccable upbringing of French girls as cooks.

In the first article of the series, he confined himself to remarking that man is only saved from being merely an animal by his intelligent selection and improvement of food, and that woman should find great pleasure in assisting in this since 'good food is in effect the basis of true happiness'.[7] He went on to say that the husband who is sure to find a simple but exquisite meal waiting for him at home will hurry back from work, and after his meal will be in good humour and not tempted to go out again to find what he knows exists under his own roof. Escoffier assures his 'gracious' female readers that he will guide them, if they wish, so that each soon becomes a true mistress in this very delicate art of cooking.

Another call on Auguste's time in 1912 was in the revision of his *Guide Culinaire* for its third edition. There were recipes to update and many more to add. To keep down the size of the book, the section setting out menus at the back was omitted. He revised these and his publisher, Flammarion of Paris, brought them out as a new book, *Le Livre des Menus*.

It was during this period at the Carlton that Auguste was offered a post at Court. He declined the honour. His reasons in his own words were: 'first, because the Carlton paid me £2000 a year, a figure which no Court could offer, and secondly, because the Court usually has a menu fixed for each day of the week, with very little variation, and a chef has no chance of showing what he can do except on special occasions'.[8] Good reasons, but had Edward VII still been on the throne Auguste might well have accepted the offer. King George V, quiet living, even austere and certainly no gourmet, had no attraction for a chef.

In mid-January 1913, Auguste did his usual post-Christmas trip home to Monte Carlo. He stopped off overnight on the 15th at Avignon, where he stayed with friends at the Restaurant Lance. On Friday 17th he met some more friends, Louis Perdrier and Arsène Dard, in Monte Carlo and went with them to the *station oenologique* where they tasted wines. In the afternoon he went to the Musée de l'Hôpital and to some of the principal vintners.

As for the evening, he says: 'I had been invited to dinner by Mme Martini-Rosé who wanted me to try out some new dishes. I arrived about seven o'clock. M. and Mme Perdrier were among the guests.' (If Mme Escoffier was also there, she doesn't get a mention.) 'If the wines which accompanied the courses were of the best growths, the dishes did honour to the mistress of the house. The menu, simple but quite bourgeois, had for me, always on the lookout for novelties, quite a special attraction.' The speciality was a *Matelote d'anguille aux écrevisses*. He included it as *Matelote rosée* (or Rosé, after Mme Martini-Rosé) along with his *Matelote au vin rouge* and *Matelote blanche* in his *vocabulaire de cuisine*. He hasn't left us the recipe, but *matelotes* in his *Guide Culinaire* have *écrevisses* as garnish. The wines were a 1911 Montrachet and 1904 and 1908 Clos-Vougeot. Not bad for a 'bourgeois' meal, although these days I expect we would gloat over a Montrachet a little longer than two years before sacrificing it.

Auguste naturally assumes that the man of the house will be the one to choose the wines. In our own enlightened times, men still mostly make this assumption.

In Edwardian Britain, women, almost half the work force, were paid a third or less than the men doing similar work. Divorce was one-sided; a woman could be divorced for infidelity, while a man had to have reinforced his extra-marital adventures with attacks on his wife, or to have totally deserted her. The father had first claim on the children. Women had a rough time in other ways too. Gynaecology was technically at an unsophisticated level and contraception was associated with prostitution. Women were indeed second-class citizens. But change was in the air. Women were fighting for their rights and had some doughty champions. Emmeline Pankhurst, the arch-suffragette, and her fiery daughter, Christabel, were at the forefront. Emmeline spent most of 1913 in and out of prison a dozen times between hunger strike and recovery. Like most men at the time, Auguste would not have seen the suffragette movement as the start of an unstoppable reform, and probably reacted with little more than amusement at the antics of Mrs Pankhurst.

Unrest among the women was matched by troubles in the male labour force. In 1912 over 800,000 miners went on strike – despite the fact that union members were greatly in the minority. Forty million days were lost that year (four times the loss in 1970 one of the worst years for strikes in more recent times).

In 1913 Auguste had another meeting with Kaiser Wilhelm II. It was on the *Imperator*, the largest ocean liner of the Hamburg-Amerika Line. Auguste had installed and staffed the kitchens for the Carlton Hotel Company, which was to be responsible for their management. The restaurant itself was a faithful reproduction of the Carlton Restaurant in London and, as on the previous liners of the company, was named the Ritz-Carlton Restaurant. The Kaiser was to join the liner at Cuxhaven on Tuesday 8 July for an overnight trip prior to the liner's maiden voyage across the Atlantic. He would travel the forty miles out into the North Sea as far as Heligoland – the island exchanged by the British in 1890 for some African territories, including Zanzibar – and then back to Cuxhaven. Auguste went aboard the previous Saturday to start preparations for the reception. He had appointed one of his own chefs from the Carlton, Charles Scotto, as *chef de cuisine* and Scotto had been aboard since early June and had trained his *brigade*. They had been to sea already on a trial cruise.

Guests, representing the higher echelons of the German aristocracy, started to arrive on Monday afternoon. One hundred and ten were at dinner that evening. It started with caviar and went to peaches, with saddle of roe deer and other courses on the way. One of the wines served was Liebfraumilch 1904, 'the milk of Our Lady', made by monks near the city of Worms. The 'milch' bit is supposed to have grown out of *Mönch* the word for monk. (It was different stuff then from the embittered sugar-water now malingering under that hallowed label, and comprising half German exports in the name of wine.)

The Kaiser arrived with his suite the next day and, anchor weighed, one hundred and forty-six sat down to luncheon:

Hors d'oeuvre à la Russe
Melon Cantaloup
Consommé froid Madrilène
Velouté Parmentier
Timbale de homard Imperator
Mousse de jambon au Madère
Epinards Nouveaux
Selle de veau Orloff
Pointes d'asperges au beurre
Dodine de canard en Gelée
Terrine de poulet à l'estragon
Salade de fruits à la Japonais
Aubergines à l'Orientale
Soufflé glacé framboise
Biscuit au Kirsch
Pâtisserie française
Fruits
Café, Liqueurs
Vins
Georges Goulet, Extra Dry
Clicquot rosé
Zeltinger Schlossberg
Château Giscours 1907

That sort of luncheon might have brought on a little drowsiness in the late afternoon. The party was ready, however, for another heroic menu at eight in the evening. Following a choice of caviar or soup came a fish course, chicken, saddle of mutton, quails and finally the Kaiser's favourite pudding, strawberries, served on this occasion as *Fraises Imperator*. There were of course some German white wines but, in case the guests had forgotten where real wine came from, there was an impressive thirty-five-year-old claret, from the Médoc, Château Rausan-Ségla.

After dinner there was a film show which, Auguste says, put everyone in high spirits. He mentions 'a delicious French artiste, Mademoiselle Suzanne', but she wasn't representative of the theme of the whole show. There was also a film about French naval squadrons on manoeuvre off Tunis. Auguste says, 'It could only have benefited Germany and compromised the security of France. The memory troubled me for a long time'. At the end of the show, the Kaiser said he would like to see Auguste after breakfast the next day.

At 8 o'clock the next morning the ship was back at Cuxhaven and breakfast was served. It was more elaborate than the Continental Breakfast we know today: four different egg dishes, three types of fish, ham, bacon, lamb chops, chicken, smoked tongue, roast beef and a cornucopia of fruits. Auguste and the Kaiser met in the Palm Lounge after breakfast where, so the story goes, the Kaiser said to Auguste, 'I am the Emperor of Germany, but you are the Emperor of Chefs'.[9] The press quoted this often and variously, referring to Auguste as 'The Chef of Kings, the King of Chefs'.[10] The style was a sort of joke often attributed to sovereigns – King Edward VII is supposed to have dubbed Cartier the 'Jeweller of Kings, the King of Jewellers' after he had supplied twenty-seven tiaras for his coronation.

Auguste does not mention this piece of flattery in his version of the encounter, so perhaps it came from the pen of an imaginative journalist:

> The Emperor shook hands and told me he'd been very comfortable on board and had slept as well as in his own palace. He then thanked me for coming especially from London to look after the cooking during his time on the *Imperator*.
>
> I thanked him for his interest and asked after the Empress and the children. He said they were all in good health and thanked me for my concern.
>
> I then said, 'Your Majesty, I hope that your own health will allow you to reign for a long time to come and to accomplish the greatest humanitarian act of the century: the reconciliation of Germany and France'.
>
> The Emperor assured me that it was his greatest wish and that he worked always to that end. Unfortunately, his best intentions were rarely correctly interpreted. I agreed that the motives behind the views expressed by certain newspapers were sometimes regrettable.
>
> He said, 'Yes, the press, or part of it, is not always favourably disposed towards good ideas. Despite that, I very much hope to see my wish realised, and wish also

with all my heart the greatest possible happiness for civilisation'.

'I hope, your Majesty,' I said, 'there'll be good will shown on both sides and that you will have the pleasure of seeing the coming together of the two great countries. It will be the crowning achievement of your fine reign and the good fortune of all the people of Europe, who will find peace at last in their work.'

It was not the sort of conversation one would expect between an emperor and the chef he had called to compliment on his cuisine. Auguste was showing courage and determined humanitarianism if not patriotism. But clearly the Kaiser was not put out by Auguste's overtures, or he would have cut short the interview, which in fact went on for half an hour. They parted with a friendly handshake. The Kaiser went ashore and passengers came aboard for the voyage to Southampton, Cherbourg and New York. Up another gangway came 600 *poulardes de la Bresse*, 500 *pigeons de provenance française* and 250 *pintades* – with one-way tickets. Back at the Carlton, two young cooks joined Auguste's team who were to make a name for themselves. Eugéne Herbodeau, at twenty-five, had trained in the provincial kitchens of France and then blossomed in Paris. It was Lucien Gouin of Paillard's in Paris who recommended Herbodeau to Auguste, who started him as a *commis* fish cook. A year later he promoted him to *chef saucier*. Eventually he became *chef de cuisine* at the London Ritz before returning to the Carlton to take the place of the master he had 'loved and venerated'.[11]

The other recruit was the seventeen-year-old Maurice Auguste Ithurbure. He came from Soustons on the Côte d'Argent in south-west France, where his father kept the Hôtel du Lion d'Or. Auguste took on young Maurice as *commis saucier*. He rose quickly from that lowly post to be *sous-chef* and *chef de nuit* under Auguste before leaving to open his own restaurant, Chez Maurice, in Eastbourne. Before Ithurbure retired it was said to be the finest restaurant in England.[12]

Much later, when a newspaper obituary for *le Maître* claimed he had been taken on as God's Chef, Ithurbure was supposed to have commented 'Papa could not be God's chef, he was God'. In 1991, aged ninety-five, Ithurbure could recall a great deal about his hero but he had no memory of uttering this ultimate apotheosis, but hastened to insist it was indeed true.[13] 'Like God, all things of Papa Auguste was *special*.'

Ithurbure claimed his family name was Basque for 'head of the waters' and, with an impish grin, mimed flushing a toilet. He was charming, but it was necessary to be something of an auditory gymnast just to listen to him – the words in a sentence were arbitrarily in English pronounced as French, or in French with a heavy English accent. He seemed to have forgotten how to use one or the other language alone. In translation, he said that, during his time at the Carlton, *le Maître* did no actual cooking but was constantly inventive, both in constructing menus and their component dishes. He spent a lot of time in the kitchens supervising all aspects of buying, preparation, cooking and presentation. He was a perfectionist and criticised the tiniest details of his cooks' work. Ithurbure didn't mind. 'Zap is 'owl ve learn *quelque chose, n'est-ce pas?*'

Everyone respected 'Papa', but there were a few who didn't like him – those who didn't want to do their full share of the work. But he was kind even to the slackers. He never lost his temper with them, and never reprimanded them when others could hear. He might ask someone to walk outside with him chatting normally, or on a serious matter, fix a time for the miscreant to go to his office on the first floor. He was particularly kind to youngsters. As well as showing infinite patience with the awkward or the slow learners, he would often slip a sovereign or so to one of them he had learned was in difficulties over money.

On the subject of Auguste's departure from the Savoy, Ithurbure shook his head thoughtfully for a moment or two and then said, enigmatically, that 'Papa' didn't bet on the horses. Most of those in the kitchen did, and 'Papa' turned a blind eye, but he never joined in. When it came to spare time activities, Ithurbure said that Auguste spent much of it in his office. He worked very hard and didn't waste a moment. He added, with a knowing look and a finger tapping the side of his nose, that *le Maître* was very fond of the ladies. What did he mean by that? He would only say, with another weird twist, that Auguste spent some of his spare time playing billiards at what he called the *Club de Cuisine* in Shaftesbury Avenue – this was probably the Association Culinaire Française, later at 1–3 Old Compton Street, which Auguste and his colleague Emil Fétu had founded in 1903.[14]

Ithurbure enjoyed recalling his life with Escoffier. Perhaps they were memories often recalled, grown and smoothed in repetition, but he was probably the last remaining witness of Auguste at work and able to draw a picture of him at the height of his fame. For Maurice Ithurbure, Papa Auguste was the greatest man ever to walk the earth, and he wanted everyone to know.

As for Ithurbure himself, he had recently lost his lady friend of many years and he was no longer a happy man. A great cook in his time, he now scarcely bothered with food – his staple diet was a bar of plain chocolate in a piece of French-style bread. He said he hoped one day soon he would 'wake up dead'. This he did, on 25 May 1991.

Interlude 16

Dodine and the Duck

'Vivent les dîneurs et les dodineurs auxquelles de tout coeur je me joins pour glorifier le véritable grand art que fut et doit rester notre cuisine, cette rose unique arrosé par les vins de France.'

Jean Richepin

This telegraphic toast from the poet Richepin was read out at a banquet at the Hotel Cecil in London. The occasion was in glorification of French cooking, and Escoffier dedicated it to Sarah Bernhardt. Poetic licence perhaps allows *dodineurs* – diners who were to eat a dodine. And it was more than just another banquet.

A Parisian newspaper revealed in May 1912 that the *Ligue des Gourmands* was organising a banquet to be served on a particular night 'in all the capitals of the world'.[1] The main dish, an ancient one modernised by the King of Chefs, M. Escoffier, the article said, would be *la dodine Chambertin*.

A week or so later an English national went further:

A New Delicacy

All true epicures will learn on 25 May next the secret of a new dinner delicacy created by that prince among chefs M. Escoffier, of the Carlton Hotel, London. *La Ligue des Gourmands* will hold simultaneous dinners in many cities including London, Birmingham, Strasburg, Paris, Brussels, Manchester, Marseilles, Liverpool, Berlin, New York, Lyons etc.

The menu will be exactly the same in each case, a feast for epicures drawn up by M. Escoffier and prepared from his recipes. At the end of the repast the new dish will be placed on the tables.

M. Escoffier is a founder of the League together with M. J. Bizeray, the French professor, M. R. Görög, the chef at the New Gallery Restaurant, Regent Street, and M. Th. Gringoire, a poet. The object of the league is to demonstrate the excellence of the French culinary art.

Strawberry surprise, *Fraises Sarah Bernhardt* will be the new delicacy; Monsieur Escoffier has devised something to excel even Pêche Melba. It will be a poem in luscious fresh strawberries, with a subtle flavour so exquisite as to defy analysis.[2]

'I think', Escoffier said when interviewed, 'it will cause just a little sensation. As for the rest of the dinner, it will be light, delicate, and piquant, such as will please the fastidious, without being specially noteworthy. But my *Fraises Sarah Bernhardt* will, I trust, be a masterpiece.'

The recipe was to be a secret until the banquets. The chefs abroad would receive it by registered post and were sworn not to disclose it before time. The report continued:

> After the epicures at the London dinner, at the Hotel Cecil, have tasted *Fraises Sarah Bernhardt*, M. Escoffier will divulge the secret of its making, and M. Gringoire will recite an ode declaring its qualities as incomparable as the acting of Madame Bernhardt herself.
>
> Then the cable will spread the recipe across the world, and the next day *Fraises Sarah Bernhardt* will appear on the menus of the most exclusive restaurants from St Petersburg to Rome, from Buenos Aires to New York.

The newspaper also demoted Auguste to prince and they got the date wrong, but the dinner was held, nevertheless, on 18 May 1912.

The affair went well. It was a Press occasion in London, and the world was told the same evening of the: 'greatest celebration in honour of *la Cuisine française* that has ever taken place.' The main dish was described as: 'this miraculous *Dodine au Chambertin*, the last word, the supreme triumph of French cuisine.'[3] This was the menu:

Hors-d'oeuvre Mignon
Petite marmite béarnaise
Truite saumonée aux crevettes roses
Dodine de canard au Chambertin
Nouilles fraiches au beurre noisette
Agneau de Pauillac à la Bordelaise
Petits pois frais de Clamart
Poularde de France à la gelée
à la d'Orléans

Coeurs de romaines aux pommes d'amour
Asperges d'Argenteuil
Sauce Divine
Fraises Sarah Bernhardt
Mignardises
Café mode orientale
Les plus fines liqueurs
Vins: Chablis Moutonne 1902
Chambertin Clos de Bèze 1887
Champagne Veuve Clicquot Dry England 1900[4]

Why did Auguste boost his *Fraises Sarah Bernhardt* with the English newspaper and wave aside the rest of the menu as not 'specially noteworthy'? It was a simple enough dish – strawberries served on a layer of pineapple sorbet and covered with a mousse of strawberries macerated in Curaçao and brandy. Was it sheer marketing flair? Artistry over culinary skill? Or was it just that Sarah was uppermost in his mind? Whatever the case, we surely cannot follow Escoffier's lead and pass on now without a glance at the *Dodine de canard au chambertin*.

What is a *dodine*? It seems to be a word modern dictionaries consider unworthy of definition. It was in the *Viandier*, one of the earliest surviving cookbooks, ascribed to Guillaume Tirel, known as Taillevent, that Escoffier found mention of what he called 'that lovely word *dodine*'.[5] Or rather, it was quoted from the *Viandier* in a much later book discovered in 1910 in the British Museum by Auguste's friend and mentor, the poet Gringoire.[6] The meaning of *dodine* is not obvious. Escoffier, as well as others, used the word at the time as though it referred to a way of preparing food, like a ragoût or a blanquette. *Le Matin* reporting its researches uses the word similarly:

> The last *Dodine Chambertin*, or rather, *Dodine Suresnes*, since the original recipe used a wine of the Suresnes, was served at a meal which brought together three of our historic figures, Boileau, Molière and La Fontaine.[7]

Yet back in the fourteenth century there was a recipe for *dodine blanche* which was simply cows' milk spiced with sugar, salt, parsley and marjoram. That was not a process Escoffier had in mind for his duck.

Again, it was Auguste's poet friend, that *bibliophile érudit*, M. Th. Gringoire, who produced the answer from his rummaging of the British Museum Library. Blaisius Ambroisius, a Bergerac monk, produced a treatise in 1583 on kitchen pottery through the ages. He mentions *dodine* as a container for cooking food in the oven or in hot ashes. It was a large earthenware pot, like a terrine but with a lid, two to three inches thick 'to resist great heat without breaking'. The maker then was a celebrated tiler of Périgueux, Pierre Loujou. *Dodines* were used mostly for cooking boar's head.[8] The monk went on to tell a story about some charcoal burners of the forest of Verteillac who, having caught a werewolf, had enclosed it in a *dodine* which they put in the middle of a wood fire. They came back the next day to see if their werewolf was well cooked. When they took the *dodine* out of the ashes, to their amazement the lid sprang open and the werewolf ran off with frightful howls which froze them with fear. Three of them died on the spot and others remained paralysed for the rest of their lives. 'The werewolf, you see', said Blaisius Ambroisius, 'was none other than the Devil in one of his many guises. No animal in the world would have leapt out alive from that *dodine.*'

A *dodine*, then, is a thick, earthenware, cooking vessel to use for slow even cooking. It might be a little difficult to find one these days, although perhaps the earthenware *Römertopf* might be considered an effete modern derivative. But we have infinitely variable heating and thermostats, and so we can probably make do with a terrine – or even a stainless-steel casserole, its bottom thickly clad with aluminium.

How is Escoffier's dish prepared? He found recipes in Taillevent's four-teenth-century *Viandier*, which he adapted to the tastes of his day.[9] An example is his *dodine* which, Herbodeau said, he 'processed in his mind, modified and simplified to the point of its becoming a marvel capable of producing the most agreeable sensations on the most delicate palate ...'[10]

First the original:

Taillevent's Duck à la Dodine Rouge

First take some bread and grill it well. Put it to soak in some red wine. Fry some onions in lard. Sift the bread and add some spices – cinnamon, nutmeg, cloves, sugar and salt. Boil all these ingredients together with the fat from the duck which has been previously roasted and pour this sauce over the duck.

Not particularly inspiring. Herbodeau remarked: 'just to read Taillevent's version brings on nausea'.

Escoffier's rendering was not so much simplified as refined. The following recipe is taken from a 1934 printing.[11] It will be noticed that he has altered the name of the dish to conform to his new understanding of the meaning of *dodine* — the duck is now in the pot with the Chambertin:

Caneton Rouennais en Dodine au Chambertin

1 Rouen duckling
½ pint *fond de veau lié* (brown veal stock)
½ pint Chambertin

¼ pint cognac
2 shallots
pinch of coarse pepper
pinch nutmeg
½ bay leaf
1 oz butter
3 tbsp. *rouennaise* forcemeat (see below)
A few small mushrooms

For the *rouennaise* forcemeat:

2oz. fresh pork fat
½ oz. butter
4oz. ducklings' livers
salt, pepper, spice
1 tbsp. chopped onion
A pinch of parsley

Chop the pork fat and put it into a pan with the butter. Be sure to remove the gall bladder carefully from the livers. Season them with salt, pepper and spice and add the onion and parsley.

Heat up the fat, put in the livers and sauté for a few seconds, just long enough to seal them. Cool a little and then rub through a sieve.

Roast the duckling keeping it a little underdone. Remove the breast and put it on to a plate, skin side downwards (to prevent any juices running out). Partially cover the plate.

Remove the legs and the parson's nose, and pound the rest of the carcass. Add the veal stock, cover and cook over moderate heat for 15–20 minutes, then press as much as possible through a sieve.

Put the wine and the brandy into a pan, add the chopped shallots, pepper, nutmeg and bay leaf and reduce quickly by two thirds.

Add the sieved sauce, bring to boiling point and boil for a few minutes. Finally add the butter and forcemeat.

Note: the slices of duckling can be covered with slices of foie gras sautéed in butter and topped with a slice of truffle.

If you want to make the *dodine* these days it is no good thinking over your morning coffee at home that it might be a good dish to serve for dinner that evening – unless of course you stock your freezer on professional lines. There is a lot of preparation, and some ingredients may not be easy to find. A request for a Rouen duckling at the local supermarket will probably gain you little more than a tolerant smile. Even the veal for the stock may be met with a proposal that you call in next Thursday when they might have something in.

There might be a bit of a problem over the Chambertin which, at the time of writing, is selling by the case at auction at around £100 a bottle, and there is still the foie gras and the truffle to come. If you are one of those who regard as sacrilege the mere thought of using a *grand cru* in cooking even a *dodine*, you are probably in the majority. The subtler heaven-sent flavours of great wines finding themselves in a hot pot would soon be off to seek their maker – it is unfortunately also true that the diabolic tangs of a spoiled wine would be reluctant to seek theirs. Even Escoffier, writing after his retirement, when he would be using the wine from his own cellar, suggested that the Chambertin 'need not be too old'. You could go a little further and still be reasonably authentic if you used one of the satellite wines of the district, such as Gevry Chambertin. It would be an epicure indeed who could detect that you had not used Chambertin itself. You could also do without the foie gras trimming, but do not dispense lightly with the truffle, which will pervade the dish with its subtle aroma and, according to Brillat-Savarin have further advantages:

> Whoever says 'truffles' utters a great word which arouses erotic and gastronomic memories among the skirted sex and memories gastronomic and erotic among the bearded sex.
>
> This dual distinction is due to the fact that the noble tuber is not only considered delicious to the taste, but is also believed to foster powers the exercise of which is extremely pleasurable.
>
> 'Rejoice, my dear', I said one day to Madame de V.; 'a loom has just been shown to the Society for Encouragement on which it will be possible to manufacture superb lace for practically nothing.'
>
> 'Why,' the lady replied, with an air of supreme indifference, 'if lace were cheap, do you think anybody would want to wear such rubbish?' [12]

So, buy your aphrodisiac truffles while they are still expensive. Meanwhile, it may be wise to keep a weather eye out for the werewolf in case it is Apollyon seeking to avenge the singed tail.

Rouen ducklings are good for the purpose but others are not necessarily worse, just different. As far as Escoffier was concerned, there were three types of duck used in cooking: the commercial Rouen, the Nantes, and the wild duck. Wild duck were roasted and used for Salmis. The Rouen duck was killed by suffocation and not bled – a bit like hanging a man with his old-school tie. They were roasted and sometimes braised. The Nantes duck he considered similar to the English Aylesbury and less plump than the Rouen: they were more often braised, although they could be *poêlée* or roasted.[13]

Another renowned French duck is from the Vendée. It grows to 7 pounds in nine weeks. La Tour d'Argent, which claims to be the oldest eating place in Paris, dating back to 1532, when heron pie was its speciality, has them choked to death and not bled for their famous *canard au sang*. They have numbered each of these like a bottle of vintage wine since the first was cooked in 1890. Doubtless Frédéric Delair, owner of the little restaurant and originator of the splendid dish, had no. 1, but since the first records are missing we can only guess. Later entries show that King Edward VII while Prince of Wales had no. 328, the Duke of Windsor in 1938 had no. 147,888 and in 1948 the present Queen as Princess Elizabeth had no. 185,397. She didn't share it with the Duke of Edinburgh – he had no. 185,398. The name was changed to *Canard du Centenaire* for the dish's hundredth birthday in 1990. It was said that the 750,000th duckling would have its last quack throttled at the restaurant by the beginning of this century.[14] But resist the temptation to use the telephone to find out whether it did; not knowing will be an added excitement when going to eat the next one available.

Before the eighteenth century domesticated breeds of duck were not specifically named and were known generally as common duck, and probably not far removed from the mallard. But, in and around the little town of Aylesbury, a white duck was farmed, developed presumably from an albino, which often occurs naturally amongst wild duck. This was called the English White and later became the famous Aylesbury Duck. It doubtless has the swan as its role model and almost succeeds with its long slim neck in being elegant, carrying its body horizontally without a tail-dragging duck waddle, but its snake-like head gives it away. By the mid nineteenth century Aylesbury ducks were not only sold all over the British Isles but exported in quantity. Their delicate white flesh was much appreciated both for its taste and its appearance. The white feathers were a bonus much sought for stuffing pillows and quilts.

Another reason for the Aylesbury's popularity was that it could be timed nicely into the market. Plump eight-week-old ducklings were ready for market in February, after the game season and before spring chickens were available. The gap later in the year was filled by the French Rouen, which laid later than the English bird and took longer to mature. The Buckinghamshire duck industry scarcely survived the nineteenth century, at least as far as the small farmer was concerned. Some larger concerns carried on and production of the Aylesbury was taken up to some extent elsewhere in the country, although the birds were in fact mostly variously crossbred. We don't see much of the Aylesbury these days; apart from wild duck we get various crosses selected for large-scale production. One of these is the Gressingham, a mallard/Pekin cross. It was developed in Cumbria by Peter Dodds. The cross is a thick-fleshed meaty bird with a high ratio of flesh to bone. Excellent for the *dodine*.

Ask a master chef what, in one word, makes a good dish a masterpiece and he will provide you with many words. Insist on just one and he might well say, 'Extravagance'. Marco Pierre White said so when asked what made his restaurant so successful.[15] He added, 'If it needs caviar, give it plenty' – probably thinking of his famous *tagliatelle* of oysters and caviar. Be extravagant, then, and *Caneton en Dodine au Chambertin* will pay handsome dividends.

17

The Great War

'What is our task?
To make Britain a fit country for heroes to live in.'

David Lloyd George, November 1918

In Britain, in the four years after 1910, the fear of a war with Germany was constantly in the air, even though up to the middle of 1911 the Kaiser acted in friendly enough fashion. He had come to England for Edward VII's funeral and again for the unveiling of the Queen Victoria Memorial. His son, the Crown Prince, represented him at George V's Coronation. Transparently, he sought only Britain's neutrality in any German conflict with France – which was almost precipitated several times in the period. Although Britain had not guaranteed military support to the French, nobody had any doubt that Britain would be sucked into any such conflict.

If anything of the ugliness of the world outside penetrated the Carlton, there was little evidence of it. The 1 per cent of the population who owned two-thirds of the nation's wealth was well represented there and was enjoying what could be bought. It was not that the threat of revolution or war was not a worry to such people: they had the most to lose, particularly the comfort of gracious living.

The Carlton provided luxurious relaxation from the strenuous life of pleasure led by its regulars in pursuit of the great outdoors. There was shooting, fishing, and the essential worship of that class totem, the horse – hunting, or following the racing season around the country. Or perhaps they were just back from teaching the Swiss to appreciate their own mountains. The day was approaching, however, when the world would start to change for everyone. It arrived the day after Bank Holiday Monday, 4 August 1914. The war declared that day was to involve all Europe and most of the rest of the world.

On 28 June a Serbian student had shot and killed Archduke Franz Ferdinand and his wife as they drove in open car through Sarajevo, Bosnia, and precipitated a rapid sequence of international events long brewing which with hindsight seems predictable. Austria-Hungary declared war on Serbia, ostensibly to avenge the assassination of the heir to their throne. Germany supported Austria-Hungary. Russia supported Serbia. Germany responded to Russian mobilisation by mobilising themselves. They then marched on France to knock out their western enemy before Russia was able to be a threat. The Germans advanced through neutral Belgium. Great Britain, not wanting the Channel ports occupied by a hostile power, came in as a great nation protecting a lesser.

War began formally for Britain on 4 August and Lord Kitchener was soon pointing at the young men to tell them their country needed them. It took them in hundreds of thousands from country seats and farm cottages, from town houses and from under railway arches, and committed them to the mud of northern France.

The evening the Germans advanced on France, Lloyd George and Winston Churchill were dining at the Carlton, well aware of the tense situation, but doubtless not yet realising it was the day the world had embarked on a new course from which there was no return – and certainly unaware that their vegetables had been prepared by Ho Chi Minh, who years later would become a renowned and influential Communist leader, but was then a *commis entremettier* on Escoffier's *brigade*.[1]

The first change at the Carlton due to war was the introduction of military uniform amongst the dress of its clients. Then came staff shortages with men changing chef's toque for tin hat and women going to make munitions rather than beds. The clientele of the Carlton was not reduced by the war but the kitchen staff went down to a third of its peacetime strength. Auguste however, at sixty-eight years of age, had lost nothing of his vigour and prodigious dynamism. He tirelessly went around his *parties*, 'from larder to sauce section, from the roast to the puddings, seeing that everything went on as it had when the staff was complete'.[2]

With memories of his experiences in the war of 1870, Auguste followed the example of many a British housewife and stocked provisions. Unlike the Germans, who expected to be in Paris in a few weeks, he was optimistic enough to believe they would meet more resistance than they bargained for; the longer the war, the greater the shortages. The British government was similarly impressed: it introduced food rationing. Auguste and the government were right. With the miraculous Battle of the Marne in September the German's headlong advance on the French capital was halted, trench warfare started, and a long war was ensured.

The major difficulty for the restaurant was the acquisition of butcher's meat and poultry on restricted supply against ration coupons. Auguste wrote:

Only venison was exempt ... and at the Carlton minced venison with eggs became a gastronomic delight much in demand. The meat was usually tough, from old deer, but braised and served as a moussaka with rice it was quite good. Again, braised and served *à la provençale* with noodles and a chestnut purée it made an excellent dish.[3]

Eggs, fish, certain types of offal and bacon were not on coupons, so he could maintain variety in his menus.

When it came to salmon he had a problem. He needed thirty to forty a week but was lucky if he got two from his supplier – the rest doubtless fetched high prices on the black market. He went therefore to the Scottish and Irish fishermen and bought direct – essentially creating a black market source of his own. He had particular difficulty obtaining sole. The solution this time was his discovery of the *petite limande*. The little dab he considered made a fine substitute for sole. Auguste regarded adaptability of this sort to be an essential quality of a *chef de cuisine*. He liked to tell a story in this connection:

It was about François Vatel. He was *maître d'hôtel* – the first to bear the title, then one of grandeur, with fine clothes and a sword at the side – of Chantilly, the great estate of Prince de Condé. Vatel had the problem of the fresh fish not arriving in time for an important banquet he was preparing. To save his professional honour he ran himself through with his sword. He made several attempts at piercing his heart but only managed it moments before the consignment of fish arrived. Auguste claimed that at a culinary exhibition in Tours someone came up to him and asked: 'What would you have done, monsieur, if you had been in Vatel's predicament?' 'I would certainly not have killed myself over some fish', Auguste had replied. 'Quite simply, I would have fabricated some fillets of sole using the breasts of young chickens. I'll bet you what you like the finest gourmet would have been taken in.'

One of Auguste's immediate problems at the outbreak of war was that his son Paul, who had been running A. Escoffier Ltd, joined up and was sent to France to work with the Expeditionary Force's canteens. He was eventually promoted to captain and spent the rest of the war running the officers' club in Boulogne.[4] For a time, Auguste was able to keep the company going with its existing management and staff, but the inroads of conscription on experienced people soon made direction from a distance impossible. He was able to sell part of the business, but not at a good price. Shrewdly, however, he retained control of the Escoffier brand name and put the sauce and pickle production under care and maintenance.[5]

Auguste often found a way of writing about the troublesome things in his life, or of telling other people who then wrote about them. He made exceptions however. For the most part he kept deeply-felt personal wounds to himself – he has left us for example no indication of how he felt about Delphine deciding she could not live with him in England. On his successes and failures, like most people, he showed modest enthusiasm for the achievements but, from a sense of shame, seldom mentioned the problems. He has left us no hint of his feelings on the plight of his company. He did, however, refer to his concern about the difficulties of getting supplies in wartime to keep up the standards of the Carlton Restaurant. He also cared a lot about the troubles of other people due to the war. In particular, he was anxious for the wellbeing of the families left in England by his kitchen staff fighting abroad.

He didn't sit on problems; he did something about them. 'I knew only too well the sufferings of the most humble not to search for some way to alleviate them.' He persuaded the Consulat Général de France à Londres, in Bedford Square, to set up a Comité de Secours aux Familles des Soldats Français. He was himself a founder member of the *comité* with a particular responsibility for easing the difficulties of families of kitchen staff, and in particular the widows and orphans of those mown down in the slaughter overseas. He never missed an opportunity to raise money throughout the war for the cause. There is little record of such activities, but one fête he organised raised £430 for the Comité de Secours – some £20,000 in today's money.[6] He also went out of his way to prevent people losing their jobs in his kitchens.[7] At the Savoy and at the Carlton he had always carried several people above complement to avoid sacking them. That might seem to indicate a good social conscience but bad business, yet a contented staff with a feeling of security was likely to be good for business. He also guaranteed the jobs of those in the forces against their return after the war, unusual for those days.

On 8 December 1914 Auguste received a letter from the Consulat Général de France à Londres, in fact, from his own Comité de Secours, to say that his son, Lieutenant Daniel Escoffier had been 'killed on the field of honour'. Daniel had been awarded the Croix de Guerre with palm and gold star. This was another occurrence of deep personal concern on which he has left no word. Delphine on the other hand wrote and published a poem 'en mémoire du Lieutenant Daniel Escoffier' entitled 'Invocation'.* Delphine, who was already looking after her divorced sister's three children, took in Rita, Daniel's wife, and her four children. It was as well the house Auguste had bought in Monte Carlo was a large one.

With the *Carnet d'Epicure* out of publication for the duration of the war

---

* Interlude 17.

– the last issue was 5 August 1914 – Auguste missed his routine writing. He started to think again about his earlier idea of a compact little reference book on cuisine for the professional. Thirty years previously his idea had been received coolly but had then been successfully marketed by Dagouret. Colleagues and publisher had persuaded Auguste that he would do better to write a more comprehensive cookery book for professionals. This had resulted in his *Guide Culinaire*, which had indeed been successful.

He felt there was the need for an up-to-date pocket-sized book for quick reference by *cuisiniers, maîtres d'hôtel* and *garçons de restaurant*. He particularly wanted to produce a source of information for those serving the clients directly, so they could answer questions with some precision without having always to refer back to the kitchen. Gradually, as his kitchens settled down to their wartime routine, he found time to put his book together.

For Auguste, as for most civilians in England, the war was almost all 'over there'. But there were civilian casualties in England. The Germans bombed a number of English cities in December 1914, following earlier British air raids on Düsseldorf, Friedrichshafen and Cologne. The Dover area suffered from shells lobbed across the Channel by coastal artillery. Zeppelin airships were awe-inspiring and dropped some bombs – the first on London was on the night of 31 May 1915. German cruisers shelled Lowestoft and Yarmouth.

These incidents were not insignificant, but nationally the worries were mostly for men fighting a bloody war overseas, the tetanus epidemic in the trenches, and finding enough to eat. In many respects, however, life was surprisingly normal. It was clearly noticed in 1915 that Henry Ford had produced his millionth car in USA and his first farm tractor, and that motor taxis were becoming numerous on London's streets.

Auguste's war was one long struggle to provision his kitchens, keep an adequate staff and to maintain the standards of the cuisine. He gives no impression of having particularly enjoyed the tasks, although he was still proud of his ability to please clients even under the most difficult conditions. He took a lot of trouble also maintaining the morale of his staff and encouraging them in their efforts to make attractive and sustaining meals with meagre supplies. In 1916, when a number of his young French cooks were complaining that wartime food shortages made *haute cuisine* impossible, he urged them to rise to the occasion as chefs had done during the much greater privations in Paris during the Franco-Prussian War of 1870. He showed them, as an example, the menu served at Christmas in the Café Voisin on the ninety-ninth day of the siege. It was the meal that had included donkey, elephant, camel and other animals from the zoo, as well as cats and rats, all cooked and served in high style.

The Great War, as it was called until overtaken by what the participants regarded as a greater one, took over four years to play itself out until the Armistice on 11 November 1918. César Ritz, in a private hospital in Switzerland, unable even to recognise Marie, had known nothing of the war. He died a couple of weeks before the Armistice. Never surpassed as an innovative hotelier, there is probably no more lasting memorial to him than his name in adjectival use for all that is luxurious and elegant. Few have achieved distinction in such a way.

For Auguste Escoffier, Armistice Day was that 'unforgettable day, when people were at last released from a terrible nightmare'. For him the day was a wonderful memory of happy hours full of hope for the future. He saw the English, usually of such a calm temperament, acting deliriously, dancing in the streets and embracing total strangers, something he hadn't seen since peace was signed with the Boers. At the Armistice, at eleven o'clock in the morning, the Carlton regulars invaded the restaurant to book tables for a celebration dinner that night. Soon after midday all tables were booked and Auguste was committed to serving 712 places. His problem was how to make his meagre supplies, particularly of meat, stretch to the task. His assets consisted of 6 legs of lamb and 2 of veal, 15 kilograms. of pork and 10 chickens. His solution was to mix all the meats, with exception of a few chickens, through the mincer. He added to this mixture 20 kg. of *paté de foie gras* remaining from his pre-war stockpile, 10 kg. breadcrumbs moistened with tinned cream and some chopped truffles. He formed the mixture into *petites noisettes* and named the resulting dish *Mignonettes d'agneau Sainte-Alliance*.

Each helping would not have been large, probably not much more than 100gms, but to those used to wartime rations it was generous. The full menu was:

Dîner au Champagne

Consommé du Père la Victoire
Velouté Renaissance
Mousseline de homard à l'Américaine
Riz à l'Indienne
Petits pâtés de volaille à la Bruxelloise
Mignonettes d'agneau Sainte-Alliance
Petits pois à l'Anglaise
Pommes de terre Canadiennes
Faisan en cocotte Périgourdine
Salade des Capucins
Coeurs de céleri à l'Italienne

Les bombes de réjouissance
Symbole de la paix
Les douces dragées de Verdun libératrices
Friandises
Liqueurs de France, Café mode Orientale
Fine Champagne 1865, Vieille Chartreuse du Couvent [8]

In 1918 Lloyd George, who was considered to have won the war, was returned to power to fulfil his promise to make the country fit for the surviving heroes to live in. The peace treaty with Germany, the Treaty of Versailles, was signed on 28 June 1919 and Marshal Ferdinand Foch visited London for the peace celebrations. He stayed at the Carlton. Foch had been Commander-in-Chief of the Allied Armies in the last months of the war. He had set the conditions of the Armistice, which had been accepted. Auguste, having asked for an audience with the Marshal, went up to the Palm Court and waited at the edge of a crowd of notables. Foch rose from his seat and came over to the chef and, stretching out his hand, said: 'You, Escoffier, were a prisoner at Metz following the War of 1870, after fighting with Marshal Bazaine. Now we have Metz and you can go back there if you so please.' Shaking hands, Auguste replied, 'That is thanks to you, Marshal Foch'.[9]

Later in the year, on the first anniversary of the Armistice, M. Poincaré, President of the French Republic, visited England. He held a reception at St James's Palace for members of the French community in London. Auguste was invited. He knew some people were to receive a souvenir of M. Poincaré's visit but he hadn't seen the list. He was most surprised when his name was called and he was presented by the President not with just a memento but the cross of the *Chevalier de la Légion d'Honneur*. He had already been awarded the *Médaille de la Reconnaissance Française*, third class (bronze), for his work abroad on behalf of France. That had delighted him. But now he was the first chef ever to receive France's high accolade, the Legion of Honour, and the President of the Republic in person had presented it.

In 1919 Auguste published his pocket dictionary under the title *Aide-Mémoire Culinaire*. This time, *L'Art Culinaire*, in which the extract he had previously submitted had appeared as an article, published the book. Sales were helped by those of his very popular *Guide Culinaire*, by then available in various languages across the world, but the small book achieved nothing like the popularity of its elder brother, *Le Guide*.

Everyone of course recognised that the world was now a different place from that they remembered before the war. Auguste accepted, earlier than most, that it was largely a permanent change. 'Huge sacrifices will be demanded of everyone', he says in the book, recognising that countries engaged in the war were financially exhausted and economies needed to be regenerated. 'The lavish life of luxury we have known has gone and we shall have to economise and return to a simple existence. There is, however, no reason why it should not be the simplicity of good taste which excludes nothing of perfection in cooking and correct elegance in service.' He went on to say that, of course, French *cuisine* and *cuisiniers* were up to the challenge. French *maîtres d'hotel* also got a pat on the back, but he feared that the youngsters coming in after the war had a lot to learn. The book was a tired one. It was, in a sense, out of character, representing almost a guilty reminiscence, a book he felt he should have produced many years earlier. It was an unnecessary underlining, too faint to see in the light of his fame.

But he too was weary – perhaps, no longer caught up in the urgencies of war, his life was now so routine as to be boring to one so lively. Later he gave more than a hint of this. Meanwhile, early in 1919, he had started to ease off his supervisory work in the kitchens to become a sort of elder statesman at the Carlton. A new *chef de cuisine*, M. Emile Malet from the London Ritz, had been appointed. By the end of the year, at the age of seventy-three, Auguste was openly speaking of retirement.

It was at about this time that Eugéne Herbodeau, *commis* fish cook of 1913 at the Carlton, was demobilised from his regiment to return to the hotel as *chef saucier* – he stayed a couple of years before being posted to the London Ritz. He had served throughout the war without doing any cooking, but in a few years he was to be another French *chef* to receive the *Croix de la Légion d'Honneur* 'for eminent services rendered to French interests'. Auguste was very fond of 'young Herbodeau', who was thirty-one when he left the army. In his turn, Herbodeau had great respect for *le Maître*; he was not one of those who called him 'Papa'. In his will, Auguste named Herbodeau along with another respected colleague, Paul Thalamas, as his literary executors. With the papers they conserved they were able to write about Auguste with authority in 1955.[10] After a brilliant period as *chef de cuisine* at the Ritz, Herbodeau returned to the Carlton in 1928 to take his master's place. Marie Ritz said of him: 'He is a man in the true Escoffier tradition and his superb cooking is worthy of the master'.[11]

At the turn of the year, Auguste still could not quite leave the profession he had been in for sixty years. He grasped any passing straw. One was a new journal to fill the gap left by the *Carnet d'Epicure* killed by the war. It was to be called the *Revue Culinaire* with Auguste as contributor and honorary editor. The first issue appeared 1 April 1920. He gave in a few weeks later. He wrote: 'In May I was tired from overworking during four years of war and I decided to take as soon as possible my freedom to enjoy the rest I needed.' Finally, 'In July I left the Carlton Hotel taking with me the memories of the twenty years I had worked there, where I had seen the highest placed English and foreign personalities.' [12] Prosper Montagné, writing of Auguste's retirement after more than sixty years in harness, said that in all the history of cookery there was no other example of such a long professional career. [13]

Interlude 17

Invocation

En Mémoire du Lieutenant Daniel Escoffier
Cité à l'ordre de l'armée pour son superbe courage
Croix de guerre avec palme et étoile d'or.
De l'Empire Allemand, les menaces guerrières,
Ont forcé l'Univers à de cruels combats
Et, le sol est jonché vers les vastes frontières,
Des cadavres sanglants de valeureux soldats!

Les nôtres sont partis rayonnants d'espérance
Pour défendre les droits du Pays en danger;
D'une juste victoire escomptant l'assurance
Contre 'ces loups' formant les rangs de l'estranger.

Ces reîtres sans honneur, ces hordes de sauvages
Qui ne respectent rien et trahissent leur foi
Reniant leurs écrits, fourbes dans leur langage,
Et, des traités de guerre abolissant la loi!

A leur ambition, la Belgique immolée,
Souffre un martyre affreux sans se plaindre un instant
Son roi, sublime et fier, la voyant mutilée
Reste fort, malgré tout, son coeur saigne pourtant.

A Reims, ils ont brûlé l'auguste cathédrale
Où le sacre des Rois imprima sa grandeur
Et, nous n'entendrons plus cette voix magistrale
Des carillons clamant la joie ou la douleur.

Car les restes bénis de cette basilique
Semblent fumer encor tel un grand encensoir
Où l'âme des mourants en souffrance héroïque
Monte, ardente prière, au ciel rouge du soir!

Déjà, trop de héros, morts à la fleur de l'age
Ont imprégné le sol de tout leur noble sang
Pitié, pitié Seigneur, abrège ce carnage
Fais, clore un miracle, O grand Dieu tout puissant!

Que descende, ici-bas, l'ange de la victoire
Qu'un triomphe éclatant fasse jaillir la paix
Et que nos Alliés dans un rayon de gloire
Enlacent leurs couleurs à nos drapeaux Français.

Delphine Daffis-Escoffier

18

Retirement

'Faites simple!'

Auguste Escoffier

Auguste, now seventy-three years old, made the final break with formal employment in July 1920. He doubtless had the usual mixed feelings associated with the terminal act of retirement: the pleasant thoughts of leisure to follow his own whims at his own pace, free from the compulsions of doing what had to be done, tempered with the fear of the emptiness of a superficial life he had never experienced. He recorded, however, only an optimistic view of the future and nothing of apprehension. Certainly, he carried with him into retirement a healthy pride in his achievements, but with some bitter pills he had been unable to swallow. It was also soon apparent that, whatever his original intentions, the flames of ambition within him were not to be easily quenched.

He commented that his fondest memory of his departure from the Carlton Hotel was of the warm friendliness shown by the directors, managers and staff, all four hundred of them. Later views he expressed suggest this might have been something of a public-relations exercise. But he left. 'And so I left England,' he said, 'the country I had liked so much, and my many friends, to rejoin my family in Monte Carlo, and to enjoy the healthy sunshine of the Riviera.'[1] This time he was not going to be just a visitor to Villa Fernand. After thirty years he was going back, it seemed, to live a normal family life. No cooking – he took great delight in telling everyone with whimsical modesty: 'Madame Escoffier cooks better than I do.'[2] But there were a lot of grandchildren: Rita, his son Daniel's wife, lived there with her four children, as did two more of Delphine's sister's children, and Paul and his wife Jeanne would often visit from Paris with their three.

From London, he followed the familiar route to Paris, and then on to Monte Carlo, all on a one-way ticket. He managed to remain 'retired' all the way, but at Monte Carlo he met Madame Giroix and started work again. Jean Giroix was the *chef de cuisine* poached in 1884 from the Grand Hôtel, Monte Carlo, by a rival hotel, leaving a space that César Ritz had invited

Auguste to fill. Since 1898, Giroix had been running the Hôtel Mirabeau in Paris and Hôtel de l'Ermitage in Monte Carlo. His death had left the responsibility for the two establishments weighing heavily on his widow. Auguste accepted immediately her suggestion that he help with the management of the Hôtel de l'Ermitage. Soon after, he was called on to collaborate in the development of the new Riviera Hotel in Monte Carlo belonging to a company called Le Progrès Hôtelier. It was one of eighteen hotels owned by the company, which was undertaking a vast programme of hotel development across France. In a letter Auguste wrote: 'at the moment I am concerned only with the Riviera but it is possible, if I stay with the company, that I shall be concerned with all the kitchens'.³

So far, all Auguste had taken on felt to him like doing nothing. He says, 'after some months of rest, being used to an active life, I found leisure monotonous'. So he took to writing again. He started to write his memoirs, although this activity was mostly one of collecting together and editing articles he had written for journals over the years. He also wrote more articles and recipes for journals, aimed, he says, at 'keeping intact the high renown of the cuisine and exquisite wines of France'. He also suggested to Flammarion, publishers in Paris, that it was time for a new edition of *Le Guide Culinaire*. They agreed and the revision became his main task. The new edition, the fourth, appeared in 1921 and was the basis for a new version in English.

Auguste's work with the Le Progrès Hôtelier was short-lived. In May 1921, having also bowed out of his commitments to Mme Giroix, he went to Paris and stayed at his flat to be near his publisher for the final editing of the new edition of *Le Guide* – it doesn't take many children to disturb a writer's concentration.

From then on, family life began to fade into the background again. He went on from Paris to London on the track of a commercial enterprise. He had written in January to a fellow investor in an earlier venture:

My dear M. Gourier, I will not deny that I have not yet finally said goodbye to England. I still intend to start an establishment in London, not too large, but smart, and if I can find suitable premises for my business the whole thing would soon be done ...⁴

He went on from London to Ostend to see a company that was supposed to be buying Maison Guibert, a restaurant both he and Gourier had an interest in. Something seems to have gone amiss with the sale. He wrote to Gourier, 'I was hoping that the Bosch would have signed on 1 May so that we could draw, if not the full sum, at least a part ... but I fear we shall not have this pleasant surprise'.⁵ Naturally enough, he would have welcomed this explosion into new activity. It isn't easy to relax into a soft armchair after a long life of constant and intensive work, nor to ignore the call of fame. It is likely, however, that he entered this new phase of his life not from boredom or a conviction of self-importance but for money.

The board of the Carlton Hotel had voted him a pension for life. It was one pound sterling a day. Publicly he praised this act of generosity – pensions were rare in the hotel business – but his real feelings were different; it was one of his bitter pills. He wrote to a colleague: 'I am not very satisfied with the gratitude shown by the directors, managers and others at the Carlton Hotel. Truly it was not worth the trouble of working myself to a shadow as I did for the whole duration of the war. But that's life. Gratitude no longer exists. It is largely replaced by egotism.'[6] Other than this small pension, he seems to have had only the reducing royalties from his books.[7] Despite good salaries during his working life, saving had been difficult. This was due mostly to the expense of a separate large household with all its children. But such outlay was not the only drain on his wealth. Auguste's various commercial ventures had mostly been costly failures as far as he was concerned. It may be that his holdings in the Ritz Hotel Syndicate Ltd had disappeared down this capital drain. Such savings as he had made subsequently he had invested in Russian Bonds, tempted like many others by the high yield.[8] These became valueless in 1917.

Charles Scotto, the successful master chef Auguste had started on his way as *chef de cuisine* on the German liner *Imperator*, said, 'like every great artist, Monsieur Escoffier lacked money sense. The sauces he created and manu-factured made great fortunes, but not for him. The hotels he built up and staffed prospered, but others got the profits.'[9] It has been said that he lost a lot of money betting on the horses, but there is not the slightest evidence for this, nor support from contemporaries. What he had to do, by stages over the first ten years of his retirement, was to mortgage his house, Villa Fernand, up to the limit its value would carry.[10]

There seems little doubt that to Auguste money was an unfortunate necessity: it often came a poor second in his decisions. He said of himself in 1909, at the banquet celebrating his fiftieth year in his profession:

Consistent progress of *cuisine* was always my ideal, even at the sacrifice of personal interest, and I want to forget that it might perhaps have been more prudent to think of my own good a little more; but we each have our faults (whether of commission or of omission) and it is quite difficult to decide what to do on the basis of what one ought to do.[11]

His highest priority had always been to reach the top of his profession, regardless of money. Matters of sentiment, loyalty to César for example, concern for his colleagues or the poor, had also come before money, as perhaps had pride and vindictiveness. Even at this late stage in his life, when clearly money was short, he was still searching for commercial activity in London. 'It is not', he wrote to Gourier, 'a question of money, rather the satisfaction it would give me.[12] You know well that I do not have very good memories of the CH [Carlton Hotel] and it would be very pleasant to give my name to a new business.' He had not previously displayed such an attitude towards the Carlton. Doubtless dissatisfaction was growing over the small size of the pension they had voted him. He also reported to Gourier with something like glee that he had had very bad reports of the kitchen management at the London Ritz and the Carlton.[13] 'It doesn't surprise me,' he wrote, 'I know too well the mentality of the people there.' He then went on conversationally to say that 'dinners around Town are not now very dear. It is easy to entertain pretty girls under such conditions.'

He wrote to Gourier later from Paris regretting he was unable to find him a job for the winter season in Nice or Monte Carlo; the seasonal jobs were booked well in advance and he had not been able to get back there in time.[14] He continued, saying that the Maison Guibert business had finally failed and he had lost not only the income he had relied on but also the capital involved. He and his son Paul had also been trying to sell the residue of A. Escoffier Ltd, and a company, Maison Liebig, had agreed to purchase and take Auguste into the business as well. At the last minute they had backed out. Putting the matter in the hands of his solicitor had cost him 2000 francs to no avail.[15]

Auguste took these setbacks in his stride and eventually the way cleared for him. The world sought him out. His professional prestige was high, and suddenly he was in demand across Europe and in the United States to lecture, to advise and to open culinary exhibitions and hotels. Invitations came so fast he scarcely noticed that his business had been sold, and didn't even register who had been the buyer.[16] His grandson Pierre said: 'He was invited to anything of importance – he was a great draw.'[17]

He didn't neglect business altogether. He was approached, for example, by Julius Maggi and collaborated with him in the introduction of the famous Maggi bouillon Kub for use in commercial kitchens. His association was apparently only transient. He seems not to have negotiated any lasting financial benefit for himself.

For years he was associated as a celebrity with a constant stream of culinary exhibitions. At one of these in Copenhagen, in 1923, he was welcomed by King Christian X and received the Cross of Denmark, the first artiste-artisan, as he puts it, to do so.[18] For the banquet given to celebrate the occasion –

produced by a French chef – Auguste created a dish, *Soufflé Princesse Renée*, tinted red and white, the Danish colours.

In 1926 he was *président du jury* at an exhibition in Grenoble, and at another in 1930 in Zürich he was delighted to find they had named the route through the immense hall it was held in 'Boulevard Escoffier'. On this occasion he was shown around the Maggi factory and marvelled at the complex soup-making operation, starting with vegetables mostly grown in a vast area around the building and finished using the most up-to-date machinery at an 'amazing speed and in perfect cleanliness'. It made what had been his own operation in England seem trivial.

It was late in 1922 when Auguste met Sarah Bernhardt for the last time. Now seventy-eight years of age, she was in Monte Carlo on tour in Louis Verneuil's *Régine Arnaud*. Back in Paris she started work on another play, but just before Christmas she fell ill with an attack of uraemia. By mid January she was up and working again, and in March shooting started for the film *La Voyante*, in which she had the title role of the fortune-teller. The scene was set in her own house on Boulevard Péreire that had been transformed for the purpose. She collapsed during a take and was carried to her bed. On 26 March the world's press encamped outside the house saw a window open. The doctor leant out and called, 'Messieurs, Madame Sarah Bernhardt est morte'.[19]

Auguste, by his repeated efforts to be where he could meet Sarah, had made clear his deep feelings for her; but he always wrote of her in bland terms. He wrote, for example, 'I have for this brilliant *tragédienne* the most respectful and affectionate memories. Sarah Bernhardt had a heart of gold.'[20] In depicting her charming character he tells a simple little story of Bizeray, a teacher of French in London. Monsieur Bizeray taught young girls and had spoken to them of Sarah Bernhardt. They wanted to see her, speak to her, touch her dress. But how could this be arranged? How does one approach divinity? Bizeray knew Auguste well and, aware of his friendship with the great lady, asked him for help. Her response to Auguste's request was immediate and she visited the children with him the next evening. He was sure the girls' memory of their meeting with the goddess Sarah Bernhardt would be engraved on their hearts. That was all. Perhaps the story, and that he should retail it, reflect as much his character as Sarah's.

In 1926 Auguste made his third trip to New York at the invitation of Cunard Line on board the *Berengaria*. The ship was originally the *Imperator* of the Hamburg-Amerika Company in which Auguste had directed the installation of the kitchen and restaurant nearly twenty years earlier. The liner had been handed over to Cunard as part of German war reparations

– an act of making the punishment fit their crime of sinking the *Lusitania*.
America was not as he remembered it from his pre-war visits. It had finally
succumbed to Prohibition after combating it since it first arose in religious
revivalism a century earlier. With this amendment to the Constitution came
the gangsters and their bloody wars. Al 'Scarface' Capone from his fifty-room
hotel suite directed his gunmen against Bugs Moran and his entourage to
fight to the death for the rights to make and distribute alcoholic drinks. The
law, bribed and threatened, kept its eyes sufficiently averted to allow murder
to go unpunished. The speakeasy also thrived where the demon drink in its
crudest forms still tempted the thirsty from the paths of abstemious righteousness. Nothing, however, is all bad. The speakeasy nurtured jazz, born
in the brothels of New Orleans, and refined it to its classical form.

Auguste stayed at the Ambassador Hotel in New York City where he was
overwhelmed by the enthusiasm of his welcome by the team from the kitchens, many of whom, he says, 'had worked under my orders at the Savoy,
the Carlton and even in Monte Carlo'. He was sheltered from the seamy
side of NewYork, but as a Frenchman he could not come to terms with a
dinner served with iced water and no wine. He made no mention of this,
however, in a talk one evening at dinner in the New York Carlton to members
of *sociétés culinaires françaises* and their American equivalents. He finished
his speech telling them that if they did their best to preserve the high
standards of French cuisine they could call themselves *cuisiniers* rather than
cooks. 'A *cuisinier*,' he said, 'is a man with professional competence, personal
initiative and experienced in his craft: a cook is a man who, too often, has
only one tool, a tin opener.'[21] The chairman of the proceedings that evening
was Charles Scotto, who was later to chide the press for referring to Auguste
as a cook. 'He is the Master', he said. At the end of the meal he presented
Auguste, on behalf of the societies, with a gold medallion, engraved with
two laurel branches tied with the Legion of Honour.

Back in France, Auguste found that Delphine, who had suffered for a year
or so from what he referred to as neuritis, was now finding it difficult to
walk. He accepted immediately that professional care would be more and
more necessary for her and set about ensuring that he would continue to
be able to afford it. While in America he had noticed that while Prohibition
drove distilled spirits into illegal markets the law varied from place to place
in its application to wines. The snag, he found, was that such wines as could
be bought were usually unpalatable. Obviously, French wines were needed
and marketing them could be a source of income. He had already talked
about this to Charles Scotto who had said that, if Auguste would arrange
supply, he would set up an agency for distribution under the label 'Escoffier
Wines'.

Auguste alerted Scotto, who contracted a company, Gigoux, as sales agent. Auguste was of course well acquainted with wine wholesalers in France and had soon arranged with Maison Bellegarde of Gaillac, in the Tarn, to supply three hundred cases of the local wine in which they specialised. The wine was crated by Maison Bellegarde and labelled 'Escoffier Sauces', doubtless to discourage pilfering. The consignment arrived in New York at the end of June 1928 and was taken in for inspection by the Prohibition Agency.

Meanwhile Auguste, now in the wine business, looked around to see where profit might be made elsewhere in the field. For a start he discussed with his publishers, Flammarion, the possibility of republishing his culinary dictionary, handled eight years previously by the publishers of *L'Art Culinaire*. This time it would have an addendum on wine, what it was and how to choose it. Flammarion agreed and Auguste immediately got down to research on the subject. The little book was published in 1928 with a long title, *L'Aide-Mémoire Culinaire Suivi d'une Etude sur les Vins Français et Etrangers à l'usage des Cuisiniers, Maîtres d'Hôtel et Garçons de Restaurant.*

Busy as he was, Auguste still noticed that a certain M. Delsaut was trying to gain commercial advantage by printing in his prospectus and other advertising material that he was a student of Escoffier. As the gentleman was unknown to Auguste, he sued – and won.[22] It was the start of a whole series of attempts at unauthorised use of the name.

Auguste's wines were kept by the Prohibition Agency for a month but were then released to Maison Gigoux.[23] By this time Maison Bellegarde was getting anxious about being paid, since they had heard nothing from New York.[24]

Auguste was warned by a friend in Marseille that an end to prohibition was foreseen in the USA and that this would certainly see the end of his wine business.[25] The change might come rapidly with the November presidential election. He meant that the Democrat, Alfred E. Smith, the so-called 'Wet' Catholic, would make the change if he won the election rather than Herbert Hoover, who would keep the US dry.

Apart from Delphine's increasing incapacitation, 1928 was not too bad a year for Auguste. The highlight was 22 March when, in the presence of personalities of the hotel and restaurant world, the Press, and 350 other guests, Auguste Escoffier was promoted from *Chevalier* to *Officier de la Légion d'Honneur*. Again he was the first chef to receive promotion to this level. Edouard Herriot, Ministre de l'Instruction Publique et des Beaux-Arts, in presenting Auguste with his new rosette, said to the assembled guests: 'And do you want to know why it is such a pleasure for me to come here to present this high distinction to a man you venerate? It is not only because he is a true artist in his profession, it is because he is (and I can judge this for myself) what I appreciate more than anything else, a kindly, good-hearted man, *un homme de coeur*.'[26]

An English journalist who interviewed him before the event wrote:

A little old gentleman, with the rosette of the Legion of Honour in the buttonhole, opened the door of a modest flat in the centre of Paris and welcomed me in. I had pictured a very different figure. The proverb about those who drive fat oxen should apply with even greater force to those who cook good dinners, but Escoffier is thin, and he is remarkably alert, both physically and mentally. He reads and writes without glasses and he is always working – I found him composing a recipe for a new edition of one of his books.[27]

In the USA Hoover was elected President. Smith was defeated mostly as a result of the strong campaigning of the anticatholic bodies, notably the Ku Klux Klan. The economic boom of the twenties continued, Prohibition remained the law and Auguste's wines gained a reprieve.

Now aged eighty-two, Auguste still had the commercial urge. Whenever he stayed at his little flat in the Rue Boissy d'Anglas in Paris he would visit his son Paul and family, who lived near the Etoile.[28] He got on very well with Paul's wife, Jeanne, and discussed with her endlessly the making of sauces and pickles and of starting new companies to market them. His enthusiasm was, however, dimmed a little when his wine business in partnership with Charles Scotto started to go downhill. Within weeks of the inauguration of President Hoover the Stock Exchange crashed, shares quickly lost 40 per cent of their value and continued on down. The Great Depression descended on the United States. Unemployment was soon on its way to encompassing a quarter of the work force, and those in work were often on maintenance salaries. It was not much of an atmosphere for luxuries like wine. Then another blow fell. One of Hoover's anti-depression treatments was to increase or impose import taxes. Wine went to 35 per cent. It was too much for the frail business. Auguste offered to forgo his interest for the time being, but the lifting of Prohibition a couple of years later found nothing of the Escoffier wine business to diminish.[29]

Early in 1929 Paul Thalamas sent a document to Auguste that Philéas Gilbert had sent him. In this, Gilbert claimed to be the main author of *Le Guide Culinaire*. Auguste wrote a lengthy rebuttal.[30] Auguste's letter was in Thalamas's house when it was wrecked in an artillery bombardment of the fort at Cap Martin by the Italians in June 1940. At the head of the letter is a note by Thalamas: 'crumpled in the looting – recovered from the wreckage'. The second page is missing. Auguste counter-charged Gilbert with being responsible for his idea for a pocket dictionary of cooking being stolen by

Dagouret, for not completing the work he was paid to do on *Le Guide*, and so on. His main point was, however, that none of the ideas for recipes in *Le Guide* were Gilbert's so he could not have been the author. Gilbert was a collaborator along with Fétu in the work. 'By his work and Fétu's', Auguste wrote, 'my thoughts were expressed and my numerous creations conveyed.' Auguste went on to write,

> *Le Guide* has always given returns, not only to me but to Gilbert and to Mme Fétu. The benefits are divided equally into three, but my collaborators did not share the annual expenses of advertising, which on average amounted to 500 francs and fell to me alone to pay. When Gilbert receives cheques of 10,000 to 12,000 francs he should remember that it is entirely because of the name Escoffier this manna falls from Heaven, since he gets no such return from his own books or from his collaboration with Montagné.

Auguste was aware that Gilbert had been collaborating with Prosper Montagné writing his *Larousse Gastronomique* as Montagné had sent him the first draft, asking him to write a preface.[31] Auguste added:

> I have seen with my own eyes, and Montagné cannot hide from me the fact, that he has used *Le Guide* as a basis for his new book, and has certainly used numerous recipes – always easy to fake by changing the names and some little details – and called them his own.'

There is a postscript to the letter, lightly crossed out:

> Don't think it is only *Le Guide Culinaire* alone and the collaboration of Gilbert from which I have acquired world renown. I have behind me a reputation which, despite anything that might now be said or desired, cannot be demolished.

It is noticeable that, in denying Gilbert's claim to authorship, Auguste only says that the recipes were not Gilbert's, not that he didn't write any of the book. Gilbert who essentially edited the work before printing must undoubtedly have done some of the writing. The extent to which this was necessary would only be known to the two of them. Used to standing on his own two feet, Auguste seemed concerned that he needed any such help. He inserted a telling sentence in the letter: 'But if I am fortunate enough to survive for a few years I can promise them a surprise.' This clearly referred to the fact that he was working on a book he intended to be of similar magnitude to *Le Guide*. It was to be about everyday cooking and suitable for the housewife, while serving as an *aide-mémoire* to the *restaurateur*. He was going to write it without their help, or anybody else's.

Writing the letter was probably Auguste's way of letting off steam: Gilbert apparently never received it. In fact, Auguste finished the letter saying: 'This letter must remain between you, Herbodeau, and me, and be used only if M. Gilbert or others of his entourage come out in criticism of me on the subject of *Le Guide*.' Montagné's book was published after Auguste's death with Escoffier's preface followed by another by Gilbert with no sign of rancour in either.

There the matter died, but Herbodeau wrote a quarter of a century later, perhaps a little tongue-in-cheek: 'none of those loyal collaborators ever thought of disputing Escoffier's right to the well-deserved glory'. He added that it was 'natural that the author of a monumental work of this kind (which with Carême's writings forms what we might term the New Testament of contemporary cookery) should call on his friends and colleagues for their assistance'. He mentions Caillat, Reboul, Suzanne and Dietrich as those consulted in addition to Gilbert and Fétu, who were more intimately concerned.

Gilbert must have been of great assistance to Auguste, particularly in the early days. They started working together on the book in 1898 after Gilbert had published his own considerable work, *La Cuisine de Tous les Mois* in 1893, and his experience would have been invaluable. In his turn Gilbert gained experience on *Le Guide* for re-editions of his book, and doubtless for his assistance to Montagné on his *Larousse Gastronomique*. There is nothing new under the sun, particularly if it is a food recipe.

In parallel with his work on his new substantial book, Auguste had also been writing two small books in which he was concerned to advise those less than wealthy how to eat well but cheaply. 'To know how to eat is to know how to live', he said. The little books were published by Flammarion in 1930. One, *Le Riz: L'Aliment le Meilleur, le Plus Nutritif*, gave 130 recipes using rice. The other, *La Vie Bon Marché: La Morue*, detailed eighty-two ways of using cod. The latter title was the subject of some ribaldry since *morue* is also slang for prostitute.

In October that year Escoffier was off again to New York, to *le pays du dollar* as he put it, for a 'hotel exhibition', entailing a seven-day Atlantic crossing on the *Paris*.[32] He stayed for five weeks with Scotto now at the new Hotel Pierre. The proprietor of the hotel had asked Auguste to preside at the 'Grand Opening' dinner. Every evening after that he went to a dinner in another hotel – 'in my honour', he said. The most memorable of these, he wrote, was the one on 28 October for his eighty-fifth birthday in the 'grand salon' of the Hotel Pierre.[33] As usual he kept the menu. One of the dishes, *Pommes d'amour aux huitres pimentées* uses Auguste's favourite name for tomatoes.

From subsequent letters it is clear that during his stay Auguste had

intended to discuss with Scotto many aspects of their 'business'. Since the
wine side had died down, there had been continuous correspondence between them on the production of sauces and pickles to Auguste's recipes,
although whether or not Auguste still had a financial interest is not clear.
He certainly had gone into a great deal of detail in his letters, not only about
the constituents and mode of preparation of the products but about the
design of suitable containers and their packing. What is strange is that they
did not get down to talks on these matters. Auguste wrote to Scotto later
saying: 'It would have been necessary to spend at least three months with
you to study these questions, but during the little time I stayed at the Hotel
Pierre, you were always so busy on the telephone that we were never able
to speak on our business and that is why I have had to fall back on the post
to communicate my ideas.' Probably, if there was any business, it didn't
amount to much. What mattered at the American end was the commercial
draw Auguste represented for the new hotel.

Auguste returned on the *Aquitania* to Liverpool, and spent a few days in
London visiting old friends before going on to Paris. At a luncheon there
he handed over to the Président de la Société Mutuelle des Cuisiniers
10,000 francs for l'Ecole des Cuisiniers, the sum of gifts from people and
organisations in the US.

One of his thank-you letters, which after his trip he didn't get round
to writing until early in the new year of 1931, was to Raymond Orteig at
the Hotel and Restaurant Lafayette in New York – for his lunch at the
restaurant.[34] He enclosed some proposals for menus, including one for a
ladies' luncheon, the Catharinettes, with an anecdote for each item – risqué,
schoolboyish and allusive, rather than frankly rude in the modern manner.
There were such dishes as:

> *Rouget en papillote* (red mullet in a sheath of greased paper or pastry) These
> seductive Catharinettes, in order to avoid certain misadventures must savour the
> delicious *rouget* provided with its *petit bonnet*.

> *Asperge à l'huile* (asparagus dressed with olive oil). It is more than probable that
> many of these young ladies will no longer need such an additive.

There was more along these lines.

In May, writing to his old friend, Gourier, Auguste said he was in good
health but had been suffering for some time from sciatica. It didn't disturb
his sleep but walking was painful.[35] Two months later he began to notice
blood in his urine. He went to see a specialist in Paris and was taken into
the Clinique de St Jean de Dieu in the Rue Oudinot for an operation to
remove a polyp from his bladder.[36] All went well.

While the USA and then most of Europe had suffered deep economic depression from 1929, France, snug behind its high-tariff walls, had remained an island of relative prosperity. By 1931, however, the chill winds of an impending slump were blowing across the land and depression in France was soon as deep as anywhere. For Auguste, additions to his income that came from his appearances at exhibitions and inaugurations were much reduced. He concentrated on his new book but the shortage of money worried him. In a letter to Gourier and his family, he complained:

> We are going through an era in which we have to put up with whatever mere existence demands. Don't think, my dear friends, that I am free from anxiety. Mme Escoffier has for four years now spent her distressing existence in her bed or wheelchair and, despite all sacrifices, without hope of cure. With such heavy costs and with the fall in the English pound I lose fifty francs a day. All is not rosy in life.[37]

At the time Delphine still had the use of her right arm but over the next few months her condition further deteriorated and she lost even that mobility. Her grandson Pierre remembers visiting Villa Fernand as a young man: 'My grandmother', he says, 'was in bed, paralysed. She had grown very fat and lay immobile in her lace-trimmed nightgown. The bedroom was very feminine and smelled of lavender soap.'[38] In fact nurses got her into her wheelchair each day, but she could not help herself in any way.

Auguste went to Paris mid February 1933 to attend the Carême Centenary celebrations lasting from 19–28 February. They were a little belated since the great chef had actually died on 12 January 1833. His fame stems from his inventive cooking and writing about it, but he is also credited with the introduction of the high toque, under which chefs even today like to be seen by their clients. Auguste stayed in Paris for a week or so after the festivities in discussion with his editor at Flammarion on the first draft of his new cookery book. The rest of the year was then taken up with the book, which involved him in several visits to Paris for periods of a few weeks at a time. He stayed at the Hôtel Garnier on the Rue de l'Isly – his flat had been one of his cost savings. The final session on the book in Paris was in December and he got back to Monte Carlo on Christmas Eve. In his periods in Monte Carlo, doubtless awaiting edited drafts from Flammarion, he got to grips again with his memoirs, which he hoped to publish.

His cookery book was published in the spring of 1934 with the title *Ma Cuisine* with around 2500 recipes and a splendid index.[39] It was his seventh publication but only his second big one. It was an exciting time for him. So much so that he seemed not to notice a communication from Denmark forwarding cheques for 65 and 149 francs, royalties on earlier books sold. The cheques still exist, not having been paid in.[40]

To add to the excitement, Charles Scotto turned up in September with proposals to have another go at a sauce-and-pickle business. It is incredible that, at his age, Auguste should have been wildly enthusiastic for a project similar to those he had burned his fingers on so often in his long life. But he was. Scotto went back to New York to raise, at Auguste's suggestion, a number of the best chefs in the city to join in the project. Then the correspondence started up again: long letters from Auguste packed with many recipes, secret processes for keeping the flavour of mushrooms when preserving them, suggestions on the design of bottles, metals to be avoided in utensils with tomatoes to keep their colour, and so on, in dozens of pages of close-written script.

Very much the schoolmaster, he wrote: 'All I have written are only notes from which you can gather my ideas. After you have considered them you can ask questions to which I will reply by return of post.'[41] He continued: 'Now, my dear Scotto, let us talk a little about our future plans.' That from an eighty-seven-year-old.

As it turned out, Scotto was not able to get the required backing. Auguste blamed the critical period following the recession. 'Germany wants war', he wrote, and went on to give a lecture on the perfidy of the Germans, backing disarmament while secretly arming so that they might easily defeat France.[42]

Writing to a friend after Christmas, he apologised for not being able to see him in Paris in November. He said, 'On the advice of my doctor, after the shaking I have just had which put me into the Clinique de Belvédère in Nice for three weeks, I must resign myself to delaying my trip until next spring so that I can publish my memoirs of seventy-five years of work. I hope I shall be able to pay you a visit.'[43]

On 16 January 1935 Auguste wrote to Louis Rampoldi at the Hôtel de Paris:

> My dear Friend, What must you think of my silence. Don't think it is forgetfulness. Since my last visit I have had to keep to my room on doctor's orders and be very careful not to make the least effort. This is because I have had a little recurrence of the haemorrhaging, but if I am a little late in sending you my good wishes for the New Year they are none the less sincere, since every day they have had a place in my heart.
>
> When we spoke on my last visit I warned you that I was expecting M. Heursel, of the Maison Bruck, who make *patés de foie gras de Strasbourg*, and that we would certainly come to lunch at the Hôtel de Paris.
>
> I am expecting M. Heursel this morning. Unhappily, I shall not be able to come with him but I am sending this letter which will tell you the reason for my silence.

Please accept, my dear friend, my regrets. I send all my best wishes for your good health and hope that 1935 will see the realisation of your most cherished desires, for you and your family. My best regards, A. Escoffier.

P.S. My hand trembles still a little and it is difficult for me to write.

The letter was typed and it was probably the last one Auguste sent.

Delphine, who as Delphine Daffis had been 'a French poetess of distinction and an officer of the Academy' became very ill. On 6 February 1935 she died.[44] On 12 February, as though he had been awaiting release, Auguste Escoffier, *Officier de la Légion d'Honneur*, died too.

Up the hill from Villeneuve-Loubet's village square, stumble up two hundred steps, each more or less a pace or two wide, up thin, steep streets, past the backs of neat stone houses supporting curly-tiled Romanesque roofs, to the church below the château. A little higher is the gate to the old, walled cemetery. From there, in the warm light of the southern sun, survey the new town below, still with its van Gogh cypresses, deep-green steeples on every spare patch between the red roofs of the villas, encompassing the old village which registered both the beginning and the end of Auguste Escoffier. The cemetery itself is too old to have retained any aura of death. The well-kept graves are mostly stark and impersonal. Even where they are garnished, it is with incongruous artefacts: a china posy of flowers with the factory's name on the back; or a faded-brown snapshot of the incumbent in life, feigning, it seems, enjoyment of death. On flat marble slabs the names of various Escoffiers are chiselled, as well as those of the Blancs and the Bernodins, families tied in by marriage from the time of Auguste's grandfather born in the eighteenth century.

Squeezed in with others near the south wall is a mausoleum, slightly grander than the rest. Entry is through wrought iron gates to a small vault with white marble plaques on the walls. One plaque is inscribed:

Auguste Escoffier

Officier de la Légion d'Honneur
Octobre 1846 – 12 Fevrier 1935

Three more have names: Daniel, Auguste's second son killed in the First World War; Delphine, Auguste's wife, and Paul, their first-born. There are two blanks, stonily patient.

Back in the village, a white marble bust of Auguste Escoffier guards the entrance to the car park: Auguste Escoffier, the King of Chefs, a man of great distinction, fêted and decorated, revered even, whose services and advice were sought across the world. More than that – much more: he dispensed, in partnership with César Ritz, the great hotelier, luxury and gracious living to High Society, which became aims for all, and their standards have filtered down into our ordinary lives. Because of Escoffier and Ritz we live better.

Notes

Notes to Chapter 1: Origins

1. 'Villeneuve-Loubet et sa region', *Guide Pratique: France*, magazine edition (1987–88).
2. Auguste Escoffier's birth registration, Villeneuve-Loubet.
3. Auguste Escoffier, *Souvenirs Inédits* (1985), p. 12.
4. Ibid., p. 13.
5. Escoffier's speech at the celebration for his fiftieth year as a *cuisinier* held in London at the Monico Restaurant, Shaftesbury Avenue, *L'Art Culinaire*, 1 November 1909.
6. Ibid.
7. Auguste Escoffier, *Souvenirs Inédits* (1985), p. 15.
8. *L'Art Culinaire à Londres*, 1, November 1909, p. 242.
9. Auguste Escoffier, *Souvenirs Inédits* (1985), p. 15.
10. Ibid., p. 16.
11. Tobias Smollett, *Travels in France and Italy* (1766; new edn, 1907).
12. Auguste Escoffier, *Souvenirs Inédits* (1985), p. 15.
13. Ibid., p. 18.
14. Auguste Escoffier *The Complete Guide to Modern Cookery* (1990), biographical note by Auguste's grandson, Pierre Escoffier, p. xix.
15. Auguste Escoffier to Philéas Gilbert, 10 and 13 September 1893.
16. Auguste Escoffier, *Souvenirs Inédits* (1985), p. 17.
17. The *patron* of a restaurant, La Rapière, near Auguste's boyhood home in Villeneuve-Loubet, lays his tables with pewter plates in respectful memory of *le Maître*. He whisks them away when the meal is served.
18. Auguste Escoffier, *Souvenirs Inédits* (1985), p. 18.
19. *L'Art Culinaire à Londres*, 1, November 1909, p. 244.
20. Auguste Escoffier *Souvenirs Inédits* (1985), p. 19.
21. *L'Art Culinaire à Londres*, 1, November 1909, p. 245.

Notes to Interlude 1: A Drink to Open the Mind

1. Auguste Escoffier, *Souvenirs Inédits* (1985), p. 11.
2. Ibid.
3. Auguste Escoffier, 'Le Café', *L'Art Culinaire*, 1 (1883–84).
4. Ibid.
5. For example, *Encyclopædia Britannica* (15th edn), iv, p. 818.

6. Claudia Roden, *Coffee* (1981), pp. 21–22.

7. *Nouveau Dictionnaire Etymologique et Historique* (1971).

8. Auguste Escoffier, 'Le Café', *L'Art Culinaire*, 1 (1883–84).

9. Claudia Roden, *Coffee* (1981), pp. 21–22.

10. Anthony Wild, *The East India Company Book of Coffee* (1994).

11. Edward Robinson, *The Early English Coffee House* (1972).

12. Auguste Escoffier, 'Le Café', *L'Art Culinaire*, 1 (1883–84).

13. Eliza Acton, *Modern Cookery for Private Families* (1845).

14. Elizabeth Ray, *The Best of Eliza Acton* (1968).

Notes to Chapter 2: A Foot on the Ladder

1. Esther B. Aresty, *The Exquisite Table: A History of French Cuisine* (1980), p. 123.

2. *L'Art Culinaire*, 1, November 1909.

3. Auguste Escoffier, *Souvenirs Inédits: 75 Ans au Service de l'Art Culinaire* (1985), p. 19.

4. *Le Jubilé Escoffier, l'Art Culinaire à Londres. Noces d'Or Culinaire*, 1, November 1909, p. 242.

5. Pierre Andrieu, *Fine Bouche* (1956), p. 103.

6. Auguste Escoffier, *Souvenirs Inédits* (1985), p. 20.

7. Pierre Andrieu, *Fine Bouche*, trans. A. L. Hayward (1956), p. 103.

8. Eugéne Herbodeau and Paul Thalamas, *Georges Auguste Escoffier* (1955), p. 65.

9. *Le Jubilé Escoffier, L'Art Culinaire à Londres. Noces d'Or Culinaire*, 1, November 1909.

10. Auguste Escoffier, *Souvenirs Inédits* (1985), p. 20.

11. Eugéne Herbodeau and Paul. Thalamas, *Georges Auguste Escoffier* (1955), p. 23.

12. Musée de l'Art Culinaire, Villeneuve-Loubet, France.

13. Jean-Anthelme Brillat-Savarin, *La Physiologie du Gout* (1825); published as *The Philosopher in the Kitchen*, trans. Anne Drayton (1970).

14. Auguste Escoffier, *Souvenirs Inédits* (1985).

15. Ibid.

Notes to Interlude 2: Primeval Soup

1. Boulanger's claim to priority is not undisputed. Messieurs Roze and Pontaille opened a 'House of Health', essentially a restaurant, in Rue des Poulies in 1766; immediately successful, they moved up market to the Hôtel d'Aligre, Rue Saint-Honoré.

2. Pierre Andrieu gives a clear account of the history of the guilds in his *Fine Bouche* (1956), pp. 22f.

3. Gregory Houston Bowden, *British Gastronomy* (1975).

Notes to Chapter 3: Cooking under Fire

1. *L'Art Culinaire* (1893/4), part 1.
2. Ibid.
3. Ibid., part 2.
4. The preservation of food by heating and sealing within a container was the invention of a Parisian confectioner, Nicolas Apper, in 1809. He used glass jars. The tin can was introduced thirty years later.
5. *L'Art Culinaire* (1893/4), part 2.
6. *L'Art Culinaire* (1893/4), part 3.
7. Ibid.
8. *Le Petit Journal* (May 1894).
9. *L'Art Culinaire* (1893/4), part 3.
10. Ibid.
11. Ibid., part 4.
12. Ibid.
13. Eugéne Herbodeau and Paul Thalamas, *George Auguste Escoffier* (1955), quoting from Escoffier's *Mémoires d'un Soldat de l'Armée du Rhin*, mostly reproduced as a serial in *L'Art Culinaire*, 1893–96.
14. *L'Art Culinaire* (1894), part 5.
15. Ibid.
16. Ibid.
17. Ibid., part 6.
18. Ibid.
19. Ibid.
20. Ibid., part 7.
21. Ibid., part 8.

Notes to Interlude 3: Lobster Tales

1. Esther B. Aresty, *The Exquisite Table: A History of French Cuisine* (1980), p. 123.
2. Robert Courtine, *The Hundred Glories of French Cooking* (1973), p. 50.
3. Ibid., for example: Escoffier talking to Philéas Gilbert, his collaborator in writing *Le Guide Culinaire*.
4. Philéas Gilbert, *L'Art Culinaire* (1889).
5. Eugéne Herbodeau, *A Few Culinary Recipes Classical and Regional*, produced in 1944 by the London restaurant, A l'Ecu de France, for its *habitués* – reproduces the Gouffé recipe.
6. Le Musée de l'Art Culinaire, Villeneuve-Loubet, near Nice, France, page 9 of a hand-written letter, undated – the rest of the letter has not been found. The writing and style suggest the letter was one of a series Escoffier wrote to M. Scotto in New York in the early 1930s.
7. Jane Grigson, *Good Things* (1973), p. 38.
8. Anne Johnson, *The Illustrated Escoffier* (1989), p. 58.

9. Peter Gray, *The Mistress Cook* (1956), p. 4.
10. Elizabeth David, *French Provincial Cooking* (1965), quotes Dr de Pomiane's *Vingt Plats qui Donnent la Goutte.*
11. Edouard de Pomiane, *Cooking with Pomiane* (1976).
12. Robert Courtine, *The Hundred Glories of French Cooking* (1973).
13. Esther B. Aresty, *The Delectable Past* (1965), p. 163. She quotes from *Culina Famulatrix Medicin* (1804).
14. Barbara Flower and Elisabeth Rosenbaum, *The Roman Cookery Book*, a translation of Apicius, *The Art of Cooking* (1958).
15. Prosper Montagné, *Larousse Gastronomique*, English version (1961).
16. Auguste Escoffier, *The Complete Guide to the Art of Modern Cookery* (1990).
17. Ibid.

Notes to Chapter 4: Prisoner's Dilemma

1. *L'Art Culinaire* (1895), part 8.
2. Ibid., part 9.
3. Ibid.
4. Ibid., part 10.
5. Ibid., part 11.
6. Ibid.
7. Ibid., part 12.
8. Ibid., part 13.
9. Ibid., part 14.
10. Ibid.
11. Ibid., part 15.
12. Auguste Escoffier, *Souvenirs Inédits* (1985), pp. 66–70.

Notes to Interlude 4: Solea Solea and Other Flatfish

1. *L'Art Culinaire* (1883/4), p. 165.
2. Elizabeth Cleland, *A New and Easy Method of Cookery* (1759).
3. 'Les Trésors Culinaires de la France', *Le Carnet d'Epicure*, 4, 15 September 1911.
4. Jules Gouffé, *The Royal Cookery Book* (1973; first published 1869), pp. 437–38.
5. Elizabeth David, *French Provincial Cooking* (1966; first published 1960), p. 295.
6. Pierre Andrieu, *Fine Bouche* (1956), p. 107.
7. Prosper Montagné, *Larousse Gastronomique* (1961), p. 107.
8. Auguste Escoffier, *A Guide to Modern Cooking* (1907), p. 290.
9. Articles in book form from the *Pall Mall Gazette*, published as *The Feasts of Autolycus: The Diary of a Greedy Woman*, ed. Elizabeth Robins Pennell (1896), pp. 88–90.
10. Auguste Escoffier, *Souvenirs Inédits* (1985), p. 172.
11. Ibid.
12. L. Saülnier, *Le Répertoire de la Cuisine*, trans. E. Brunet (15th edn, 1979).

13. *L'Art Culinaire* (1895).
14. Auguste Escoffier, *A Guide to Modern Cooking* (1907), pp. 310–16.

Notes to Chapter 5: Rat au Vin

1. Marie-Louise Ritz, *César Ritz: Host to the World* (1938), p. 38.
2. Ibid., p. 34.
3. Pierre, Andrieu, *Fine Bouche* (1956), p. 168.
4. *L'Art Culinaire* (1895), part 15.

Notes to Interlude 5: Take Six Eggs

1. Auguste Escoffier, *A Guide to Modern Cooking* (1907), p. 164.
2. Elizabeth David, *French Provincial Cooking* (1966), p. 181.
3. W. Kitchiner, *The Cook's Oracle* (1829). Thomas Moore, *The Fudge Family in Paris* (1818).
4. Auguste Escoffier, *Le Guide Culinaire* (1902; 4th edn, 1921).
5. Auguste Escoffier, *A Guide to Modern Cooking* (1907).

Notes to Chapter 6: A Goal Achieved

1. *L'Art Culinaire*, 16 (1895).
2. Jeanne and Paul Neyrat, ed., *Auguste Escoffier*, a booklet produced by le Musée de l'Art Culinaire, Villeneuve-Loubet, France.
3. Eugéne Herbodeau and Paul Thalamas, *George Auguste Escoffier* (1955), p. 77.
4. Ibid., p. 76.
5. Author's discussion with Pierre Escoffier, grandson.
6. Auguste Escoffier, *Souvenirs Inédits* (1985), p. 77.
7. Ibid., p. 78.
8. Auguste Escoffier, 'Causeries Familières', *Carnet d'Epicure*, 8, 15 January 1912, pp. 253–54.
9. There is an example of Doré's work on a monument to Alexander Dumas *père* in Place Malesherbes, Paris.
10. Ruth Brandon, *Being Divine* (1991).
11. Auguste Escoffier, *Souvenirs Inédits* (1985), p. 79.
12. Ibid., p. 80.
13. Ibid., p. 81.
14. Ibid., p. 80.
15. The first sealed tin-plate container for the preservation of food was patented in England in 1810 by Robert Durand and sold to Donkin and Hall for provisioning the Royal Navy.
16. Eugéne Herbodeau and Paul Thalamas, *George Auguste Escoffier* (1955).

Notes to Interlude 6: Four and Twenty Blackbirds

1. English translation, 1598, of the *Epulario quale tratta del modo de cucinare ogni carne* (1549).
2. 'Pocket', as in 'pocket full of rye', was a grain measure at the time.
3. Iona and Peter Opie, ed., *The Oxford Dictionary of Nursery Rhymes*, quoting John Nott, cook to Duke of Bolton.
4. Esther B. Aresty, *The Delectable Past* (1965), p. 86, quoting Robert May, *The Accomplish'd Cook* (1660).
5. Brillat-Savarin suspected that *garum* (expensive in his time) was 'nothing more than soy ... known to be an extract from fish fermented with mushrooms', *Physiologie du Goût* (1825).
6. More accurately, *nid de salangane.* The salangane is a bird of the genus *Colocalia* that makes an edible nest.
7. *L'Art Culinaire*, 1 (1883).
8. Auguste Escoffier, *The Complete Guide to Modern Cookery* (1990), p. 450.
9. *Birds and the Law*, the Royal Society for the Protection of Birds (Sandy, Bedfordshire).
10. *L'Art Culinaire*, 2 (1885).

Notes to Chapter 7: César Ritz

1. Several cousins and forebears of Ritz were sculptors, carvers of wood or artists. One ancestor was doubtless responsible for the Ritz 'crest' which decorates the large stove in the room in which César was born. The emblazoned shield is still used as a logo by the Paris Ritz on their notepaper and advertisements.
2. Marie-Louise Ritz, *César Ritz: Host to the World* (1938).

Notes to Interlude 7: What Goes with a Trou Normand?

1. François Rabelais, *The First Book of Gargantua and Pantagruel*, chapter 4.
2. Auguste Escoffier, 'Les Trésors Culinaires de la France', *Carnet d'Epicure*, 4, September 1911.
3. Len Deighton, *Action Cookbook* (1965).
4. Auguste Escoffier, *Ma Cuisine* (1965).

Notes to Chapter 8: Marriage

1. Auguste Escoffier, *Souvenirs Inédits* (1985), p. 83.
2. Ibid., p. 84.
3. Ibid., p. 85.
4. Ibid.

Notes to Interlude 8: Faites vos Jeux

1. Xan Fielding, *The Money Spinner* (1977).
2. Monte Carlo built itself on the back of the Casino, but these days the tables contribute only a small fraction of the Monaco budget. There is still no income tax – most of the income derives from purchase tax, postage stamps (mostly for collectors) and tobacco.

Notes to Chapter 9: Climbing

1. A note in Ritz's little book of memoirs, a mere sketch in an exercise book which he dictated when he was ill towards the end of his life.
2. Marie-Louise Ritz, *César Ritz: Host to the World* (1938).
3. Elizabeth David, *French Provincial Cooking* (1960).
4. Urbain Dubois, who had been chef to the German Court, did not entirely desert *service à la Française* for *service à la Russe* and still wrote of both styles as late as 1889. He often visited the Grand Hôtel and he and Escoffier became firm friends.
5. Urbain Dubois, *Ecole des Cuisinières* (7th edn, 1889).
6. Jeanne and Paul Neyrat, ed., *Auguste Escoffier*, booklet produced by le Musée de l'Art Culinaire, Villeneuve-Loubet, France.
7. Cerises Jubilé was a dish created by Escoffier for the Jubilee Year of Queen Victoria.
8. Marie-Louise Ritz, *César Ritz: Host to the World* (1938), p. 122.
9. Auguste Escoffier, *Souvenirs Inédits* (1985).
10. Eugéne Herbodeau and Paul Thalamas, *Georges Auguste Escoffier* (1955), p. 39.
11. Marie-Louise Ritz, *César Ritz: Host to the World* (1938), p. 83.
12. Auguste Escoffier, *Souvenirs Inédits* (1985). Not all the dishes listed survived, so named, to reach Escoffier's *Le Guide Culinaire*.
13. Eugéne Herbodeau and Paul Thalamas, *Georges Auguste Escoffier* (1955), p. 43.
14. Auguste Escoffier, *Souvenirs Inédits* (1985).
15. Letter from Escoffier at Villa Fernand, Monte Carlo, to Paul Thalamus, 5 February 1929.
16. Eugéne Herbodeau and Paul Thalamas, *Georges Auguste Escoffier* (1955), p. 41.
17. Auguste Escoffier, 'Les Trésors Culinaires de la France', *Carnet d'Epicure*, 2, 11 July 1911.
18. Marie-Louise Ritz, *César Ritz: Host to the World* (1938), p. 128.

Notes to Interlude 9: The Strand

1. *The Times*, 29 May 1889.
2. Ibid.
3. Advertising brochure for the Savoy Hotel, 1893. Schweizerisches Gastronomie-Museum, Schloss Schadau, Thun, Switzerland.

Notes to Chapter 10: The Savoy

1. Marie-Louise Ritz, *César Ritz: Host to the World* (1938), p. 127.
2. Ibid., p. 138.
3. Helen Simpson, *The London Ritz Book of Breakfasts* (1988).
4. D'Oyly Carte's invitation to the opening was to both Marie and César and it has been assumed elsewhere that both attended. Marie reports otherwise in her biography of her husband.
5. Marie-Louise Ritz, *César Ritz: Host to the World* (1938), p. 143.
6. *L'Art Culinaire à Londres, Le Jubilé Escoffier*, 1 November 1909.
7. Auguste Escoffier, *Souvenirs Inédits* (1985), p. 100.
8. The Savoy continued the policy of noting customers' preferences and in 1982, after almost a century, transferred some quarter of a million references to the computer.
9. The cook's white hat, a copy of that worn by Orthodox priests, is said to have originated in Greece where cooks sheltered in monasteries to escape persecution.
10. Eugéne Herbodeau and Paul Thalamas, *Georges Auguste Escoffier* (1955), p. 79.
11. French cooks still seem to think of the English this way. An eminent chef, Pierre Koffman of the Tante Claire, said on BBC Radio 4 in 1992 that most English people are content to eat from cardboard and tins.
12. *New York Times*, 13 February 1935.
13. George Criticos, *George of the Ritz* (1959).
14. Paolo Contarini, *The Savoy was my Oyster* (1976).
15. Marie-Louise Ritz, *César Ritz: Host to the World* (1938), p. 153.
16. An innovation in hotels that started the big band era, which was to blossom in the twenties with bandleaders such as Carroll Gibbons, Roy Fox, Bert Ambrose, Geraldo and Lew Stone – now degraded in many places to cheap imitation, intrusive musak.
17. Robert Courtine, *The Hundred Glories of French Cooking*, trans. Derek Coltman (1973).
18. Pierre Hamp (pen name of Pierre Bourillon), *Mes Métiers* (1931).

Notes to Interlude 10: The Princely Frog

1. Jean Anthelme Brillat-Savarin, *The Philosopher in the Kitchen* (1970).
2. Robert Courtine, *The Hundred Glories of French Cooking*, trans. Derek Coltman (1973).
3. Auguste Escoffier, *Souvenirs Inédits* (1985).
4. After Escoffier's death in 1935, his son, Paul, found the draft memoirs. His grandsons, Pierre and Marcel. arranged for publication in 1985. It formed the basis of *Auguste Escoffier: Souvenirs Inédits* (1985).
5. *Carnet d'Epicure*, 9, March 1912.

Notes to Chapter 11: High Society

1. Marie-Louise Ritz, *César Ritz: Host to the World* (1938).
2. Author's dicussion with Pierre Escoffier, May 1991.
3. Stanley Jackson, *The Savoy: A Century of Taste* (1989); previously entitled, *The Savoy: The Romance of a Great Hotel* (1964).
4. Marie-Louise Ritz, *César Ritz: Host to the World* (1938).
5. Auguste Escoffier, 'Les Trésors Culinaires de la France', *Carnet d'Epicure*, 6, November 1911.
6. Stanley Jackson, *The Savoy: A Century of Taste* (1989).
7. Ruth Brandon, *Being Divine* (1991).
8. Marie-Louise Ritz, *César Ritz: Host to the World* (1938), p. 191.
9. Ibid.
10. Ruth Brandon, *Being Divine* (1991).
11. Letter from Auguste Escoffier, Villa Fernand, Monte Carlo to Paul Thalamus.
12. Pierre Dagouret was not the only one to run with the idea of a pocket reference book for the professional. Louis Saulnier and Edouard Brunet produced *Le Répertoire de la Cuisine* in 1919, but dedicated it 'To the Master of Modern Cookery, Auguste Escoffier, our respectful admiration.' This useful little book with over seven thousand succinct recipes has been kept up to date in English by Léon Jaeggi and Sons, London.
13. Letter from Auguste Escoffier to L. Badin, 5 February 1892.
14. Ibid.
15. Eugéne Herbodeau and Paul Thalamas, *Georges Auguste Escoffier* (1955).
16. Marie-Louise Ritz, *César Ritz: Host to the World* (1938), p. 150.
17. Auguste Escoffier, *A Guide to Modern Cookery* (1907), preface.
18. The Duke of Orléans, banished from France in 1886 as pretender to the throne, lived in Twickenham near London. He was imprisoned for a few months when he tried to return to France. A traveller and adventurer, he was also a bit of a playboy and loved the good life.
19. Marie-Louise Ritz, *César Ritz: Host to the World* (1938), p. 195.
20. Ibid., p. 192
21. Escoffier's Food Preparations Syndicate Ltd was incorporated in 1898, company no. 58732, Companies House, Cardiff.
22. Marie-Louise Ritz, *César Ritz: Host to the World* (1938), p. 203.
23. E. B. Page and P. W. Kingsford, *Master Chefs: A History of Haute Cuisine* (1971), p. 183, quoting J. B. Platina, 1474.

Notes to Interlude 11: The Frying Pan

1. Harold McGee deals with myths such as these in his *The Curious Cook* (1990). He doesn't merely inflict more myths, he performs some nice, tidy experiments.

Notes to Chapter 12: Fall and Rise

1. Eugéne Herbodeau and Paul Thalamas, *Georges Auguste Escoffier* (1938), p. 56.
2. Prosper Montagné, *Larousse Gastronomique* (1938).
3. Eugéne Herbodeau and Paul Thalamas, *Georges Auguste Escoffier* (1938), p. 56.
4. Marie-Louise Ritz, *César Ritz: Host to the World* (1938), p. 205.
5. Ibid., p. 206.
6. Ibid., p. 200.
7. Helen Simpson, *The London Ritz Book of Breakfasts* (1988).
8. Auguste Escoffier, *Souvenirs Inédits* (1985), p. 118.
9. Marie-Louise Ritz, *César Ritz: Host to the World* (1938), p. 219.
10. Ibid., p. 212.
11. Ibid., p. 248.
12. Ibid., p. 208.
13. Aluminium was first isolated from its ore in 1826, but it was sixty years before a commercially viable process for its extraction was developed.
14. Helen Simpson, *The London Ritz Book of Breakfasts* (1988).
15. Philéas Gilbert, 'Auguste Escoffier', *La Revue Culinaire*, February 1935. Escoffier wrote similarly in the foreword to the 1903 edition of his *Le Guide Culinaire*.
16. Place Vendôme was originally named Place Louis-le-Grand. When kings went out of fashion it became the Place des Conquêtes. The present name derives from a love child of Henri IV, the Duc de Vendôme, who lived on the site.
17. The second hotel in the world with the distinction of a bathroom to each bedroom – after the Grand in Rome, which Ritz had also organised.
18. Swiss Gastronomy Museum, Schloss Schadau, Thun, Switzerland.
19. Marie Ritz, *César Ritz: Host to the World* (1938), p. 226.
20. Booklet of La Fondation Auguste Escoffier, Villeneuve-Loubet, *Auguste Escoffier, 1846–1935*, ed. Jeanne et Paul Neyrat.
21. Marie Ritz, *César Ritz: Host to the World* (1938), p. 227.

Notes to Interlude 12: Little Devils

1. *Carnet d'Epicure*, 16, December 1912.
2. Diablotin is also the name of the black-capped petrel peculiar to Hispaniola in the West Indies.
3. George Courteline, humorous novelist, 1858–1929.

Notes to Chapter 13: The Carlton

1. Marie-Louise Ritz, *César Ritz: Host to the World* (1938).
2. Auguste Escoffier, *Souvenirs Inédits* (1985).
3. Auguste Escoffier, *Souvenirs Inédits* (1985).
4. Marie-Louise Ritz, *César Ritz: Host to the World* (1938), p. 264.
5. Ruth Brandon, *Being Divine* (1991), p. 397.

6. Foreword to the first edition of *Le Guide Culinaire* (1903).

7. The Carlton, bombed in the Second World War, was replaced in 1957 by the present New Zealand House.

8. Marie-Louise Ritz, *César Ritz: Host to the World* (1938), p. 263.

9. Eugéne Herbodeau and Paul Thalamas, *Georges Auguste Escoffier* (1938), p. 56.

10. Marie-Louise Ritz, *César Ritz: Host to the World* (1938), p. 259.

11. Ibid., p. 268.

12. *New York Times*, 14 February 1935, p. 3.

13. Maurice Ithurbure, one-time *chef de nuit* under Auguste Escoffier at the Carlton. Discussion with the author at Eastbourne, 13 March 1991.

14. Ibid.

15. Marie-Louise Ritz, *César Ritz: Host to the World* (1938), p. 275.

16. Ibid., p. 274.

17. Pierre Escoffier, Auguste's grandson, London, 1991.

Notes to Interlude 13: Out of the Jungle

1. Reay Tannahill, *Food in History* (1988; first edn, 1973).

2. Barbara Flower and Elisabeth Rosenbaum, *Roman Cookery* (1958). A critical translation of *The Art of Cooking* by Apicius.

3. Auguste Escoffier, *The Complete Guide to Modern Cookery* (1979), p. 383.

4. Auguste Escoffier, *Ma Cuisine* (1989), p. 424.

5. Marie-Louise Ritz, *César Ritz: Host to the World*, (1938).

6. *L'Art Culinaire*, 1 (1883–84).

7. Elizabeth David, *French Provincial Cooking* (1960), p. 392.

Notes to Chapter 14: The Summit

1. Kitchener had half a million men against 80,000 Boers. He won in the end by herding those supporting the guerrillas into what were the original concentration camps. Total army losses, on both sides, were about 10,000. Three times that number of women and children died in the camps.

2. Letter from Auguste Escoffier to Paul Thalamus from Villa Fernand, Monte Carlo, 5 February 1929.

3. Ibid.

4. Foreword to the first edition of *Le Guide Culinaire* and reproduced in Cracknell and Kaufmann's translation of the 1921 edition: Auguste Escoffier, *The Complete Guide to the Art of Modern Cookery* (1979).

5. Marie-Louise Ritz, *César Ritz: Host to the World* (1938). Quoted by Marie from a newspaper cutting in her scrapbook.

6. Ibid., p. 291.

7. Ibid.

8. Ibid.

9. Ibid., p. 298.

10. Daphne Fielding, *The Duchess of Jermyn Street* (1964).
11. Ibid.
12. Ibid.
13. Ibid.
14. Maurice Ithurbure, in discussion with the author, Eastbourne, 13 March 1991.
15. Eugéne Herbodeau's introduction to the 1961 edition of Escoffier's *A Guide to Modern Cookery*.
16. Eugéne Herbodeau and Paul Thalamas, *Georges Auguste Escoffier* (1955).
17. Jules Gouffé, *The Royal Cookery Book*, trans. Alphonse Gouffé (1869; reprinted 1973).
18. *Daily Telegraph*, 14 February 1935.
19. Letter from M. C. Monteille, of Maison Lenoble, Arcueil, France, to Auguste Escoffier, at the Carlton Hotel, London.
20. A small farmhouse (dialect, south of France).
21. Auguste Escoffier, *Ma Cuisine*, trans. Vyvyan Holland, ed. Marion Howells (1965). First published in French by Flammarion (1934).
22. Marie-Louise Ritz, *César Ritz: Host to the World* (1938), p. 298.
23. *Bavarois*, a Bavarian, but on menus it is a moulded, chilled cream sweet, usually incorporating various fruits, for example, *Bavarois diplomate*, which is vanilla flavoured and dressed with chocolate and strawberries.
24. *Daily Telegraph*, 14 February 1935.
25. *Le Pot au Feu*, first issue, 15 April 1893.
26. *Le Carnet d'Epicure*, 25, September 1913.
27. *New York Times*, 14 February 1935.

Notes to Interlude 14: Peaches

1. Auguste Escoffier, *A Guide to Modern Cookery* (1907).
2. *L'Art Culinaire*, 15 June 1907, p. 133.
3. *The Governable of Health: With the Medicyne of the Stomacke*, c. 1490. Quoted in *Mrs Groundes-Peace's Old Cookery Notebook*, ed. Robin Howe (1971), p. 74.
4. Platt, *Widows' Treasure*, quoted by Anne Wilson, *Food and Drink in Britain* (1973), p. 351.
5. Marie-Louise Ritz, *César Ritz: Host to the World* (1938).
6. Eugéne Herbodeau and Paul Thalamas, *Georges Auguste Escoffier* (1955).
7. *L'Art Culinaire*, 15 June 1907, p. 133.
8. Nellie Melba, *Melodies and Memories* (1980), pp. 163–64; first published in Australia (1925).
9. Auguste Escoffier, *Souvenirs Inédits* (1985).
10. *Le Carnet d'Epicure*, 2, 11 July 1911.
11. *La Revue Culinaire*, June 1928.
12. Marie-Louise Ritz, *César Ritz: Host to the World* (1938).
13. Auguste Escoffier, *A Guide to Modern Cookery* (1907), p. 797.
14. Ibid., p. 777.

15. Auguste Escoffier, *The Complete Guide to Modern Cookery* (1990), p. 556.
16. Ibid. *Sabayon* is from the same Latin root as the Italian *zabaglione*.
17. Auguste Escoffier, *The Complete Guide to Modern Cookery* (1990), p. 556.
18. *Le Carnet d'Epicure*, 31, March 1914.

Notes to Chapter 15: Celebrity

1. *Le Carnet d'Epicure*, 4, September 1911.
2. Letter to Auguste Escoffier from Comte Becheval, 15 August 1906.
3. Marie-Louise Ritz, *César Ritz: Host to the World* (1938), p. 302.
4. Auguste Escoffier, *Souvenirs Inédits* (1985).
5. Marie-Louise Ritz, *César Ritz: Host to the World* (1938), p. 302.
6. *Un Cuisinier Français en Amérique, Joseph Donon, 1888–1982: Commemoration du Centenaire de sa Naissance*, Institut Joseph Donon, Villeneuve-Loubet, France.
7. Letter of commendation for Joseph Donon from Auguste Escoffier at the Carlton Hotel, 3 May 1912.
8. *The Gentlewoman*, 7 July 1906, p. 15.
9. Discussion with Paul Escoffier's son, Pierre, May 1991. Companies House records show Escoffier (1907) Ltd as company no. 93909.
10. Dinsdale Landen and Jennifer Daniel, *The True Story of HP Sauce* (1985).
11. Booklet of La Fondation Auguste Escoffier, Villeneuve-Loubet, *Auguste Escoffier, 1846–1935*, ed. Jeanne et Paul Neyrat.
12. Archives, Musée de l'Art Culinaire, Villeneuve-Loubet, France.
13. *L'Art Culinaire de Londres: Noces d'Or Culinaire*, 1 November 1909.
14. Auguste Escoffier, *Souvenirs Inédits* (1985).
15. Ibid.
16. Ann Barr and Paul Levy, *The Official Foodie Guide* (1984).
17. Paul Levy, *Out to Lunch* (1986).
18. Auguste Escoffier, *Souvenirs Inédits* (1985).
19. Letter to Auguste Escoffier at the Carlton Hotel from Harrison, the Natal Agency, London, 15 June 1909.
20. C. Monteille to Auguste Escoffier at the Carlton Hotel, 21 March 1909. Archives, Musée de l'Art Culinaire, Villeneuve-Loubet, France.
21. Auguste Escoffier, *Souvenirs Inédits* (1985).
22. Ibid.
23. Eugéne Herbodeau and Paul Thalamas, *Georges Auguste Escoffier* (1955).
24. Auguste Escoffier, *Souvenirs Inédits* (1985).

Notes to Interlude 15: Pommes d'Amour

1. Auguste Escoffier, *Carnet d'Epicure*, 'Causeries Familières', August 1911.

Notes to Chapter 16: Phoenix

1. Auguste Escoffier, *Souvenirs Inédits* (1985).
2. *Le Carnet d'Epicure* 12, July 1912.
3. Ibid.
4. Archives, Musée de l'Art Culinaire, Villeneuve-Loubet, France.
5. *Le Carnet d'Epicure*, 10, April 1912.
6. *Le Carnet d'Epicure*, 9, March 1912.
7. *Le Carnet d'Epicure*, 1, July 1911.
8. *Daily Telegraph*, 13 February 1935, and the *Morning Post* of the same date.
9. Prosper Montagné, *Larousse Gastronomique* (1961), p. 404.
10. *Carnet d'Epicure* 25, July 1913.
11. Eugéne Herbodeau and Paul Thalamas, *Georges Auguste Escoffier* (1955).
12. Allan Hall, ed., *Great Dishes* (1988). Chez Maurice is now a fish and chip shop.
13. Maurice Ithurbure, Eastbourne, March 1991.
14. The association moved again in 1991.

Notes to Interlude 16: Dodine and the Duck

1. *Le Matin*, 6 May 1912.
2. *Daily Mail*, 15 April 1912.
3. *Le Carnet d'Epicure*, 12, June 1912, p. 435.
4. Auguste Escoffier, *Souvenirs Inédits* (1985).
5. *Le Carnet d'Epicure*, 11, May 1912, p. 380.
6. Pierre Pidoux, *La Fleur de Toute Cuysine*.
7. *Le Matin*, 6 May 1912.
8. *Le Carnet d'Epicure*, 13, July 1912.
9. Taillevent, born in 1326, was cook to Philippe VI de Valois, and then master of the kitchen to the Duke of Normandy, the first Dauphin, and remained with him as head cook when he became king as Charles V. He left the king's service in 1371 and got down to compiling the *Viandier*.
10. Eugéne Herbodeau, and Paul Thalamas, *Georges Auguste Escoffier* (1955).
11. Auguste Escoffier, *Ma Cuisine* (1934).
12. Jean-Anthelme Brillat-Savarin, *La Physiologie du Gout* (1825); published as *The Philosopher in the Kitchen*, trans. Anne Drayton (1970).
13. Auguste Escoffier, *A Guide to Modern Cookery* (1907).
14. Drew Smith, *Modern Cooking* (1990).
15. BBC Radio 4, *Desert Island Discs*, 1 June 1991.

Notes to Chapter 17: The Great War

1. Ho Chi Minh's original name was Nguyen That Thanh. After the First World War he joined the French Communist Party. In 1945 he became President of the Democratic Republic of Vietnam, later North Vietnam.

2. Eugéne Herbodeau and Paul Thalamas, *Georges Auguste Escoffier* (1955).
3. Auguste Escoffier, *Souvenirs Inédits* (1985).
4. Discussion with Pierre Escoffier, London, 28 May 1991.
5. Licence to use the Escoffier name was under the control of the Fondation Auguste Escoffier, Institut Joseph Donon, 06270 Villeneuve-Loubet, France. A case heard in recent years by a court in Paris was lost and full rights to use the name were accorded to the Hôtel Ritz in Paris, controlled by Mohamed Al Fayed.
6. Postcard from Auguste Escoffier to Paul Thalamas, archives, Fondation Auguste Escoffier, Villeneuve-Loubet, France.
7. Auguste Escoffier, *Souvenirs Inédits* (1985).
8. Ibid.
9. *Caterer and Hotelkeeper.*
10. Eugéne Herbodeau and Paul Thalamas, *Georges Auguste Escoffier* (1955).
11. Marie-Louise Ritz, *César Ritz: Host to the World* (1938).
12. Auguste Escoffier, *Souvenirs Inédits* (1985).
13. Prosper Montagné, *Larousse Gastronomique* (1961).

Notes to Chapter 18: Retirement

1. Auguste Escoffier, *Souvenirs Inédits* (1985).
2. *New York Times*, 13 February 1935.
3. Letter from Auguste Escoffier to M. Gourier, 20 January 1921.
4. Ibid.
5. Ibid., 2 May 1921.
6. Ibid.
7. Discussion with Pierre Escoffier, Villeneuve-Loubet, France, March 1991.
8. Ibid.
9. *New York Times*, 13 February 1935.
10. Discussion with Pierre Escoffier, Villeneuve-Loubet, France, March 1991. Villa Fernand in Monte Carlo is one of the few buildings in the town that has remained virtually unchanged since it was built in the middle of the nineteenth century.
11. *L'Art Culinaire de Londres, Noces d'Or Culinaire*, 1 November 1909.
12. Letter from Auguste Escoffier to M. Gourier, 20 January 1921
13. Ibid.
14. Ibid., 30 October 1921.
15. Ibid.
16. A booklet by Brown and Polson Ltd, *Something a Little Special*, published by *Good Housekeeping* (1966). They wrote of Escoffier's bottled sauces: 'These original recipes are still being used today.'
17. Discussion with Pierre Escoffier, London, May 1991.
18. Auguste Escoffier, *Souvenirs Inédits* (1985).
19. Ruth Brandon, *Being Divine* (1991).

20. Auguste Escoffier, *Souvenirs Inédits* (1985).
21. Ibid.
22. Auguste Castel, *avocat*, Nice to Auguste Escoffier, 16 June 1928, notifying the court's findings.
23. C. Scotto to Auguste Escoffier, 3 August 1928 (from the Ambassador Hotel, New York City).
24. E. Bellegarde et Cie, Gaillac (Tarn) to Auguste Escoffier, 6 August 1928.
25. A. Caillat, Marseille, to Auguste Escoffier, 21 August 1928.
26. Auguste Escoffier, *Souvenirs Inédits* (1985).
27. *The Times*, 17 March 1928.
28. Discussion with Paul Escoffier's son, Pierre, in London, April 1992.
29. Auguste Escoffier to Charles Scotto, New York, 14 October 1930.
30. Auguste Escoffier to Paul Thalamas, 5 February 1929, from Villa Fernand, Monte Carlo.
31. Prosper Montagné, *Larousse Gastronomique: The Encyclopedia, of Food, Wine and Cooking*, first published in English in 1961.
32. Auguste Escoffier, *Souvenirs Inédits* (1985).
33. Ibid.
34. Auguste Escoffier to M. Raymond Orteig, Hotel and Restaurant Lafayette, New York, 3 January 1931.
35. Auguste Escoffier to M. Gourier, Cannes, 12 May 1931.
36. Ibid., 6 July 1931.
37. Auguste Escoffier to M. and Mme Gourier *et petite famille*, Cannes 26 January 1932.
38. Discussion with Pierre Escoffier, London, May 1991.
39. Auguste Escoffier, *Ma Cuisine* (1934). The first edition in English of a translation by Vyvyan Holland (1965).
40. Fondation Auguste Escoffier, le Musée de l'Art Culinaire à Villeneuve-Loubet, France.
41. Auguste Escoffier to Charles Scotto, New York, 23 September 1934.
42. Ibid., 14 November 1934.
43. Auguste left notes for his memoirs, arranged in date order, which were preserved by his son Paul. Paul died during the Second World War. His sons, Pierre and Jean-Bernard, intending to edit them for publication did not complete the task by 1970 when Jean-Bernard died. Pierre and his cousin Marcel put the book together. (Marcel was one of Daniel's children who, with his mother, two brothers and a sister, went to live with Delphine when his father was killed in the First World War.) The book was published in 1985 as *Souvenirs Inédits*. It is often quoted in this volume.
44. *Daily Telegraph*, 13 February 1935.

Glossary

aboyeur: barker; shouter of waiters' orders to kitchen staff.
agneau de lait: young lamb, milk-fed.
aiglon: young eagle.
aigre-douce: bitter-sweet.
aile: wing.
alouette: lark.
aloyau: rosbif d'aloyau, sirloin.
amande: almond.
âne: donkey.
anguille: eel.
asafoetida: an onion smelling gum from a plant root.
asperge: asparagus.
ananas: pine-apple.
arrosé: sprinkled, moistened, basted.
auberge: inn.
bardées: covered with slices of bacon fat (breasts of poultry etc).
bains de mer: sea-bathing.
bar grate: with the introduction of coal, iron bars were built in across the fire for cooking – end of seventeenth century.
batraciens: frogs and toads.
bavarois(e): Bavarian, custard cream made with almond milk.
béarnaise: rich white herbal sauce, thickened with egg yolk.
Beaux-Arts: fine arts, painting, sculpture etc.
bécasse: woodcock.
béchamel: white sauce; **béchamel grasse,** meat-stock based; **béchamel maigre,** milk based.
Béhague: Southdown mutton in England; **pré-salé** (q.v.) in France.
beterave: beetroot.
beurre de Montpelier: savoury herb butter.
bigarade: bitter orange (Seville).
blanquette: ragoût of veal, lamb or chicken with onions and bound with egg yolks and cream. Variously garnished.
blé: wheat, corn.
blinis: Russian pancake made with buck-wheat flour.

bombe Nélusko: ice cream from conical mould, lined pralinée, chocolate inside.

bouchées: small patties of puff pastry, a mouthful.

boucher: butcher.

boudin: French style black pudding.

bouquet-garni: herbs tied together as a faggot for ease of removal when cooking is complete.

bouquetière: flower seller, flower-girl.

brasserie: beer saloon.

brocheé, la: spit-roast.

brochet: pike.

brouillés: scrambled.

cabillaud: cod.

caille: quail.

canard: duck.

caneton: duckling.

cassoulet: haricot bean stew with pork, mutton, or duck etc. Originally from Languedoc. Name derived from *cassole d'Issel.*

causerie: chat.

céleri: celery.

cèpes: flap mushroom, *boletus edulis* – yellowish, rich nutty flavour.

cerise: cherry.

Chambord (à la): a method of cooking fish in a white-wine *court bouillon.*

chameau: camel.

champignon: mushroom.

Chantilly (à la): usually with whipped cream.

chapons: pieces of bread rubbed with garlic.

chateaubriand: a thick fillet steak or a porterhouse.

chaud-froid: chicken, game, cutlets etc served cold with a sauce and garnished with savoury jelly.

cheval: horse.

chevreuil: roe-deer.

chou: cabbage.

civet: brown stew of game.

coeurs de laitues, d'artichauts: lettuce, artichoke hearts.

colonne: column (also apple-corer).

commis: assistant.

concombre: cucumber.

confiture: jam.

coque, oeufs à la: boiled eggs.

côtelette: cutlet.

coulibiac: Russian dish. Flaked fish mixture baked in brioche pastry.

coulis: juice from cooked meat, liquid purées, or even veal stock.

court-bouillon: A marinade or cooking medium used for meat or vegetables, but mostly for fish; made variously with red or white wine, vegetables and herbs and seasoning.

couvent: convent.

cresson: cress.

crevettes: shrimps, prawns.

croustades: shapes of bread or paste fried or baked – to serve delicate entrées on.

croûte: crust of pastry etc. or fried bread on which entrées are served.

cru: raw, locality of a vineyard.

cuillère de cuisine: wooden spoon.

cuirassier: mounted soldier.

cuisinier: cook.

cuisse: thigh.

cuisses de grenouilles: frogs' legs.

cuit: cooked.

culinaire: culinary.

cygne: swan.

daim: deer.

dariole: small entrée; paté baked or steamed in moulds.

defrutum: grape juice, reduced.

demi-glace: thin brown sauce.

dépecés: carved, cut in pieces.

diablé: devilled, dish with very hot condiments or highly seasoned spiced sauce.

dinde, dindon: hen, cock turkey.

dindonneau: young turkey.

doré: gilded, browned meat; glazed cake.

douce, doux: sweet, smooth, soft.

downhearth: hearth for cooking in a wood-burning fireplace.

dragées: sugar almonds.

écrevisses: fresh-water crayfish etc.

émincé: cut in thin slices.

encensoir: censer

entremets: side-dish, second course.

éperlan: smelt (fish).

épicerie: spices, grocer's shop.

épigramme: small fillet of poultry, game, breast of lamb.

épinard: spinach.
espagneul: spaniel.
estragon: tarragon.
esturgeon: sturgeon.
étampé: stamped.
faisan: pheasant.
faites vos jeux: place your bets.
familière: domestic, household.
farci: stuffed (with forcemeat etc.).
feuille: leaf, thin sheet.
Flamande: Flemish style.
fond de veau: veal stock.
fonds d'artichaut: artichoke hearts.
fraise: strawberry.
fraise des bois: wild strawberry.
framboise: raspberry.
friandise: tit-bit.
fricassée: a stew of white meat.
frit, frite: fried.
fromage: cheese.
Frontignan: strong sweet muscat wine from the Midi.
fumet: reduced (concentrated) game or fish stock.
galantine: dish of white meat glazed, served cold.
galettes: flaky pastry, round flat breakfast roll.
garçon: waiter.
garde-manger: stock or larder keeper on kitchen staff.
garum, liquamen: a sauce made from fermented fish as favoured by the
   Romans.
gauffrettes: wafer biscuits.
gelée: meat or fruit jelly.
gelinotte: hazel-hen (grouse family), sometimes a fattened poulet.
gibier: game, animals hunted.
glacé: cold, iced, frozen, glazed or glossy
goût: taste.
gratinée: surface of dish browned.
grenouille: frog.
grillé: grilled, broiled, toasted.
grive: thrush, fieldfare.
haut, haute: high, high-class.
hirondelle: swallow.
homard: lobster.

huile: oil.

huîtres: oysters.

immolée: sacrificed.

inédits: unpublished.

ingénue: simple, unsophisticated.

jambon: ham.

jonché: strewn, spread around.

koulibiac: see **coulibiac.**

lait: milk.

laitance: soft roes.

laitue: lettuce; **laitue romaine** cos lettuce.

langouste: spiny lobster, crayfish, crawfish.

lazannes: thin strips of noodle paste.

léger, legère: light.

levraut: leveret, young hare.

libraire: bookseller.

lié: bound.

lier: to thicken (a sauce).

lièvre: hare.

limande: dab (flat fish).

liquamen: see **garum.**

loup: wolf

Lyonnaise: Lyon style, garnish including fried shredded onion.

Madère: Madeira.

mas: (dialect) small farmhouse.

matelote: rich, brown fish stew.

mauviette: lark (bird).

médallions: small round fillets of meat.

merlan: whiting (fish).

meunière: (fish) cooked nut-brown in butter, served with parsley, lemon.

moelle: bone marrow.

Montmorency: a bitter cherry.

morilles: morel, edible fungus.

mousseline: frothed (sauce), or mashed with aeration.

mousserons: white mushroom often used in a ragoût.

naartje: Mandarin-sized orange from the Cape.

navets: turnips.

neige: snow, whipped up froth of cream or egg-white and sugar.

nid: nest.

noces d'or: golden wedding.

noisette: hazel-nut; small round pieces of lean meat, médallion.

nouilles: noodles, poached and tossed in butter.

oeuf: egg.

oiseaux: birds.

ortolan: ortolan bunting.

ours: bear.

paillettes: straws, spangles.

papillottes: greased paper or pastry cases.

partie: section of a kitchen team.

pâtissier: pastry-cook.

pauperisme: poverty.

paupiettes: forcemeat rolled in slices of meat.

pêche: peach.

perdreaux: young partridges.

perle noir du Périgord: truffle.

pet de nonne: literally, nun's fart. Classical name for a batter fritter or a doughnut.

pigeonneaux: squabs, young pigeons.

piment: pimento, red pepper.

pimentée: to season with red pepper.

poché: poached.

poireau: leek.

poissonier: fishmonger.

poivrade: dressing of oil, pepper and vinegar.

polenta: sun-dried porridge of Piedmont maize flour.

Pompadour (à la): indicative of extravagance.

pony: a small wineglass sometimes used for champagne.

pot-au-feu: stock-pot or its contents.

poularde: pullet.

poulet: young cock chicken.

praliné: flavoured burnt almonds.

pré-salé: salt-meadow: mutton raised on the salt marshes of France; see also **Béhague**.

printemps: spring.

quenelles: shaped forcemeat.

Racine, Jean: Classical French poet and playwright (1639–99).

radis: radish.

ragoût: a richly flavoured stew.

raifort: horse-radish.

rayonnant: radiant.

reître: a rough, tough and crafty person.

réjouissance: rejoicing.

retraite: retirement.
ris-de-veau: sweetbread.
riz: rice.
romaine: see **laitue.**
rôtisseur: caterer in roast meats.
rouge-et-noir: a card game, variety of poker.
rouget: red mullet.
sabayon: light frothy sweet sauce – white wine, cream, sugar, eggs.
sablé: a kind of shortbread.
safran: saffron.
salmis: *ragoût* of partly roasted game.
salpicon: a mixture of finely diced ingredients.
saucier: sauce-chef.
saucisson: sausage.
serre: greenhouse.
secours: aid.
sterlet: small sturgeon.
suc: juice.
suprême: best part, often refers to the breast of a fowl
tête: head.
timbale: (kettledrum, metal cup) round metal mould, also pie-dish.
tortue: turtle.
trou Normand: a glass of Calvados usually gulped down.
truffe: truffle; **trouffe blanche:** mostly from Northern Italy and North Africa; **trouffe noire:** best from Périgord and Lot.
truite: trout.
turbotin: baby turbot.
Valaisan: a native of Valais, one of the twenty-two cantons of Switzerland, originally with its own dialect.
vanille: vanilla.
veau: veal.
velouté: white sauce from chicken stock and cream.
vers: worms, verse.
viande: meat.
volaille: poultry.
Xérès: sherry.
zabaglione: as **sabayon** but thickened by heating and served hot in glasses.

Bibliography

All titles published in London unless otherwise indicated.

Anthony Allfrey, *Edward VII and his Jewish Court* (1991).

Pierre Andrieu, *Fine Bouche* (1956). Story of the restaurants of France from the early inns and taverns to the prestigious restaurants.

Esther B. Aresty, *The Exquisite Table: A History of French Cuisine* (New York, 1980).

Ann Barr and Paul Levy, *The Official Foodie Handbook* (1984). Where and how to eat in the world with a Who's Who of Foodies. Includes a revelation about Escoffier's departure from the Savoy.

Simone Beck, Louisette Bertholle and Julia Child, *Mastering the Art of French Cooking* (1966). Perhaps one of the best expositions in English of French cooking techniques. Cook from this and you cook French.

Sarah Bernhardt, *My Double Life: The Memoirs of Sarah Bernhardt* (1977).

Anthony Blake and Quentin Crewe, *Great Chefs of France* (1978). A history of French cooking, twelve of its chefs and their restaurants. Foreword by Auguste Escoffier's grandson, Pierre.

Raymond Blanc, *Recipes from Le Manoir aux Quat' Saisons* (1988).

Gregory Houston Bowden, *British Gastronomy: The Rise of Great Restaurants* (1975). The growth of British gastronomy initiated by Escoffier at the Savoy.

Ruth Brandon, *Being Divine* (1991). A biography of Sarah Bernhardt.

Jean Anthelme Brillat-Savarin, *The Philosopher in the Kitchen* (1970). Originally *La Physiologie du Goût* (Paris, 1826).

Marie-Antoine Carême (and Plumerey), *L'Art de la Cuisine Française aux XIXe siècle* (Paris, 1833).

Percy Colson, *Melba: An Unconventional Biography* (1932).

Jean Conil, *The Epicurean Book* (1962). How to be an epicure, by one of them who can cook; with recipes, and some new ways of cooking the familiar ones.

Paolo Contarini, *The Savoy was my Oyster* (1976).

Robert Courtine (Savarin), *Real French Cooking* (1956). The cream of French provincial cooking set in anecdote and aphorism, sonnet and doggerel, with a dressing of acrid comment on *haute cuisine* and food philistines.

Robert Courtine, *The Hundred Glories of French Cooking* (New York, 1976). A cultural history of French cooking constructed around the author's hundred favourite recipes.

Clemence Dane, *London Has a Garden* (1965).

Elizabeth David, *French Provincial Cooking* (1965). Wide-ranging, informative entertainment, pragmatic and stylish. Now a classic and a book that must be read. She liked Escoffier too.

Alan Davidson, *On Fasting and Feasting* (1988). An anthology of the author's favourite pieces of good writing about food.

Len Deighton, *Action Cookbook* (1965).

Joseph Donon, *The Classic French Cuisine* (1960).

Drummond and Wilbraham, *The Englishman's Food* (1939). A history of five centuries of English diet.

Urbain Dubois, *L'Ecole des Cuisinières* (Paris 1889). Advice on techniques and 1600 recipes. Dubois, predecessor of Escoffier, stands alongside Carême as one of the great chefs of the mid-nineteenth century.

Auguste Escoffier, *A Guide to Modern Cookery* (1907) The first translation of *Le Guide Culinaire* (partial).

Auguste Escoffier, *L'Aide-Mémoire Culinaire* (Paris, 1919).

Auguste Escoffier, *L'Aide-Mémoire Culinaire, Suivi d'une Etude sur les Vins Français et etrangers à l'Usage des Cuisiniers, Maîtres d'Hôtel et Garçons de Restaurant* (Paris, 1919).

Auguste Escoffier, *La Vie à Bon Marché: la Morue* (Paris, 1929). 82 Recipes.

Auguste Escoffier, *Le Guide Culinaire* (Paris, 1903, 2nd edn 1921. Reprinted to 1936).

Auguste Escoffier, *Le Livre des Menus: Complément Indispensable du Guide Culinaire* (Paris 1912).

Auguste Escoffier, *Le Riz* (Paris, 1927). 120 recipes.

Auguste Escoffier, *Les Fleurs en Cir* (Paris, 1885).

Auguste Escoffier, *Ma Cuisine* (Paris, 1934).

Auguste Escoffier, *Ma Cuisine*, trans. Vyvyan Holland, ed., Marion Howells (1989).

Auguste Escoffier, *Souvenirs Inédits* (Marseille, 1985). A compilation of Escoffier's notes for his unpublished memoirs.

Auguste Escoffier, *The Complete Guide to the Art of Modern Cookery* (1979). A translation of the complete French version of 1921.

Auguste Escoffier, ed. H. L. Cracknell and R. J. Kaufmann *The Illustrated Escoffier* (1989). Recipes from the *Guide Culinaire*, selected, expanded and updated by Anne Johnson; garnished with fine photographs. Introduction by Auguste's grandson, Pierre Escoffier.

Daphne Fielding, *The Duchess of Jermyn Street* (1964). Biography of Rosa Lewis.

M. F. K Fisher, *With Bold Knife and Fork* (1983). Recipes from the world, across time, with personal comment. Entertainingly chirpy and with many interesting food related facts.

M. F. K Fisher, *The Art of Eating* (1991). Stories about food, life, places and Margaret Fisher, in five books.

Ernest N. Flammarion, ed., *The Art of French Cooking* (English translation of *L'Art Culinaire Francais*, undated). An encyclopaedic collection of recipes of classic chefs, including Escoffier.

Barbara Flower and Elisabeth Rosenbaum, *The Roman Cookery Book* (1958). A critical translation of *The Art of Cooking* by Apicius. The source versions were Apicius, *De re quoquinaria* and Apicius, *Culinarius*. They were probably written by Gavius Apicius who lived in the first century AD, spent most of his fortune on food, and then, unable to face privation, committed suicide. The translators used a version compiled by an anonymous editor in the fourth or fifth century. The Latin text is included.

Philéas Gilbert, *La Cuisine de Tous les Mois* (Paris 1893).

Peter Gray, *The Mistress Cook* (Faber and Faber, 1956). A thousand classical recipes from a dozen countries over six centuries.

Jane Grigson, *Food With The Famous* (1991).

Jane Grigson, *Good Things* (1973). A collection from her long series in the *Observer Colour Magazine*. Recipes include a number of Escoffier's.

Jane Grigson, *Jane Grigson's Fruit Book* (1983).

Jane Grigson, ed., *The World Atlas of Food* (1974).

Zara Groundes-Peace, *Old Cookery Notebook*, edited from her original material by Robin Howe (1971). Food before the eighteenth century – spoons, gingerbread, cookbooks, saltcellars, medicine, the words used and recipes. A small mine with a lot of nuggets.

Bertrand Guégan, *La Fleur de la Cuisine Française, Aux Editions de la Sirène* (1920).

Allan Hall, ed., *Great Dishes* (1988).

Joseph R. Hamlen, *Flight Fever* (New York 1971).

Eugéne Herbodeau, *A Few Culinary Recipes Classical and Regional* (1944). Produced for the habitués of the A l'Ecu de France of Jermyn Street. A great chef and his own man, but clearly a disciple of Escoffier.

Eugéne Herbodeau and P. Thalamas, *Georges Auguste Escoffier* (1955). A biography by chefs who knew Escoffier, worked with him.

John Hetherington, *Melba* (1967).

Christopher Hughes, *Switzerland* (1975.

Stanley Jackson, *The Savoy: The Romance of a Great Hotel* (1964). Revised and updated as *The Savoy: A Century of Taste* (1989).

Anne Johnson, ed., *The Illustrated Escoffier* (1989). See Auguste Escoffier above.

James P. Johnston, *Hundred Years of Eating* (1977).

Dinsdale Landen and Jennifer Daniel, *The True Story of H.P. Sauce* (1985). The story from AD 43 to Harold Wilson and the readable bottle.

T. A. Layton, *Cheese and Cheese Cookery* (1971).

Alison Leach, ed., *The Savoy Food and Drink Book* (1988). A hundred glorious years illustrated from old sources. Many of the Savoy's own recipes.

Margaret Leeming, *A History of Food* (1991). A quick worldwide tour from biblical times to date, stopping to view interesting detail on the way.

Paul Levy, *Out to Lunch* (1988). A forthright view across the world of things and people to do with edibles from braised puppy to Spanish fly. Enlarges on the story of Escoffier's departure from the Savoy – see Ann Barr and Paul Levy, *The Official Foodie Handbook*.

Harold McGee, *The Curious Cook* (1992). Takes the lid off kitchen facts and fallacies.

Anthony Masters, *Rosa Lewis: An Exceptional Edwardian* (1977). A biography.

Nellie Melba, *Melodies and Memories* (1980). Autobiography.

Prosper Montagné, *New Larousse Gastronomique* (1977). A thousand-page encyclopaedia of matters culinary.

Raymond Oliver, *Classic Sauces and their Preparation* (1967). Raymond Oliver, son of Louis deals in great detail with the history and techniques for making classic French sauces.

E. B. Page, and. P. W. Kingsford, *The Master Chefs* (1971). A history of *haute cuisine*, from the Egyptians and Ancient Greeks to Escoffier.

Elizabeth Robins Pennell, *The Feast of Autolycus: The Diary of a Greedy Woman* (1896). A series of essays from the *Pall Mall Gazette*, all concerned with gastronomy.

Johannes-Baptiste Platina, *De honesta voluptate* (Venice 1475).

Edouard de Pomiane, *Cooking with Pomiane* (Oxford, 1976). Fine recipes with pragmatic, if sometimes acidulated, explication.

Cyril Ray, *The Gourmet's Companion* (1963). A splendid collection of stories, biographies of great cooks and descriptions of memorable meals. Included is Julian Street's short essay on Escoffier, a micro-biography.

Marie Louise Ritz, *César Ritz: Host to the World* (1938). A biography.

Hugh D. Roberts, *Downhearth to Bargrate* (Marlborough, 1981).

Claudia Roden, *Coffee* (1981). A fascinating tour of the world of coffee.

Waverley Root, *The Food of France* (1958).

George Augustus Sala, *Paris Herself Again* (1948), first published as despatches in the *Daily Telegraph*, 1878–79. The revival of Paris after the siege and the Commune 1870–71. Amusing coloured lithographs by Victor Ross.

E. Saint-Ange, *Le Livre de Cuisine de Madame Saint-Ange* (Paris 1927).

Timothy Shaw, *The World of Escoffier* (1994). A lavishly illustrated book on the life and times of Auguste Escoffier with a kindly view of the great chef.

André Simon, and Robin Howe, *Dictionary of Gastronomy* (1978).

Helen Simpson, *The London Ritz Book of Breakfasts* (1988).

Delia Smith, *Delia Smith's Cookery Course* (1981). The BBC's set of books on the TV series.

Drew Smith, *Modern Cooking* (1990).

Taillevent (Guillaume Tirel), *Le Viandier* (1375; first printed 1490).

Reay Tannahill, *Food in History* (1988). Wide-ranging in time and space, but detailed.

Derek Taylor, *Fortune Fame and Folly* (1977). The story of British hotels and catering from 1878 to 1978.

Céline Vence, *Cuisine du Terroir: The Lost Domain of French Cooking* (1988). Pools the knowledge of members across the world of a distinguished association, the *Maîtres Cuisiniers de France*, to record and perpetuate traditional French domestic cookery.

Richard Viner, *George of the Ritz* (1959). The story of George Criticos, the famous hall porter of the Ritz in London, as he told it to the author.

M. Warner, *The Crack in the Teacup* (1979).

Anthony Wild, *The East India Company Book of Coffee* (1994). A tiny book with a jewel of a two-page introduction about the East India Company. The rest is coffee: its origins, its production and how to use it.

Constance Anne Wilson, *Food and Drink in Britain* (1973).

Index